Purple Reign

Sexual Abuse and Abuse of Power in the Diocese of Trenton, New Jersey

Bruce Novozinsky

Linda Vele Alexander

About the Authors

Bruce Novozinsky is a technologist by trade and has been a student of the clergy sexual abuse crisis for over 10 years. He is the proprietor of novozinsky.com. Purple Reign is his first book.

Bruce resides in Upper Freehold Township, New Jersey with his wife, Maureen and their four children. He can be reached at bruce@velenobooks.com.

***

Linda Vele Alexander is founder and principal of The Alexander Law Firm and a former Deputy Attorney General for the State of New Jersey. She is currently a reserve Lieutenant Colonel in the United States Air Force Judge Advocate General's Corps and spent six years on active duty.

Linda resides in Upper Freehold Township, New Jersey, with her husband Steve, their three children and dog. She can be reached at linda@velenobooks.com.

Purple Reign - Sexual Abuse and Abuse of Power in the Diocese of Trenton, New Jersey

Copyright © 2012 by Veleno Publications, LLC

All rights reserved. No part of this book may be reproduced or transmitted in any form or by any means without written permission from the author.

ISBN-13: 978-1456500962
ISBN-10: 1456500961

Dedication

For my five strong and wonderful women. My wife, Maureen – everything that is right with me is because of you. You are every fiber of my happiness, every ounce of my strength; my mother, Constance who always tried to see the good in people even as they hurt her; Linda who makes great out of good; Emily, my muse; and Rose, my guardian angel.

-Bruce

***

In awe and appreciation of the genius of John Irving and Jonathan Franzen, who just plain nail American literary fiction;

To my parents and sister, who indulged the eccentric musings of an 8 year-old poet/playwright/librarian/private detective and sometimes air traffic controller;

To my Auntie Grace, who will promptly start a novena for me;

To my husband Steve, who does the right thing ALWAYS, but who was wrong about ground squirrels;

and mostly

To my children, Analise, Allegra & SJ, I got you right the first time - perfect works to whom no edits are necessary.

-Linda

Note on "Journal" Source

Within the book, several references were made to the "journal" of Monsignor George Everitt. The journal consists of a series of handwritten notes and papers that I found in various boxes while cleaning out Saint Joseph Hall at the time of demolition of Saint Mary Academy.

Contained in those notes were references to people, some still living, who in no way had anything to do with this book, but the identification of whom could prove embarrassing due to the sensitive nature of the issue discussed with the Monsignor, and the disclosure of which could breach the priest-penitent bounds of confidentiality.

Based on this, I *alone* decided to destroy the Monsignor's journals.

I offer no apologies.

-Bruce Novozinsky

"Who is going to save our Church? Not our bishops, not our priests and religious. It is up to you, the people. You have the minds, the eyes and the ears to save the Church. Your mission is to see that your priests act like priests, your bishops, like bishops, and your religious act like religious."

-Archbishop Fulton J. Sheen
June 1972

Table of Contents

Prologue

Introduction

1 "Saint Mary We Love Thee and Loyal We'll Be…"

2 Larry D'Oria and Father Jack: A Twisted Manipulation

3 "After Boston, There is Only Heaven:" An Examination of the Crisis

4 "No Honey, Just Bad People"

5 Trenton and Metuchen Split; The Cardinal McCarrick Syndrome

6 Larry Becomes Lorenzo

7 Bishop John M. Smith – The Great Communicator Goes Silent

8 The Priest That Refuses To Run

9 Father John Bambrick: Advocate or Adversary?

10 The Curious Cases of Patrick Newcombe

11 "Uncle Ronnie"

Epilogue

Afterthoughts

Acknowledgements

Endnotes

Introduction

"Where did it all go so wrong?"

Many people have asked me in the past four years, "Where did it all go so wrong?" To this day that question still resonates in my mind. I could be over-thinking the question and coming to some unqualified conclusions, but the question is all telling to this story.

I think for me personally it "*went wrong*" in a confessional at the altar of the much-to-be mentioned Saint Mary of the Lake Church, in Lakewood, New Jersey, during the Easter season of 1988. At the time the face-to-face confessional policy was still in its advent stages. The priests knew all the parish families and so to a young boy or girl, this was an intimidating change. But in my case and on this particular day, I was 27 years old, had not been to confession in over 10 years, and was about to be married. I wanted to start off my marriage with a clean slate and this brought me into the confessional of Father Joseph Wade.

Understanding the personality of Father Wade was a lesson in priestly psychology 101. He was well into his seventh decade at this point, had a thundering baritone voice, an accusatory tone, an arrogant demeanor and a pompous, dismissive quality that could scare lions out of a fresh kill. I had been afraid of him since I met him back in high school, but that fear had long faded come this day in 1988.

Father was a family friend. He came to our home on every first Sunday of each month for dinner precisely at four o'clock in the afternoon. He took my stepfather Gerry's place at the table's head. This gave me some pleasure because it would force my stepfather from his throne to one of the "kid spots" as we all shifted down the table, diminishing his role as the self-appointed patriarch of 5 Montana Drive. To my mother's credit, she never yielded her place as the head at the opposite end of the table, intensifying the frustration etched on my stepfather's face.

Father Wade would fill his plate. Obsequiously, we would wait with our hands clasped on our knees until he picked up his fork and started eating. Father would then begin the conversation with a topic of his choosing. He picked the topic and there were no "one-off" conversations allowed. We were young. We were Catholic. We obeyed. My stepbrother Gregory, my stepsister Deborah, and my sister Rose and I would contribute to the conversation only if invited in - children were better seen and not heard. This cycle went on for years.

For over a year my stepfather carried a tape recorder to Mass to record Father's sermons. After months of observing this, one day I finally asked what he was doing. Gerry told me he was taking his homilies and placing them in a book. Father had become close to him and my mother, so I could understand this, but I decided to show rebellion nevertheless. I was leafing through the booklet draft of my stepfather's tribute to Father's spoken words and challenged him right on the spot: "You know these are not his words?" The air was sucked out of the room. I watched my stepfather's face go ashen and he asked me to explain. "They're not his words. Plain and simple. He looks through old sermons of Archbishop Sheen and puts his voice to the words." Keeping in mind that this was the early 1980's and pre-Internet, there were very little means by which my stepfather could verify my accusations, but I was right. Father Wade would take the lesser-known texts of Archbishop Fulton Sheen and use those words as his very own. How did I know this? Easy: I was the proof. I had been writing Father Wade's bullet points to his sermons on and off for over three years. I put the unfinished tribute to this priest's leveraged words on the kitchen table and left. Gerry's project would not end, but it was hardly finished with the same enthusiasm in which it was started.

Archbishop Fulton Sheen was a hero of mine and really the reason I entered the seminary in 1975. The Archbishop was a regular visitor to the campus of Georgian Court College (now University), and one day I stumbled upon him. He looked at me and spoke to me as if I were the only child on earth; as if the future of the Catholic Church depended on what I would say next. This was 1973, I was 12 years old, and the man with a simple roman collar, tan sweater, buffed and manicured fingernails stood in front of me with his arms crossed holding a worn breviary bookmarked with a rosary. He asked questions of me and blessed me not with a final hand placement on my head, but with a closed fist and playful "knock." I stood in the presence of greatness; with every fiber of my being, I knew that I had just been blessed by a saint.

The day came to give the book of homilies to Father Joseph Wade as a gift at a birthday celebration in his honor; he opened the finished product, casually thumb-leafed through and didn't stop to give even the most fleeting acknowledgement to a single page, word or letter. He then laid it aside and moved on to his next gift. I felt a sense of sympathy that my stepfather's heartfelt gift was not as well received as he had hoped. Graphic artistry was his life and occupation and the care he took to craft this gift was an effort in the days before personal computers. The dinners eventually stopped and the superior regard that priests enjoyed in our home began to fade.

By the time I approached the confessional on that day in 1988, I had long graduated high school and been honorably discharged from the United States Navy; in a few weeks, I would be married.

"Bless me father for I have sinned..." It started out well and safe enough. For a face-to face confessional this was a "semi-private" room. The area was open and a kneeler was set up between confessor and priest that blocked the face and body. It was Holy Week and open season for part-time Catholics to come out of the woodwork for the annual absolution. "... It's been over three years since my last confession..." (lie, it was over 10). "... I used the Lord's name in vain, I missed Sunday Mass and I disrespected my mother and father and for these sins and for those I do not remember, I am heartily sorry." At this point, I assumed absolution and began the certain-to-follow demand to recite the Act of Contrition. I began, "Oh my God I am heartily sorry for having offended thee, and I detest..." Suddenly, the lion awoke and the entire church echoed with the booming voice of Father Wade: "You are asking for absolution without a proper examination of your conscience!" I was stunned. Father Ken came from his confessional to see what the commotion was. I looked at him imploringly for "a little help here" but he turned and went back to his duties. In a notably softer tone Wade continued, "Your sins will follow you if you were to die today," but then I was completely taken aback as the next series of questions were asked. I had confessed to three broken commandments and Father Wade decided to bypass the inquisition of the remaining seven and asked me instead: "Do you masturbate?" I was 27 and had sworn off sex with my wife-to-be for three months prior to marrying, so I masturbated like it was my job. As I was processing Father Wade's question, he followed quietly with, "Do you take pleasure in bringing yourself to climax?" Suddenly, I was in seventh grade again and the stories and the "near misses" I heard about and experienced came rushing back right on the very altar that I was about to be married on in exactly three weeks. I was confirmed on this altar. I served Mass on this altar and now a priest was asking me on this altar, if I jerk off? What was going on behind our partition? Was he touching himself? Was he leading me and others on to later satisfy himself in all hope that the sacred bind of the confessional would be a two-way street and my silence would be held?

I'd like to say that my outrage and embarrassment channeled into action and that I punched the old man through the divider or that I became as loud and vocal as he was when we began our session, but I did neither. I slowly got up off my knees and walked away. The thoughts that lingered as to what was possibly going on behind that divider were left at the kneeler. I was not challenged or stopped by Father Wade.

My biggest regret about the way I handled it was that as I exited the altar, a boy of no more than 12 was next in line to have his confession heard.

Three weeks later I again stood on that altar as Father Ken married me to Maureen Tighe; next to him stood Father Joseph Wade at the request of my stepfather and mother, an invitation until that moment unbeknownst to me.

Saint Mary of the Lake in Lakewood, New Jersey, in the late 1970's and March 26, 1988, is where it all went wrong for me. I don't accuse Wade of any misconduct, but I do raise the questions. Many that I've spoken to in these eight years, including one closely associated with this book, tell of the same types of leading questions in the confessional by another priest who would later become a sexual predator.

I became a student of the sexual abuse crisis in 2002. The Internet brought this world back to my life and by 2006, I decided to bring this issue back to the forefront of the Diocese of Trenton, New Jersey, where it all began for me. Trenton is not Los Angeles or Boston or Chicago. These cities were all major headlines when it came to the clergy abuse scandal of the 1980's and 1990's that continues on today, ten years into the 21st century. What was not as well publicized, because of the area's lower news profile, were the abuse cases of the Trenton Diocese.

Until now.

The Diocese and its hierarchy have covered up and protected child predators in the name of self-preservation over the course of the past 50 years. The powerful bishops split the Diocese and hid the scandal through transfers and retirement packages. My research brought these cases to light; my book gives voice to the victims.

In a calculated effort to suppress the voices of accusations against the clergy, in 1981 the Trenton Diocese "split," forming a new diocese, the Diocese of Metuchen. In one fell swoop, pedophile priests were transferred 25 miles north and into a seemingly Caligula-like concentrated area. It was done under the direction of then Bishop Theodore McCarrick (now a retired Cardinal, Prince of the Church), who had a known practice of hosting alcohol-infused weekends at his beach house on the New Jersey shore in what has become commonly known throughout the Internet as the "Cardinal McCarrick Syndrome," coined by Dr. Richard Sipe. This plan to divide the Trenton Diocese was hatched not to protect the parish youth, but to protect priests who raped boys by night and served Mass with them by day.

Does this book brand me an enemy of the Church? I've recently been accused of the same in emails, voice mails, and postal service mails - you name it - and within the walls of my children's parochial school.

I've long since resigned myself to the fact that there will always be those who believe that I am. At my first meeting with my current bishop, the Most Reverend David M. O'Connell, he assured me that I am not (however, he has taken the steps to "block" me from access to the social media the Trenton Diocese utilizes). My critics' reasoning is that as a Roman Catholic I am bringing to light the darkest moments in our Church's history and this gives more ammunition to the enemies of the Church to continue their prosecution. I have been told that I am magnifying the problem by giving water to a dying tree - and I could not disagree more vehemently. What brings condemnation on the Church are the missteps and arrogance of a hierarchy that boasts an apostolic line of succession to the original twelve followers of Christ, one being Judas, covering up these atrocities with the chain of command up to the Vatican fully in support and partially in denial of the crisis that they caused.

The sexual abuse scandal is tragic and horrific left to its own sin; the cover-up through transfers and judicial interference is reprehensible. The bishops that govern the individual sees are quick to proselytize *"If you do this to the least of my brothers you do it to me,"* particularly during the Bishop's Annual Appeal fund drive, but dismiss the same when it applies to the molestation and abuse of children by the clergy. These bishops, from George W. Ahr to the great communicator John M. Smith, were concerned solely with the preservation of their office and legacy, a hypocritical and most damning indictment to Catholic charity, sympathy towards victims, and the altruistic virtues they preached to the faithful each and every Sunday. The fact of the matter is that whereas a "small number of priests" may be guilty of actual pedophilia, towards the latter part of the 20th century we discovered that more and more bishops were guilty of the cover-up that ultimately made the victims suffer once again.

This book invites you to enter my world and the world of my friends in the 1970's, the small corner of the Diocese that is now starting to be referred to as the "Devil's Triangle" of sexual abuse. I will introduce you to a single family, their lives so deeply affected by the abuse of their oldest son, whose first three sexual encounters were with three different priests; the bishops, and the politics of intimidation they employed to secure the silence of victims and their families; and the crimes that were never prosecuted in Trenton because of the agreement between the Diocese and the Mercer County Prosecutor's Office to seal the names of the abusers due to a legal "technicality."

"Imagine for a moment," I asked Father Ian Trammell, the present pastor at Saint Gregory the Great, in Hamilton Square, New Jersey, "that you look out of your office window and towards the school building and see six boys on their way over to see you. These boys are a mix of seventh and eighth graders and all are altar boys. You greet them and the oldest tells you that the new priest in the parish is giving them cigarettes, beer and rum with coke, and taking them to the Parish Center or the beach or a nearby lake and molesting them." In present day 2010 (when I posed this question to him via email), within hours search warrants would be issued, arrests would be made and communities would be rallying in an uproar. The pastor would be questioned, his entire parish disrupted and the 24-hour news cycle would be fully employed. It was not this way in 1974 when the exact same scenario played out in Lakewood. Father Trammell expressed what his feelings were, but due to the nature of the conversation it would not be fair to him to divulge it here. Suffice to say, it was his own sincere reply, coupled with the corporate spin that is the Vatican.

I'm not versed in writing books; this is my first. You may come across language that's inappropriate and offensive to both children and English scholars. I write the way I speak and that's with candor and very little filtering. If grammar is shattered in this book then assume that it's the way I'd tell you this story if you weren't reading it for yourself.

Call it divine providence, but it's been said that people are placed in each and every situation for a reason, and when I reflect on the course my life has taken - the chance encounters, the opportunities that but for a minute later might not have been, the faces of my children here only because I ventured into an office building and met the woman that was to be my wife - I do believe it to be so. I can say with certain conviction that I do believe I was witness to the abuse and spared from such because I was meant to tell this story. Many have come forward and twice as many have stayed behind, choosing to internalize the abuse that they endured. Some feel ashamed (unrightfully so), others feel less of a person (unrightfully so), and all feel abandoned by the Church (rightfully so). It is my every hope and prayer that everyone victimized in this regard will find the peace that God intends for them.

I did not change names; however, I did not use surnames for those persons who have not responded to my consent requests for involvement in this project or those who requested that their last name be withheld. Some first-person accounts are graphic but as part of the agreement with those involved, I did not edit their contributions. I pledged that their accounts would remain authentic, and so they are. Moreover, no one has been compensated for his or her story and there are no post-sales agreements are in place.

Digest the material; form your own conclusions. As for me, this research has had a profound impact on my faith. I remain a practicing

Catholic and each of my children attended (or presently attends) Catholic schools within the Trenton Diocese, with no repercussions, owing to the "*sins of the father*" in writing this book. My internal crisis is with the hierarchy and the bed they made - most definitely not with the Christ who died for the redemption of my sins - of which there are many. I am a sinner and before I cast this stone, I confess that there is not a Commandment of Ten that I have not broken or had a part in breaking. Am I hypocritical in seeking absolution from those who were ordained by the very people I am condemning? Perhaps, but faith is a hard thing to shake. Faith in others, well, that's a whole different story.

-Bruce Novozinsky - 2012

Prologue
October 1973

In the Gilded Age of the 1920's and 1930's, Lakewood, New Jersey, was a resort town for the flourishing New Jersey shore. This densely forested area of coastal plain with inhospitable crop soil known as the "pine barrens" was the gateway to the beaches that ran along the 70-mile coastline from Point Pleasant to Atlantic City. The natural beauty of the pine trees made for a stunning holiday visual for the social elite of New York City and Philadelphia, who in the winter flocked to this pocket of climate rumored to be five degrees warmer than their cities; the names Rockefeller, Gould, Pack, Smock and Brick were all registered in Lakewood's Town Hall as "part time" or "seasonal" residents, and the legacy of their generosity and masterpiece architecture endures today.

At the recovery period of the Great Depression in the 1930's, the family of railroad tycoon Jay Gould sold the site that is now Georgian Court University to the Sisters of Mercy. The Charles Lathrop Pack Estate would follow suit and sell them the grounds that ran along Forest Avenue. It made "the Mercies" the largest single, tax-exempt landowners in Ocean County at the time, years after their community debut in 1898 with their flagship elementary school, Saint Mary Academy. Admittedly misplaced in this tight-knit Jewish community, the nuns and students nevertheless enjoyed a mutual respect with their ultra-conservative orthodox neighbors.

Contrary to the belief of many throughout Lakewood-lore, which no doubt, as most lores do, started from erroneous assumptions - here that the names were the same so they must be affiliated - Saint Mary of the Lake Church was not the parish of Saint Mary Academy. Lakewood was home to our school and the church by the same name, only two blocks away, needed altar boys; Saint Mary Academy satisfied that need and thus, a bond was forged. Beyond this convenience, none of the vast history of the school and church that by random mutual patronage enjoyed the Blessed Mother's special intercession mattered in the early-to-mid 1970's, although that Her protection would be grievously needed by those in her altar service would soon become apparent, to us at least, with the arrival of a new priest in the parish, Father John "Jack" Banko.

The lead altar boy at the time was Lawrence "Larry" D'Oria. In 1973, Larry was in eighth grade and his primary job was to schedule altar boys for weddings, funerals and the daily 7:00 a.m. Mass. Larry came from a prosperous and respected family in neighboring Jackson, and was appointed to this exalted role by Banko. Larry's father owned a family operated pharmacy in what was then the town center, building this flourishing business from the ground up. This meant a lot of time away from home and away from his eldest son.

Appointing Larry with the potential for D'Oria money lining church coffers had little to do with Banko's choice for lead altar boy; rather, Banko saw access to Larry, a circumstance of opportunity for a predator and his prey. Banko saw a busy parent (albeit not an abandonment of love for his son), an altar boy, and a well-established, well-to-do Catholic family that was seemingly loyal to the church and its priests.

Larry was slightly effeminate in his mannerisms and his speech. Back then we didn't call each other "gay" or "faggot," but Larry just seemed "different." He avoided branding by our inclusion of him at recess, and because he was not entirely unathletic, bringing to the table some enviable competitive swimming skills. "Father Jack," as he was known, was also somewhat effeminate and had a nervous habit of tilting forward on his toes when he became uncomfortable, be it on the altar or in the playground where he spent a lot of time during recess hours at Saint Mary Academy. But Father Jack was also the "cool" priest. He smoked and gave cigarettes to the kids on the playground "for after school and don't get caught." He drove a very unpriest-like Dodge Charger (olive green with a spoiler) and he was not above using his status as a priest to intervene on behalf of one of his "favorites" to the teachers even if it were done so in front of other students. With a Beatles haircut and an aloof way about him, his entire persona begged playground legend, and we were very willing to crown him. Others were not so sure.

Indeed, Father Jack was developing another reputation and "cool" had nothing to do with it. More than a few worried phone calls went from the school administration to the Church administration. Some lay teachers knew that something was "off" in the relationship this new priest was forming with the boys of the school and some were very vocal about it to the school administration. Father Jack was smoking. Father Jack was cursing. Father Jack was picking up boys after school in his flashy car – all of which was heard and politely dismissed by the receiver of the calls at the church. However, the indomitable Sister Harold Phelan was the principal of Saint Mary Academy and primary liaison between our school and Father George Everitt, the pastor of Saint Mary of the Lake Church, and her street-smarts were telling her that there was something to be concerned about – very concerned about - with this new playground presence, who was not one to be unsupervised himself.

In October 1973, lead altar boy Larry scheduled William "JR" Giebler and me to serve the 7:00 a.m. Mass. Back then, 7:00 a.m. Mass was served in week intervals on a rotating basis, spanning Monday morning through the following Saturday. You were accumulating "points." These points counted toward your wedding and funeral schedules. The more points you accumulated the more paid ceremonies you received. A wedding was $20.00 and a funeral was $10.00. In the mid-1970's this was a lot of money for a boy to have in his pocket so it was rare that you missed a rotation. It was even more rare that you would not try to tell Larry that you served more Masses than you actually did. Larry was very aware of the "point-ploy" and more often than not played along with our money grabbing scheme, but after Banko came to the church, Larry seemed more and more business-like in his approach to his administrative duties and this caused some resentment among those that were clearly in the wrong and not open to change.

JR and I were not close. He was in the eighth grade and I was in seventh. He was left back a grade so he should have been in the ninth grade at Saint Joseph High School in Toms River when we served Mass that morning. Looking back not so many years later, I thanked God that he was left back because of that one October morning – though at the time I hardly realized the bullet - or priest - I was about to dodge because of his courage.

When my father died in 1968, JR was good to me. I'm sure that this was at the direction of his parents, Bill and Denise, who were close to my parents until my dad died and my mom remarried. JR dated my stepsister Debbie from time to time and he, like me, hated my stepfather all the time. He taught me a certain way to bend my Holbrook Little League hat, break in a baseball glove using saddle soap and shoestring, and once gave me a used Sears bat because it was imprint-signed by Ted Williams of the Boston Red Sox, who were my favorite team.

JR was okay to hang around with and talk to about girls and baseball. He knew basketball, as well, and we'd spend time after Mass shooting hoops on the playground before the buses pulled up and he went with his friends and me with mine. He was a good-to-great looking kid and other kids wanted to be like him, hang out with him, and be recognized by him. I was no different. I didn't idolize JR, but I wanted to be in that circle of friends he had. Yet, I was always on the fringe and never made that step "inside." When JR's mother dropped us off for morning Mass, she'd instruct him "Look after Bruce," and it gave me a sense that I may be "in" with JR a bit closer, and I liked that.

JR looked after me because he liked Debbie and because his sister Tracie was friends with my sister Rose. He also liked that I was the epitome of a smart-ass. I was quick with humor and that humor was often biting. I wore my hair in a tight crew cut, had freckles and could curse with a cornucopia of profanity, and actually understood what my foul mouth was saying. My cutting edge wit almost always worked with the teachers in a charming way that endeared me to them and bolstered my Eddie Haskell-like image. But JR knew something the teachers did not; I was a kleptomaniac around the church poor box and I was developing a healthy drinking habit at the age 13.

Kids learn by example and the example set for me in the 1970's was not good. My mother, Connie, began drinking heavily at the age of 15 and had a child when she was 16 as a result being raped. She ran away from an emotionally abusive father and when she returned to give birth, the baby was taken from her by the nuns at the hospital as soon as the umbilical cord was cut, separating mother from child – in their case, forever.

My mother married my father Walter in 1957 and had my sister Rose a year later. She left my father briefly but came back when my sister was born in September 1958. My mother's life was far less than perfect but it made her a stronger woman as she went on. People gravitated towards her, trusted her, depended on her, and she rarely let them down. If you needed two dimes and she had three, you'd get all three "just in case." Unfortunately, my mother's best qualities were only but a glimpse. I only wonder how amazing she would have been but for her victimization at the hands of the men she was involved with and her resulting spiral into life-long dependencies.

I was born in 1961 and my dad died of lung cancer in 1968 within twelve hours of Dr. Martin Luther King's assassination. My last memory of my father was at his funeral when the car procession route was rerouted because of the Lakewood riots in the King assassination aftermath. I remember the hearse being stopped by black protestors and looters who had no concern for King's murder as they carried televisions and stereos in their arms that were stolen from local appliance store windows. I can still see the friends of my father - Fred Capper, Harold Bennett (a bear of a man with a heart to match), Jerry Moore, Stan Drumme, Bill Lohewing, and Jimmy Groff - leaping out of the cars on Madison Avenue in Lakewood and clearing a path for the procession.

The years between my father dying and my mother remarrying in 1972 were hard for my sister and me, but we survived by watching out for each other, Rose more so than me. Rose was a rare combination of street-smart, book-smart, personality and toughness. What she lacked in outward beauty she made up for in her ability to make friends with steadfast loyalty. This trait lasted a lifetime. When it was time to sign up for Little League, it was her babysitting money that paid for my registration fee and when it was our parents' turn to work the concession stand, she worked the register.

Rose was nothing short of brilliant. She ran a string of straight-A's from third grade through high school. Her ambition, to be an attorney, was anachronistic for the time and place we grew up, but her lack of self-confidence was an insurmountable obstacle. She was her father's daughter and he was gone. She never forgot her devotion to him and never allowed a replacement to fill that hurting, empty spot in her life or her heart.

My mother is an alcoholic. Her dependency on alcohol and pain medication lasted her lifetime. Her once vibrant personality and toned body is now a shell of itself. There is no blame here whatsoever. My mother was a pillar of the community and steadfast in her love and support of her faith. She faced the tribulations of the world around her and at times she succumbed, but to have "Con" as a friend, was to have a friend for life.

My mother had a difficult childhood and was prone to abusive relationships after my father passed. She remarried in 1972 to a demanding, mentally abusive, manipulative, and self-absorbed man. He would beat me on a whim and had his own son by a previous marriage committed to a boys' home while he was in high school for what could be written off as normal boy behavior even in these times of hovering parents and overbearing political correctness. He insisted my sister and I call him "dad" because in his logic, he paid the bills now and he would be given that respect. He also drank and the more he drank the more abusive he became. His was a mental anguish. A classic misogynist, He isolated my mother from her friends that were there for us when my father died. They divorced in the 1990's and the life that my mother once had was coming back but the physical toll of years pressed on her; today, after suffering a series of strokes, she remains in assisted living, but is still a loving and caring soul.

Rose settled on being a court stenographer and real estate agent. She worked for years for a divorced attorney and father of two girls and Rose eventually moved in with him. I felt it was my turn to look out for her. I tried. I warned her that the attorney was not going to marry her and she was pouring her money into his house and the day he left her she would be without a job, a boyfriend and a home all in one day. He became a prosecutor, left his struggling law firm and eventually left Rose. She was left without a home, a boyfriend and a job. Her once brilliant mind and spirit deteriorated on a slow balance thereafter.

Following these weekday Masses, JR and I would follow an established ritual; he would stash an open bottle of altar wine outside and retrieve it afterwards. I would take the money from the "drop-box" and we'd split it on the way to school. We'd walk along Lake Carasaljo swigging and when we reached the exit point of North Lake Drive and Forest Avenue we'd toss the remains in the lake.

This Thursday morning things were running pretty much the same. As we left Mass, Sister Mary Theresa offered us a ride back to school. We declined and laughed on how "messed up" it would be if we were caught by our friends in the "nun car." We decided that risking the crossing of a busy highway during the morning rush hour was better than the social suicide of being escorted back to school by a car full of nuns.

As the last car left the parking lot, JR and I took our book bags and placed the bottle of altar wine in his. I was fumbling with a transistor radio and getting mad that he would not walk the one block north to Taylor's drug store so I could use my new found cash to get the batteries needed to listen to the New York Mets and Oakland Athletic World Series game that afternoon. The wine came out as we descended the embankment leading to the lakeside. What we didn't notice was the Lakewood Police car that drove up. When we did, I panicked and threw the bottle in the direction of the lake and it shattered against one of the pine trees that enhanced the landscape of the lake area. The thundering crash, I thought, must have surely woken up all of Lakewood.

The police officer was Fred Capper. His brother, Danny was in my class. His dad was one of the pallbearers at my dad's funeral and I tried to leverage both bits of information to get us a pass on underage drinking and littering of a public park. JR stood his ground and let me do the talking. Fred recognized us from our school uniforms but he had already "called it in" and was forced to do something, anything, to bring the matter to closure. Basically, there were three options offered to us: 1) take us home to our parents; 2) take us to the nuns at school; or 3) take us to the church and have Father Jack deal with us. While all of the options involved adult intervention, JR opted the latter on our behalf and so we were taken back to Saint Mary of the Lake Church. My turn to do the talking was over, and JR took the commanding lead at that point.

As we approached the church, Father Jack was coming out. Cigarette already in hand, he listened to Officer Capper. He never made eye contact with Fred who was dismissively thanked by the priest as he left. Father Jack was already tilting on his toes. *"What was HE nervous about?"* I thought, as tears streamed down my cheeks. I looked at JR. He remained calm, almost ice-like, and with his stare fixed on Father Jack's face, said coolly, "So that's it, Jack?" My body went numb. JR had just called a priest by his first name – his nickname no less - and completely disregarded his formal title. Father Jack didn't return JR's glare, but instead flicked his cigarette against the brick wall of the church. I watched the ashes form into an explosion of orange sparks and land back at Father's foot. He stubbed the butt out and with a sharp motion of his thumb directed JR to, "Go." I was motionless and scared. My tears resumed and quickly became sobs. JR stood his ground and said, "Let's go, Novozinsky." I looked at what were now two combatants and felt Father Jack's tobacco-stained hand on my shoulder; I remember the smell of his nicotine breath from years of chain smoking. At the same time JR had my hand. He held it like we were going to take a walk. He remained calm and focused even as two ladies came to clean the church and passed us with a smile and a wave. I was about to be placed in a human tug-of-war when Father Jack exploded, "Leave now Mr. Giebler, I'll take this one back to school, don't make any more trouble for either one of you." At that second, JR tugged me and my uniform tie fell to the ground. Not only was I going to get in trouble for drinking, getting caught by a police officer and my parish priest, but now I had lost my school tie! JR didn't let go of me until we reached the other side of Route 9 and by this time my sobbing was uncontrollable, and I fell to the ground.

"Stop it! Stop it and shut up! You're making it worse. Just take your stuff and let's get back to school," JR kept repeating to me over and over again. I dared to look back only once, and Father Jack was smoking another cigarette, tilting on his toes and just looking in our general direction. Finally, as we reached the wrought iron gates that surrounded the south end of Saint Mary, JR put both his hands on both my shoulders and said, "Bruce, listen. He will never tell your parents. He will never tell my parents. It's over. He's a fag." Then he told me to wash my face and handed me his tie. We went to the boys' room in Saint Joseph Hall and I cleaned up. I leaned over and without a word offered JR his tie back. He didn't look from the mirror. "You keep it; it'll keep you from crying again." Then he looked at me and threw a playful elbow at my ear. We laughed and I asked, "Banko is a fag?" JR didn't even look at me and said, "He just is. Shut up."

JR was right - Father John "Jack" Banko never told my parents because he had secrets of his own to keep, and most of them at the time involved lead altar boy, Larry D'Oria.

1
"Saint Mary We Love Thee and Loyal We'll Be..."

*"...Saint Mary we love thee and loyal we'll be.
Our Alma Mater we hail, hail to thee.
The Blue and the Gold hold a sweet memory;
Now and forever we pledge loyalty.
Saint Mary forever, hail, hail to thee."*

-Saint Mary Academy School song

When Catherine McAuley opened the House of Mercy on the corner of Lower Baggot and Herbert Streets in Dublin, Ireland, in 1827, she had no intention of founding a religious institution but rather a place for a well-intentioned group of laywomen to instruct the poor. Having lived the orphan life after the early death of her parents before she reached adulthood, Catherine was well acquainted with the needs of the destitute and inclined to charitable works, and used the large inheritance left to her by her guardians to permanently house her "mercy" mission. Catherine was piously committed to Catholicism despite the Protestant forces which battered her for conversion throughout her life, so it was only natural that Catholic clergyman were her advisors in this endeavor, and only a matter of time before the conduct of the house resembled a monastery and the Archbishop of Dublin asked that the "Sisters of Mercy" declare their intentions as a religious congregation. In September 1830, Catherine, along with Anna Maria Doyle and Elizabeth Harley, began the formal training necessary to establish a new order of religious women and, in December 1831, the Order of the Sisters of

Mercy was born when the three women made their Profession of Vow to minister to those in need.[1]

Mother Catherine died in her sleep in November 1841, just a few months after Pope Gregory XVI formally approved the Mercy Rule and Constitutions. In just ten years, Mother Catherine had established ten foundations in Ireland and two in England, prodigious growth foreshadowing a mercy mission that would soon spread worldwide:

[T]he ten short years of her own religious life were but the seedling-time; it was only after her death that the full fruitfulness of her life began to show itself. At the time of her death there were little more than 100 Sisters of Mercy; fifteen years later there were 3,000 ... one hundred years later there were 23,000.[2]

In 1843, Mother Frances Warde, one of the first Sisters of Mercy professed by Catherine McAuley, established in Pittsburgh, Pennsylvania, the first of many foundations in the United States. The Sisters' energy in ministering to the sick and economically poor attracted many new members and spread throughout the country, from New York to San Francisco, inspired by the words of their foundress: "Mercy, the principal path pointed out by Jesus Christ to those who desire to follow Him, has in all ages excited the faithful to instruct and comfort the sick and dying poor and in them they find the person of our Divine Lord." In 1873, Mother Warde settled in Bordentown, the New Jersey foundation of the Order, with five other Sisters.[3]

"The Mercies" were here to stay.

The Sisters of Mercy opened Saint Mary Academy in Lakewood on September 8, 1898, with less than ten pupils in the scarcely Catholic town. The building, located at 503 Lexington Avenue at the corner of Lexington and Fifth Streets, was a large double house that the Sisters leased until 1905 when they purchased it.[4] In 1908, the Sisters founded what is now Georgian Court University. The lavish estate of millionaire George Jay Gould I, son of railroad magnate Jay Gould, "Georgian Court" was sold to the Sisters of Mercy in 1924 after his death. While the details of the estate's payments are unclear, legend that it was completely donated by the Gould's to the Mercies is certainly not true.

In 1950, after the Sisters of Mercy purchased the Pack estate and the James estate, Saint Mary Academy moved from Lexington Avenue to 250 Forest Avenue. By this time, the Gould fortune was depleting and the cost of living in Lakewood was on the rise. In 1951, the grounds Saint Mary Academy occupied on Forest Avenue was purchased by the Mercies for $20,000 (on top of the property already obtained for $17,000) and the "Academy," as it would henceforth be known, was open for business, one that would be in the service of Catholic education for 40 years until it was torn down in the 1990's to make room for additional middle-income housing for the large Orthodox Jewish population.

Colorful and rich in history, the Sisters of Mercy were not the stereotypical sisters swiping rulers across our knuckles; in my experience, these nuns truly lived up to their calling of mercy and compassion. In Sister Simon Robb's first grade class in September of 1967, we were seated in alphabetical order, putting me right in back of Debbie Mazzella and in front of Alice Pasquale. Sister was young and she sang to us all day. She had a song for everything and learning was fun. In April of 1968, she comforted my sister and me in our living room the night my father passed away and stayed the night on our couch because she could not get back to Lakewood. It was the same night that Dr. Martin Luther King was killed and the burning of Lakewood had begun.

Sister was at my wedding and she carried the gifts to the altar at my sister's memorial Mass in 2008. Sister Simon was a good and thoughtful person. She'd wake every morning at 4:30 a.m. to have her "hour with Christ" that she modeled from the teaching and sermons of the charismatic Bishop Fulton Sheen, and she remained in customary habit when other abandoned theirs because she served the elderly, a population that recognized her from her traditional religious dress.

We grew up in the climate of rebellion and the nature of the conservative church was to suppress that urge to protest, to grow hair, wear loud colors and above all, to question authority. Our teachers, the nuns and lay alike, were the authoritative figures and our parents accepted that. We lived in the fear that if we got in trouble at school, we were in twice as much trouble at home. The nuns knew this as well and leveraged it. It was an unspoken understanding between all involved, and so the status quo was maintained, mutually beneficial to everyone.

We were not used to having any "dignitaries" coming onto our grounds with the exception of the Mother Superior from Mount Saint Mary College from Watchung, in upstate New Jersey. In my first seven years at the Academy it was rare that a priest ever came over to the school from the church.

Father George Everitt was the pastor of Saint Mary of the Lake Church. When he passed in 1994, he had served as church pastor for over 30 years as well as the Vicar General for Ocean County for the Diocese of Trenton. George Everitt was a good and decent man, revered by the parishioners and respected by his peers. The admiration stemmed from the fact that it was his parish and his church by infrastructure only; it was our parish and our church as a place of peace and prayer, a tradition of the church long forgotten by today's clergy that are ordained with an entitlement clause.

When people came to Father Everitt for a job, there was work to be done. When the call came to the rectory at three-o'clock in the morning for last rites, he got up and went to the nearby Paul Kimble Hospital. When anyone looked for guidance he always had the time. Father was not challenged in the everyday life of running his Parish. He had the money and the support staff. But what he didn't have was a school to call his own. This was always an area of concern for the Sisters of Mercy. The Mercies were an island onto their own and did not want to fall under formal diocesan rules of answering to the Bishop. The Bishop, however, wanted a diocesan school in the Lakewood area to form a line of continuity from neighboring parishes, Saint Veronica (Howell), Saint Dominic (Brick) and Saint Joseph (Toms River). The Mercies may have been tenants in the regard that they secured a non-interest bearing mortgage of $10,000 for the renovation of the Forest Avenue campus, but they did not want to be beholden to the Diocese; they were content on maintaining their own private sovereign nation in Lakewood, collecting tuition and donations and being accountable to the Mother Superior administratively and to the Diocese only on ceremony.

Father Everitt was not a vindictive man by any means but he was a "company man." He raised money for his bosses in both Trenton and Rome and the school was a part of this objective, and he would see it through. The main reason for him absenting himself from the grounds of Saint Mary Academy was because of a business objective; the priest did not want his face associated with being the root cause of eventually putting this school up for sale. In truth, Father was the de facto spiritual advisor to the students of Saint Mary Academy and a gracious host to all of the liturgies and ceremonies that required his church and his Parish Center. He loved the children of his parish and surrounding areas above all. If invited to a student function, he came. The seniors from the budding retirement villages sprouting up in Ocean County at the time supported him but the children gave him strength. He championed the first "latch-key" program as well as educational, religious and scouting programs that did not discriminate based on creed. Father took what and who the Diocese sent him. He had a flock that tended to itself and the associate pastors largely said Mass and administered the sacraments as needed.

There was no denying that Father Everitt was the greater-among-peers within his brothers' circle of priests in Ocean County and the proper respect was shown to him by the many that sought his advice. If you were the "new guy" in Ocean County you would be expected to seek out Father and get his advice. Father personally selected hopeful candidates that came to him, with mothers and fathers in tow, for slots in the two minor (high school) seminaries in the Trenton Diocese - Divine Word in Bordentown and Saint Joseph in Princeton. Father had a way of identifying those that would be a fit and those that would fail in these environments.

George Everitt was progressive by today's standards. His was a congregation that welcomed divorced individuals who remarried back into the church and into the sacraments. He counseled those that had a deep faith to maintain their relationship with their God and not depend so much on what was said in Rome; "Let that be my problem," he was fond of saying and I heard him say it often.

Once in the summer of 1972, a man walked up to Father as he stood in the parking lot after Mass. The United States Olympic Basketball Team just lost in the gold medal game to the Soviet Union and men were lingering outside the church to talk about the game. A man stood by patiently and when he saw his opportunity, approached the pastor and said, "Father, I'm gay," with his chin lowered to his chest. Even an 11 year-old observer such as myself could tell that the man rehearsed his introduction a thousand times over, but when the moment arrived for him to deliver it to the priest, only three words could be mustered. Taking his forefinger and lifting the man's chin so their eyes met, Father Everitt offered, "I'm Father Everitt, do you want to come inside?" Thirty years later, that man is still a parishioner and still honors "my Monsignor." That was George Everitt.

This not to imply that Father didn't have a firm streak of discipline in him but rather that he didn't display it for the benefit of chest thumping. If you were a child that showed disrespect in Mass or in the confessional line, you were singled out and called to task. His confessional penance was deemed harsh to a large degree because it went beyond the rote five Hail Marys and five Our Fathers; it was not rare that the bearer of the penance Father dispensed would be required to work the weeded field on a Saturday in back of the main parking lot of the church. The more perceptive kids from our school who worshiped at Saint Mary of the Lake Church avoided Father Everitt's confessional each first Friday of the month between September and June.

Saint Mary of the Lake was considered a plush assignment, but what it was becoming in the mid-to-late 1970's was not a fair thing to befall George Everitt. It had become a breeding ground for sexual abuse and inappropriate behavior by a priest assigned to him.

By this time, Father Everitt was Monsignor Everitt and he had begun to keep a journal.

Sister Harold Phelan did not keep a journal. She didn't have to. Sister had a photographic memory. Even though she was a constant presence at the Forest Avenue campus, her unannounced visits to a classroom were always a welcome treat and the correct answer to a religious question was worth a Jolly Rancher or red-hot jawbreaker candy hidden in her worn sleeve. The sleeve of the nun was often compared to the "loaves and fishes" from the Sermon on the Mount for the endless supply of confection that seemed to be there. Sister's outward persona - a ready smile, giggle, and laugh combined with a loving, motherly demeanor - were not to be mistaken for a lack of administration skills or tough street-smart know-how and her warm smile could turn to ice with the split timing of a misplaced word. Sister dealt with the parents at her school firmly, letting them know "who's boss" and it was not them.

Though an advocate of community involvement, Sister never mandated volunteer time from the parents. She didn't have to. The parents were ready to work for her in any capacity whatsoever. She did not subscribe to the "service points" in place at many of the private institutions today, but in a day where telephones and overhead projectors were the leading edge of technology, Sister only had to "put out the word" and the parents fell over themselves to help. When a bus driver jumped a curb with "her kids" onboard she came on the bus in the afternoon, fired him, and proceeded to have a parent with a bus license drive the route, never mind that the she had no authority to fire the man much less commandeer the bus that belonged to the Township of Manchester. When she found out the man was an alcoholic she made sure that the Lakewood Parks and Recreation Department employed him because it was near his home and he didn't have to drive to work. This was Sister Harold. You didn't say "no" because she didn't accept "no."

The relationship between Sister Harold Phelan and Father George Everitt by today's standards would be called "strictly professional." In Sister, Father saw his opposite gendered-peer. When they greeted each other it was always with a barely noticeable head-bow, a handshake and slight brush of the cheek on both sides. Sister was very proud of her French heritage and Father respected that and made certain that his traditional greeting acknowledged her proud background. Father Everitt stood 6 feet 2 inches tall, a full twelve inches taller than the short and rounded nun, but in the religious community of Ocean County across all denominations, both stood as equals at the top of the pecking order.

Sister and Father had another common ground to stand on - both ran a business. One was looking to expand and the other was looking to stay afloat. Tuition at Saint Mary Academy in the 1970's was 90% less than the cost of Catholic grammar school tuition in 2011 in the greater Trenton Diocese area. The four anchor buildings were in major disrepair and kept intact by two retired maintenance men, Frank Grover and Bill Lohewing. All of the buildings were laced with asbestos that was covered with mere plywood and shingles. At that time, Saint Mary Academy was on borrowed time and how it lasted upwards of another 20 years is in itself a miracle if not a living and breathing monstrosity of health code violations.

Saint Mary the church didn't have a school and Saint Mary the school was without a church. The straight flush was in the hand of the (now) Monsignor and it was up to Sister Harold to call a bluff. Conventional wisdom of the time and all the brain trust of the official Saint Mary Academy Father's Club (an active working organization that was a mandatory "join" at the school) wagered that the church would purchase the school and its properties and the employment of staff and administration would be maintained. The mayor of Lakewood at the time was George Hoffman and his daughters, Jane and Gae, were students of the school. George was one of the first Eucharistic Minister at the church, and very close with the clergy there. It stood to reason that this would be a seamless transition.

What did not enter the equation was the fact that neither Monsignor nor the then Bishop of Trenton, George W. Ahr, wanted the Forest Avenue property. In a journal entry, Monsignor Everitt was adamant when he wrote: "… RSM (Sisters of Mercy) believe that the property is safe and not in need of demolition. Disagree. Trenton (Bishop Ahr) interested only in (the) (C)onvent loc(ation) … no value or use to me. GH (George Hoffman) assessment and opinion valued but biased, (his) girls went to sm (Saint Mary)…." The Monsignor and the Bishop were going through the motions but had other plans for a school in Lakewood that was far removed from Forest Avenue.

In 1970, Monsignor Everitt broke ground on a Parish Center. It served as a multi-use facility for everything from youth basketball to hall rentals for weddings. It was "home" to Saint Mary Academy Laker basketball games and it also shared the sub-church facility of Holy Family Church. All these belonged to the Catholic community of Saint Mary of the Lake. Ever the good neighbor, Saint Mary Academy was never charged a rental fee for the children's events.

Monsignor's plan (with the blessing of the Bishop) was to allow Saint Mary Academy to be condemned, swoop in, take advantage of the displaced students, and attain immediate enrollment objectives based on the fact that parents from neighboring Brick would send their kids to a closer facility, that Jackson had no other option, and that Lakewood would break the doors down to keep the continuity of their kids Catholic education in town in place. Margin notes in Monsignor's journal included surprisingly accurate and precise student enrollment from the Academy for a three-year span. It was broken down by gender and town demographics, with space planning for the building of his new school. If he remained patient (and this could take years to fruition), he would fill his school within three years instead of the "norm" of four to six years in a new building plan.

When Monsignor Everitt announced in 1972 that he had intended to build an ultra-modern school facility to be attached to his newly built Parish Center/gymnasium between Brick Township and Lakewood, the message was clear: Saint Mary Academy would not close down right away but they also would not survive the millennium.

Monsignor Everitt's plan was to open a small "transitional" school called Holy Family School in September 1975 with 200 planed enrollees (he got 174 that year) for kindergarten through third grade. Classes were held in Holy Family Hall and the Parish Center. In 1977, the school expanded to add fourth through eighth grades, and the Saint Mary Academy deathwatch was on.

Through it all, the cordial relationship continued with the Sister Harold administration. By and large it was not just a show – the admiration one had for the other was genuine but only to a point, and that point was about to be tested with the arrival of one Father John "Jack" Banko.

In 1972, Father John "Jack" Banko was assigned to Saint Mary of the Lake Church. He came from Saint Mary Seminary in Baltimore, Maryland, founded in 1791, the first Catholic seminary established in the United States. On its website the seminary boasts: "A community of diocesan priests dedicated to the formation of priests.... Embodying the values of the Sulpician tradition, St. Mary's offers the very best programs possible in preparing the next generation of diocesan priests." In actuality, this marketing, which capitalizes on their 200-year specialization in "forming" priests, masks an alternative curriculum than you or I would expect for a priest training for vocation; there are those, including insiders, that attest that Saint Mary Seminary is a counter-culture that provides both ample opportunity and encourages the homosexual lifestyle to take root, be active and flamboyant.

Father Andrew Walter, ordained for the Diocese of Bridgeport, Connecticut, in 2000, spent several semesters at the Baltimore school as a seminarian for the Diocese of Paterson, New Jersey. According to Father Walter, the situation at the Baltimore seminary was so bad that the vice rector delivered a lecture "in front of at least 150 people" acknowledging, "Yes, we accept openly gay seminarians; that's our policy." Father John Trigilio, proprietor of the well-respected blog "Black Biretta," observed while visiting the Baltimore seminary: "There was no discretion at all. The few times I was there, some of the seminarians would literally dress like gays from [Greenwich] Village. They would even go so far as to wear pink silk; it was like going to see La Cage Aux Folles."[5]

Father Trigilio explained that the problem was so bad when he was there that "some of the students and faculty used to get dressed up in leather to go to "the block," Baltimore's equivalent to 42nd Street in Manhattan. Seminarians, sometimes accompanied by faculty members, would do this regularly: "They would meet in the foyer, and then head for the gay bars." The *New York Post* reported in a March 24, 2002, interview of Father Walter: "The Rev. Andrew Walter was tossed out of Baltimore's St. Mary's Seminary five years ago after a psychological evaluation at a church-approved treatment center concluded he was "homophobic" and had a "histrionic personality disorder." Father Walter claimed his traditional view on sexual orientation led to lower grades and other forms of harassment, although it was supposed to be a "celibate" environment, a level playing field for everyone eventually subject to the vow. "I know for a fact guys were protected," Walter said. "Activities and agendas on the part of homosexual guys were protected."[6]

In a clear cut traditional, conservative church one would have the faithful believe that it's the homosexual agenda that breeds the pedophilia syndrome. If those making that argument pointed to the Trenton Diocese, their poster boy would be Father John "Jack" Banko.

When Banko came to Saint Mary of the Lake Church in the early 1970's he was a standout that could not fit in. The priest with the goatee mustache, hot rod car and bell bottom pants did not fit into the conservative rectory and stood in sharp contrast to the man he was replacing, the Reverend William Dunlop.

From the start, Banko was a misplaced misfit that was incapable of carrying on a prolonged adult conversation, delivering a sensible homily or administering to the elderly or sick of the parish. It was not long before Father Everitt discovered the lack of maturity in his new charge and Father Jack was taken off of the daily rotation of priestly obligations, save for Sunday and weekday Mass, funerals and the occasional wedding, but only when he was requested.

The homilies delivered by Banko were in monotone and sometimes fragmented sentences. When he was questioned about the meaning of his words, he balked and became defensive. In the months following Banko's arrival, it was not uncommon to see Father Everitt in the back of the church taking mental notes of Banko's delivery and "rush-job" through the Mass. In a quick journal entry, Everitt noted, "FJB" (Father Jack Banko) "mistakes are made." As later entries are made it became obvious that Father Everitt was not focusing on Banko's slip-ups during the liturgy but rather his actual vocation and homosexual tendencies. Most notable in Father Everitt's journal was the following insert in pencil and long hand:

Jack is a sociopath who is incapable of accepting responsibility for the job he needs to perform. He has a way about him that in a young priest could be seen as charming but in his case it's not and it's getting worse by the day. He leaves (the) rectory early and stays out late. No accounting for his traveling and he would not answer if I asked. He walks past us at dinner without a word and brings nothing to the church. He answers to no one and has formed no nitch in the parish. He identifies with the altar boys and many of them are (more) worldlier in 8th grade then he is in his 20's. If he has a vocation it was missplaced [sic] and he needs a prolonged mission retreat or assignment to figure it all out. All I can do is recommend...(it's a) shame what we are making for priests now....

Due to his insecurity and immaturity, Banko was unable to put in a full business day's work and found his daily escape as "Father Jack" at the recess time of Saint Mary Academy. The parking lot doubled as the playground for the upper grades, and Father Jack would slowly and deliberately drive through the lot/playground with his Dodge Charger smiling, with full cognizance of the attention he was generating with the boys and girls alike. He would park, and in his best James Dean, open his car door, light a cigarette and run his hand through his Beatles-cut hair.

Kids swarmed to the car. It was something "new" to see this hip priest and as time went on, he would let the kids at recess sit in his car. For others he brought cigarettes and promises of alcohol-fueled "retreats" and after-school drives. From her window that overlooked the schoolyard, Sister Harold Phelan, already predisposed to feeling uneasy about Banko because he refused to acknowledge and respect her authority, witnessed this conduct most atypical of a priest. In the early days of January 1974, after Father Jack took Stephen [last name withheld by author upon request] from school early in order to prepare for a Mass that evening, Sister Harold decided it was time to make a phone call to the rectory.

In his journal, Father Everitt noted the initial phone call (or at least the first one he entered in the journal). Indented after the initials "FJB" was, "S Harold concerns from lay-teach (lay teachers) observing inappropriate contact and prolong touchg [sic] on JB part... Picking up altar-boys before (end of school) day and driving to lake (Lake Carasaljo which was adjacent to the SMA property)."

Teacher Doris Kessler was no fool. Outspoken, attractive and political for the time, the Jewish Mrs. Kessler was as close as she could be to the students without overstepping boundaries. She also believed in being candid and not insulating kids from the world that went beyond Catholic dogma. But in 1973, Kessler saw in Jack Banko right away what it took others longer to surmise; Banko was a predator and not only did she convey the same to the administration, but she also went out of her way to let her "boys" know of her suspicions. She had her favorites and this was obvious. She also saw that there was certain gravitation of her favorites to this rebel priest and she took every precaution to make certain that we took every precaution. She'd demand of us, "Don't be alone with him and if you can, just stay away from him totally." The contempt in her voice ("What do you want here?") and in her eyes when passing Jack Banko in the halls was discernible even to the youngest in our school as we single-filed from room to room.

Once while classes shifted, a seventh-grader was talking to Father Jack in the hallway when the bell rang prompting Mrs. Kessler to pull the student away from him and into the classroom slamming the door behind her and leaving the now humiliated priest on the outside looking in. Undeterred, Father Jack opened the door and made no attempt to mask his wounded ego and anger. When met at the door with a curt and almost dismissive, "Yes?" from Mrs. Kessler, Father Jack replied with, "Yes, Father?" and "This is an altar boy issue." Likewise undeterred, and making no effort at hiding her disdain for the priest, Doris Kessler snapped, "It's always altar boy business, isn't it?" The point was made and Jack Banko knew from experience when to retreat and run. He knew the script to this play because it's the fallout plan for a predator - run when the slightest suspicion is raised. As she took her seat, she looked up at Scott Neuner and me sitting directly in front of her and muttered, "One tough Jew. Don't mess with me, got it?" breaking eye contact and stacking papers while regaining her composure within seconds. Then she flashed her beautiful smile that launched a thousand schoolboy crushes and began her lesson plan and Father Jack Banko would have to wait another day to discuss "altar boy issues" with his senior altar boy, Larry D'Oria.

2
Larry D'Oria and Father Jack: A Twisted Manipulation

"How much filth there is in the church, and even among those who, in the priesthood, ought to belong entirely to him. The church often seems like a boat about to sink, a boat taking in water on every side. The soiled garments and face of your church throw us into confusion. Yet it is we ourselves who have soiled them! It is we who betray you time and time again."

-Pope Benedict XVI

No one could predict on June 6, 1960, when Lawrence D'Oria Jr. came into this world how far astray his life would detour from his middle class American upbringing. The second of four children born to Carol and Larry Sr., he had every opportunity that suburbia had to offer. He attended the best schools available, his father having built a successful and well respected pharmacy in Jackson, that still stands today after almost 45 years, preferred by the locals despite the encroachment of bigger drug store chains.

Larry is HIV positive, owing to years of unprotected sex with men in the United States and Europe and needle-fed drug abuse. He offers no excuses for his mannerisms or lifestyle. He doesn't need to; he is happy, spiritual and in the company of good friends. He is also the victim of rape at the hands of one man he loved, one he despised and feared, and one that returned no physical gratification to him whatsoever. All of this started at the age of 13.

I lost track of Larry for 35 years, however I had heard the stories that funnel through the rumor mill of a small town and close-knit Catholic community: "Larry is gay…; " "A priest molested Larry…;"

and, "Larry is dying/dead." All of these are true.

For the past four years I had been wondering *"whatever happened to…"* as I read more and more on the sexual abuse crisis in the Church, particularly with regard to the Diocese of Trenton. I wondered what Larry was doing today, and if the rumors were true about him and Father Jack Banko. After 30-plus years, I got in my car one fall day in 2009 and decided to put my curiosity at rest.

Larry D'Oria Sr. was behind the counter of his pharmacy, head down, hard at work as it had been for the past 40 years. Long retired, he sold the business to his daughter, Laura, and he was now the weekend fill-in. Despite the passing of decades since he last saw me, he greeted me warmly and asked about my family and after a few exchanges I said to him, "I know about what Larry went through and I am going to nail these people." His eyes told a story of guilt, frustration, anger and defeat. All he could muster was, "Bruce, they destroyed my son." I asked him if I could come back and give him a letter to pass onto Larry Jr. and the next week I handed this distraught father the following missive:

Larry,

I don't know if you remember me, but about a month ago I ventured in the pharmacy (where I had not been in 25 years) and saw your dad. Within 3 minutes we were talking about Saint Mary Academy and Saint Mary of the Lake Church. Larry, I had a close-call with John Banko and an encounter in a hotel room with Jerry Brown in the late 1970's. The Diocese would not acknowledge it, let alone discuss it.

As the years went on and the focus on sex abuse among clergy came to light in Boston, Chicago and Louisiana, I began my therapy and my healing – I wasn't alone. I have battled the Diocese and clergy to release the names of the 9 priests that sexually abused children; but through an agreement with the State, the names are sealed due to age or statutes of limitation. My fight has not ended.

I know that you had similar experiences. Your family fought a brave battle when those fights were swept under the Bishops' carpets and the victims were made to feel like the accused. I strongly believe that my research (after 8 years) is complete and it's time to put it all down on paper. Trenton is no different that the larger "more flashy" archdiocese's and our voice needs to be heard.

I'd like your story. I want you to be heard, as I will be. I am outlining the case against Banko and what brought him from Baltimore to Trenton and onto Metuchen. My feeling is that he left a long string of boys from SMA who have not been heard. I'd like you to write your story and the effect it has had on you decades later and allow me to interview you and your family. I hope that you will consider this. My attention will focus as much on the abuse as it will on the cover up from Bishop Ahr through today with Bishop Smith.

Jack Banko will most likely die in prison but if he doesn't, he will live 2 blocks from the grammar school where my kids currently go. You have suffered at the hands of a vile and reprehensible individual and owe nothing to anyone. I have a strong voice in the Diocese and the Central New Jersey area with my website (www.novozinsky.com) and owe it to you to express that voice. I hope (and yes, still pray) that you will join me. We have a voice!

A month later I spoke to Larry and our professional, yet very personal endeavor, began.

The next several chapters tell a tragic story of molestation, violence, and rape, bringing you to a very dark place indeed. But you will also read about love and commitment and a family once torn, now reconnected and rebuilding. These are the worlds and words of Larry D'Oria, which are presented exclusively without editing or commentary. Larry writes as he speaks. He has a flare for the dramatic and at times is difficult to follow. His experiences are as real as they seem unbelievable. He writes from midnight to 8 in the morning and his tire, no doubt from haunting memories as much as physical exhaustion, is evident. Whereas he has free reign on what he writes, as per our agreement he does not go unchallenged.

Larry D' Oria (unedited):

What do I say when asked to write about affairs that went on quite some time ago? Something that would change me forever, in many ways, some subtle, some more pronounced. My innocence and belief in trust were almost irrevocably damaged. I was a warm and trusting boy who would turn into a young man who was unable to trust men. The fall of the Nixon Administration was happening all around us. Watergate and Viet Nam were shown daily on Television. I grew up knowing what the "Body Count" was for the day. A member of the first generation to grow up knowing how many soldiers had died that day on the field in combat. Looking back, it was strange. We rehearsed Bomb Shelter maneuvers at school. The Cold War was fun.

During the Cold War I lived in an area of New Jersey that had many Russians. I had several close friends whose parents were of Russian birth. They were all wonderful people. I often wondered who came up with these stupid ideas that Russians were all bad. We knew the drill of crouching under the desk for safety in case of a nuclear bomb attack from Russia. Like that would have protected us? Right. All of my friends were either Catholic or Jewish.

I was a precocious child. My first historic memory is of JFK's Funeral Broadcast on television. I was rather annoyed that it was interfering with whatever it was that I wanted to be watching on the TV at that time, which no doubt was cartoons or Shari Lewis. It's not my earliest memory, just the first historic one. I remember always getting up in the morning, and checking the one large fish tank my father had, to see if any of the fish had committed Hari Kari during the night. It was the morning fish patrol. I still do that now, except that I'm in charge of my own fish, and of different kinds. My fish are much larger than the fish my father bred, for the most part. It's worlds away from what I remember from early childhood.

When I was four I knew I was somehow, fundamentally, different from the other boys I'd met. If a man visited our home, and he was alone, with no wife or girlfriend, I wanted to leave with him. It wasn't that I didn't love my parents. I simply would have preferred to have left with the man. Whoever he was.

Even as a four year old child I knew that the way I was wired was not going to be acceptable to many people. I figured I'd better break it to my parents slowly and soon. I started with my Mom. I remember specifically asking her on at least three occasions, "But Mom, what if I don't find the right girl?" She always lovingly insisted that it would happen just as it was supposed to, and not to worry about finding the right girl, she was out there, of course. It was simply a matter of meeting her. If I didn't get this through to my Mom, telling Dad was going to be out of the question. The lack of communication was due to my already learned sense of boundaries with the outside world. I already knew they (the world) disapproved of me, or would because I didn't see myself represented anywhere around me in my 4 year old body, so I learned to hide in plain sight, as well as cover my butt. I didn't have a word for what I was, but I'd eventually find one. I didn't like people who asked too many personal questions. I never saw any images I could relate to, so Dick Van Dyke, Paul Lynde and Vincent Price became my idols. I had a sharp witted (read: vicious) tongue and enough well pronounced consonants to challenge the Queen of England.

I didn't like getting dirty. I had a fear that if I wasn't perfect, and got my clothes dirty I wouldn't be loved.

In first grade, at St. Mary Academy, my teacher Sister Simon Robb, always kept an eye out for me. She was my guardian angel. Once when the boys were making fun of me for jumping rope with the girls, she defended me, by telling the group that had gathered, that Cassius Clay, The World Heavyweight Champion in Boxing, jumped rope too, and that they'd better watch out for me, I was going to be a boxer. I knew I was a boy, but that I was different from the others. I never thought of myself as a girl in any way, I didn't want to be a drag queen. I wasn't effeminate. I didn't get into my mother's clothes. I was somewhat affected and a little bit prissy. That was a manifestation of my fear of getting dirty. I had to stay clean, and for the most part I did. One of my nick-names in grammar school was "Lord Fauntleroy". That was not said in an insulting manner either. It was usually used in a loving but teasing way. I was no worse than Tony Randall in "The Odd Couple." Everyone knew me and that was all there was to it. I was just me.

Today, I no longer care about that much. Actually I think I've been making up for lost time. I love to get covered in dirt in the garden, or working outdoors in Florida in the sun, looking like a wet rag when I'm done, or at least some kind of an Indiana Jones going on with me and my machete; a tool that is indispensable in the tropics and the subtropics. Today getting dirty is a reflection of my masculinity. It's butch to work outdoors, conquer the land! I created an Eden from virtual scratch. I control what lives and what dies, sometimes. I am the ruler there, and usually get what I want. Sometimes you just don't get what you want, or deserve no matter what you do…Just like in real life.

I remember being attracted to Catholicism, and most certainly the clergy. What more fun could you have than to live with just men? I knew I was a homosexual one day when I was at the public library and found the word somehow in a psychology book and made sense of it. I'm not completely sure what year that was. There were differing opinions of course. I didn't feel like there was anything wrong with me, but I was sure the rest of the world was wrong in their rejection of me. There were always people who you knew loved you unconditionally, and then there was everyone else. The numbers ratio, of those who loved you unconditionally, and the rest, is of great disparity at that point in time. Stonewall hadn't even happened yet. And besides, I found things supporting homosexuality as something normal and also things that portrayed it as an abomination. I tended to agree with the people who supported the view it was ok to be gay, small wonder! Remember they used to do "Electro Shock Therapy" and "Aversion Therapy" on homosexuals to straighten them out. We don't know how many lives were ruined because of the misuse of the treatments as a "cure" for something I know to be fluid but yet immutable.

When I was 8 I believe that I joined the Altar Boys of St. Mary of the Lake Church in Lakewood, NJ. At that time I joined I was much younger than most of the boys. I loved the pomp and circumstance. I loved the incense, and also the garments. However, my main interest was in the stained glass. We had moved to Central Jersey from North Jersey in 1966. I would dutifully do 7:00 AM Masses during the week, even with some of the early morning drunkards who made up the priests of St. Mary of the Lake. Some reeked of liquor early in the morning. That was not enough of a deterrent to me. I was taken with the mysticism and symbolism of the Catholic Church. I heard the message that "God/Jesus loves you!" I could imagine Jesus loving me as I was, because that was how I was made. I really related to the apostle John, the youngest of them when he has his head on Jesus' chest. And C'mon and become a priest. Being an altar boy was step number one!

The altar boys of St Mary were a colorful lot. I don't remember ever disliking any one of them. Now the priests, that's another story. I remember liking Msgr. Everet , Father Robb, and then Fr. Jack Banko. There were several I didn't like at all i.e. Fr. Eelman (sp) an alcoholic who said the Mass faster than anyone else and consequentially had crowded Masses. They were fast. Also, Fr. Jerry Brown, whom I distrusted and found effeminate, revolting and pitiful from the first moment I met him. He had the personality of a scared possum. At the moment only those gentlemen come to mind.

I believe that Fr Robb was in charge of the altar boys when I began. I remember watching the older boys getting their secondary sex characteristics, like facial hair and body hair sometimes. I was already looking at the older boys and wanting to hang with them. The eventually younger altar boys were of no interest to me. Somewhere along the line I remember becoming "Head Altar Boy". I believe that was when Fr Robb was around. If my memory serves me correctly Jack Banko came to St Mary's as a replacement for Fr Robb. That would seem logical. Jack Banko arrived there some time in 1972.

I had liked Fr Robb. He was a great guy, and he would be missed. I used to talk to him about having a vocation to the religious life. He left the church to marry a woman eventually. Obviously he was straight. Exactly what we actually did as altar boys, other than drink altar wine, set up the altar for Mass and participate in general rituals, be boys etc., is still somewhat vague in my mind. We occasionally went somewhere. Exactly where I don't remember. But they were always kind of informal, compared to school trips or God Forbid the Boy Scouts! I had been to a Boy Scout's meeting. I was bored out of my gourd. Altar Boys had much more fun than Boy Scouts, and we had better clothes too.

I was enthusiastic as a young Catholic boy. I didn't really like girls much, so the idea of becoming a priest seemed a logical choice. I loved God and He loved me, and I loved men. Girls were ok at a distance. What a winning combination. Priesthood here I come!

Of course, when you decide you may have a vocation to the priesthood, the priests and nuns pay a little extra attention to you. I was interested in a possible vocation from as early as nine or ten. No one pushed me that way. It just made sense to me. I was deeply involved in my faith and I had a personal relationship with Jesus. I even wanted to become a missionary and travel to exotic, strange Central and South American Countries, speak foreign languages, save or adopt pagan babies and meet people from everywhere! I wanted to be a missionary, a warrior for Christ wrapped up in "liberation theology" and fabulous vestments by Gianni Versachi. Not to mention I would feed the poor and hungry as well as comfort the sick and dying simultaneously. I delivered the Eucharist to a nursing home on Sundays when I eventually got a license to drive. That was working for Sister Virginia McGary, arguably the teacher who left the largest thumbprint on my life. I really wanted to be a priest, somewhere along the line. But of course I would have to finish High School. During my sophomore, junior and senior years of High School I was a Candidate with the Maryland Province Jesuits. I went on retreats with the Maryland Province Jesuits and found myself out in Reading P.A. I remember being very busy at night, as visitor after visitor would check in on me, or I visit them around the monastery. Somewhere along the line we parted ways. I needed to go 'have more experience' in life matters (translate: girls). I took that as a direct order from God to go out and see the world. But, I was not Jesuit material. They suggested that I'd make a better Franciscan.

I believe that I was in 4th Grade (Sister Yolanda) when I joined the altar boys that would have been in 1969 or so. As I said, I was for a short period of time the youngest. I was a good boy. I was always a peacemaker, not that I never got into a fight. I had a few. However I never started even one of them! Sr. Yolanda was the most socially advanced of the women I had as teachers at SMA. In 4th grade she instilled into us a sense of Social Justice and an interlinked world economy. She was actually teaching 'Liberation Theology' before I believe it really had a name.

Jack Banko entered my life somewhere in 1972. I do remember our first meeting. He made my 11-12 year old heart flutter. He was young, 27, I believe, at the time. I'd had experience with boys my own age, which is pretty normal up to that point, even a few who wound up 'coming out' as gay eventually. But I had yet to have a sexual experience with that obsession of mine, an older man. There were a multitude of older men, some straight, some gay, whom I worshiped and wanted so to emulate. I wanted to be with them and around them. I was smitten with quite a few.

I was also a 13 year old kid, precocious in many ways, already interested in sex. The development of my secondary sex characteristics had begun. I never believed that I was going to hell for masturbating. I will say that I was probably looking for a father figure. My Dad was a workaholic. He didn't know any other way of being. Banko knew I was already gay by the time he first molested me, that made me all the easier to target. I was also socially mature and infinitely presentable. I had looks, manners and smarts. I was already a swimmer with the Central Jersey Aquatic Club. In the summer we worked out swimming sometimes 11 miles a day. We practiced all year round. I had a toned swimmers body, with a tan line. I was physically maturing rapidly and because of so much swimming, as well as farm work, I had a lot more muscle than many of the boys my age. They wanted me to join the wrestling team in HS. That would have been HELL to me. Great! Rolling around humping a bunch of hunky guys! (This is where you put yourself in the opposite situation re: sexuality; If you're a heterosexual male, imagine being set loose in the girls locker room. If you're a woman, I don't know if you'll relate, but just think about it!) Just what I needed, wrestling. No Way!! I would have gotten an erection out on the mat that wouldn't have been an 'accident'. I would never live that one down.

At first when Jack arrived I was already one of the 'senior' Altar boys. He paid a fair amount of attention to me, something I so desperately wanted. I always got the Masses I wanted on the schedule. We would go out for ice cream sometimes. I remember going out to dinner many times with him. He would pick me up from first our home on Mohawk Place, and later our home on Cross Street. He sometimes came in and talked to my parents. We became closer and closer, especially as the time spent alone and together, became more frequent. My parents were leery about him. But I wasn't. He was my buddy. He was 27, and if I must say, at the time he was rather handsome, he had a cool goatee and a really great muscle car, a 1972 Dodge Charger, dark green all over with tinted windows. I really loved going out driving on what I perceived as "our dates".

I remember a trip up to somewhere up near Lake Hopatcong with the altar boys. That was with Jack Banko. I think that trip was the first time I became really aware that a man I knew was interested in me in a sexual way. We had all brought our swim suits and most of the boys got changed and went running off to the lake. For some reason we had our lockers in another part of the locker room. I had worn a Speedo. I was a competitive swimmer, that's what we wore. The inner linings of a men's Speedo swim suit has the jock strap "built in", so you didn't need to wear jock straps competitively. I remember Jack having a boxer type suit and he had his jock strap on as well. We didn't have to shower to get into the lake but I watched him watching me out of the corner of my eye. I was trying to be modest, which was deeply ingrained in me because I didn't want to be getting erections in locker rooms. Fortunately I had my towel too. I made a run for the lake and cold water. Shrinkage, yes. Saved by the bell!

I think some of the guys were perhaps wondering what we were up to. I remember being asked, by one, what was taking us so long. He looked at me kind of funny. I wanted to reply "young love", but I knew he would definitely not understand! Homosexuality was definitely not cool yet. I had yet to hear anyone I knew ever talk about it openly. I remembered hearing about the "Stonewall Riots" in 1969 on the news, and watching "A Star is Born!" for the first time. It was the same weekend as Judy Garland's funeral and all three television networks were doing Judy Garland Memorials of one type or another. I saw a bunch of strange people on the news, the police were inside this bar, *located in Greenwich Village, and people were making a fuss and being arrested, and they were……homosexuals. I started to read the Village Voice, on the slide. Those guys I was looking for weren't that far away from me! They were just in the City. They were "Downtown" where all the lights were bright and everything was wonderful. They had taken themselves "Over the Rainbow" and out of Kansas. I thought it was rough in New Jersey. Only in Lakewood, New Jersey is New York so far away.*

After he'd established close trust with me he began to hug me after Mass on Sunday or when we got back after one of "our dates". I already knew what an erection was, I had my own, and this was no mystery to me. I remember the day exactly that he pressed his full erection into me while hugging me after Mass, alone, in the altar boy's room of the Sacristy. It was Easter Sunday, 1972. He got me all hot and bothered. My hormones were raging out of control. I began to smell like a man at this period in time. I cannot say his advances weren't appreciated by me. They made me a bit nervous; I didn't want to get caught doing the things I knew others didn't approve of. He groped me too that day, almost to orgasm. Also for the first time, I was kissed on the mouth, in the arms of a man I was enthralled with. He also made sure he spoke to me about how "our kind of love" was special and that society was judgmental. Of course I knew not to talk to anyone about it. It had to be kept a secret! We had "to guard our love." They simply "would never understand what we do". I lost three cherries that day and hadn't even taken my clothes off. Man was I excited! I felt rather mature, and of course there was the music in the background and birds chirping, that only played inside my head and young heart. I already was aware of my sexuality at an early age and had come to similar conclusions, as he had said they were. "They" wouldn't understand"; he was correct. "We" had to stick together to protect one another. One small problem, I was twelve years old.

People didn't like Homosexuals then. They hadn't become gay yet! I knew my father would never go for me being gay. That story is an Opera of its own, with a happy ending. I knew most people wouldn't like me if I was gay. I didn't know I was almost like a canary in the coal mine.

After that Easter Sunday, things really heated up between us. He'd call on the phone. We went out to dinner or ice cream more frequently and I fell deeper in 'puppy love' with him. It was around this time that we talked more about how important it was to keep our love a secret because people "wouldn't understand." I cast myself in the role of a star crossed lover, protecting his beloved. Also, it was at this time that he'd decided he could not only trust me, but also count on me, to keep my mouth shut. He knew that I understood that it was not just about him, it was about "us." It was about me too. I was now between a rock and a hard place ethically. I knew society and the official church position on homosexuality was not in my favor.

However I knew that Jesus loved me. If it had been important to Jesus that people NOT be gay he would have said so. Jesus never even mentions the word itself or any euphemisms for it either. You have to go back to the Old Testament to find written statements of laws against what was translated as "homosexuality". If it had been important to Jesus he would have said something, one word at least. Don't you think??? Also, I was quite sure that you couldn't pick and choose what you wanted to believe. You needed to accept or reject all those rules, lock stock and barrel. There were an awful lot of things there in the Old Testament I was sure many people weren't paying any attention to.

From this new found relationship came a sense of urgency. Urgency in my adolescent loins to find out what this was all about, as well his urgency called out to him to hunt, trap and score. My sense of privacy became extreme. I didn't like people asking me too many questions. My lonely, isolated heart was under stress. The first real stress of its life.

One day he told me he had a "beach house" in Surf City on Long Beach Island that he rented every summer for a month or so. He told me he wanted to have me down early when he got the house so we could spend five days there together. I, of course loved the idea. Convincing my parents to let me go was a monumental task. They definitely didn't want me to go. My mother was very suspicious. The last thing she said to me before I left there with Jack was; "If he wants to do anything you don't want him to do, call me, I'll be there in 40 minutes. I love you!" I knew she was "onto" him. I kissed her goodbye and told her not to worry; I said I'd call if there was anything amiss.

We took a few minutes to relax and unwind in his car when we hit the road. I didn't tell him what my mother had said to me just minutes before. In not too long a period we were relaxed and I was off on the vacation of a life time with my boyfriend. I was still nervous. I knew this was my personal *"Summer of '42"*. This was less than one month after my 13th birthday.

We arrived, and as all good Jerseyites know, you need to shop when you get your beach house. So we went shopping. He bought special cake mix to make me a cake and made me his special *"Strawberry triple layer cake,"* with Strawberry preserves in between the layers. We bought other groceries, although I don't remember anything about food from that weekend other than the cake, which was a great way to soften me up. Then of course while the cake was being baked we had to have a drink to celebrate our holiday together. I'll never forget that drink. It was Pimm's Cup # 2. That was a whiskey based liquor. It was from England and ceased to be produced in the 70's or the early 80's. However it was a drink I will never forget.

The first one got me loosened up a bit. He toasted to our friendship and to our being friends for a long time. In the middle of the second drink was when he started to make his move. I was shy, I was a virgin, and I had no experience with a real man, just boys. Now I had hit the big time. I already knew the look in a man's eye when he undresses you with his eyes. It's called lust. It was right in front of me. I felt mature, lightheaded, giddy, independent, adult, as well as nervous, inexperienced and excited. Nervous won out first. I ran off to the bathroom. He finished the cake. I came back from the bathroom in my Speedo and the cake was ready. However it needed to cool. He made me a fresh drink.

He asked me to model the Speedo for him so he could see the

whole suit. Then he asked me to show him some un-tanned skin so he could make a comparison. I pulled down one side an inch or two. That's when he asked me to remove the Speedo. However by this time it was a foregone conclusion to him, and to me, that I was in the bag, just not quite yet. The lion would play with his prey before pouncing. I was still shy and waiting for "it" to eventually happen. He moved in for the score. I was nervous, but getting excited. He reminded me about our 'special love' and that I was 'very special' to him. He led me into the bedroom and laid me out on the bed and so it began. When it was over he'd convinced me I was a "Man" now. He told me that I was very important to him, and that he loved me. A very neat package of lies. I was no longer a virgin, and I hadn't entered High School yet. Talk about a swollen head! Holy Confusion Batman!*

Losing my virginity was not traumatic to me in and of itself. I had absorbed the societal double standard that it was ok for males to go out and sew their wild oats. If girls did that they were whores! If men did that they were "experienced". This was the event that triggered a cataclysmic conflict period between my father and I. I felt that I was old enough to be a man and have sex, and that my father was now fairly insignificant to me, disregarding the fact that he put a roof over my head, food in my stomach and paid my tuition to private schools. We never got along for many years from the date of the loss of my virginity. Obviously, since I was a "Man" now, this changed my thoughts about my Father's authority. We were on equal footing now.

I couldn't tell anyone the truth. It was too dangerous. They couldn't find out because if they did, we were both in trouble. If they found out the truth about Him, they would have to find out about me too. There was no way for me to hide the fact of my own sexuality from whoever found out about what happened between us. If it had been a nightmare for me that would be one thing. However, I spent five days there and hardly put clothes on. That was partially due to the storm that blew in. It was the storm the islanders refer to as the "Storm when the Ocean met the Bay". It was June or July of 1973. I remember looking out the windows during part of the storm, as well as going outside into it while it looked like one continuous body of water. At the same time, deep within me, something changed.

Jack did the cooking and I didn't do much except "play" as I would refer to it today. It was seemingly idyllic. It was my personal Summer of '42. A lot of playing went on those few days. I knew there were other altar boys coming during his stay on LBI. I wasn't jealous though. I figured the others were going to be there in groups. I was probably lied to. I'll never get to the entire truth until one day we (the altar boys from that time) all sit down together and put all the pieces together. After my trip to the beach house on LBI other altar boys started to 'fish around' searching for information. I automatically knew what they were searching for. They were looking for clues about what had gone on between Jack and I at the beach house. I saw Jack a few times after the beach house that summer. However he had overplayed his hand with me.

As the summer ended I started to hear stories, about other people having 'experiences.' Virtually all of us went to school together at St Mary Academy. Most of us would go on to St Joseph High School called Msgr. Donovan HS today. I was somewhat isolated from the other altar boys. I didn't participate in any of their sports, I was a swimmer. I was into singing and playing the piano, and it was already obvious to me that I was the only one of us that was gay at that point, as far as I knew.

After the 'summer house' trip there was one other. We went to spend the night at his mother's house in Trenton. I don't remember the reason we made the trip. His mother was nice, but obviously firmly in denial about her son and his behaviors. We were sleeping in a single bed there. She chose to not notice. She simply had to know, and chose to ignore it. I guess she was protecting her son. I dumped Banko, when I found out he was messing around with other boys. I decided to play the scorned lover. I don't remember who told me what he was up to. I do remember JR, Billy and one of the other altar boys having some discussions with me about it. They never told me that they had been molested. They told me about the partying they had been doing at the beach house, booze and cigarettes. They hinted around that they were suspicious. However it might work out, they were suspicious about me. Was I a homosexual too? They wanted to know If I had been molested. Of course, I said no, I hadn't been molested. I had lost my virginity, but I didn't tell them that. I entered St Joseph HS not a virgin which made me feel mature and experienced. The virgins could wonder what they'd missed. I didn't see myself as someone who'd been a victim. I was never sure why keeping one's virginity intact was a virtue, unless you wanted to be like the Blessed Mother.

Finding out that Jack was 'cheating on me' with other guys really made me feel angry and I felt cheep and betrayed. I thought we were going to be something special! I didn't think of myself as just another 'piece of posterior.' I was special and how dare he not treat me as such. I was livid. I believe it was around this time that Banko got transferred to somewhere in Central Jersey, not Metuchen yet. The Metuchen Diocese didn't exist yet.

After his transfer he'd call if he was going to make a quick visit. This usually consisted of dinner and fooling around in the car. Eventually I heard that he had been spending time with lots of other boys. I just decided I would not speak to him anymore. So if he called I would simply not answer the phone. That was my plan.

I was practicing piano when the phone rang. I never answered the phone while practicing piano. I had my own number and I knew it wasn't for me, so I didn't answer when it rang. Very simple arrangement. One day while I was practicing the piano after dinner, the phone rang. It was Jack Banko, my mother took the call and tried to hand me the phone. I refused and we had an argument about whether or not I was going to answer the phone. I stated simply, but quite agitatedly, that I don't answer phone calls while I am practicing. She handed me the phone and then listened with every fiber of her hearing. I'm sure my father was doing about the same; he said I was being disrespectful to a priest and I was going to answer the phone. 'No son of his' was going to be disrespectful to a priest. 'No Son of his' was going to be gay either. It didn't quite work out that way.

They had never seen me react to Banko like that. The jig was up, I was now officially busted. What could cause such a nice boy to be rude to a priest? I could have thrown Banko under the bus, but that would have been to throw myself under the bus too. Yes I had been molested, but yes, I was also gay myself. I had loved him, even if he did turn out to be a louse. He lied to me and he cheated on me. That was my beef with him; not that he took away my innocence and my virginity. He'd told me I was the only one. I believed him. I was gullible and thirteen and that hurt like hell. I wasn't ready for the whole truth yet. I still figured it put me ahead of most of the other boys. I'd had sex. I wasn't a clueless virgin. I was sophisticated "Man" now. My problems with my Dad reached a crescendo when I was about 16. It had to do with many different things, however the fact that I thought of myself as his equal, after the onset of sexual activity, was the primary reason. Thanks Jack.

3
"After Boston, There is Only Heaven:"
An Examination of the Crisis

"Unfortunately there are priests that aim at becoming bishops, and they succeed. There are bishops who don't speak out because they know they will not be promoted to a higher see, or that it will block their candidacy to the Cardinalate. This type of careerism is one of the greatest ills in the church today. It stops priests and bishops from speaking the truth and induces them into doing only what pleases superiors."

-Carlo Maria Cardinal Marini

      To say that the Catholic Church abuse crisis started in January 2002 in Boston, Massachusetts, is naïve and simply not true. Sexual abuse and the abuse of power in the Church have been around since Adam bit the apple, but never truly outed until the newspaper was delivered on the doorsteps of New England homes the morning of January 6, 2002, when the *Boston Globe* dropped with a veritable thud, delivering a jolt to its readership their morning cups o' Joe couldn't match; Part I of a two-part series that exposed the theretofore veiled sexual abuse of minors by clerics in the Boston Archdiocese. Even worse - not only had the men called to priestly vocations egregiously violated the trust of both God and man, but those in direct line of succession to the Apostles were keeping that secret.

      In the Catholic faith, it is believed that a bishop is a successor to the Twelve Apostles. In Roman Catholic theology, the doctrine of apostolic succession states that Christ gave the full sacramental authority of the Church to the Twelve Apostles in the Sacrament of Holy Orders, making them the first bishops. By entrusting of the Sacrament of Holy Orders to the Twelve Apostles, they were given the authority to transfer the Sacrament of Holy Orders onto others, thereby consecrating more bishops in a line of succession tracing its origin back to the Apostles and Christ himself. This direct succession of bishops from the Apostles to the present day bishops is referred to as apostolic succession, and is reaffirmed in the Nicene Creed with the words, "we believe in one holy and catholic and apostolic church...."[7] - Implicit in the principle of apostolic succession is the understanding that one bishop does not overtly criticize another, and an archbishop should preserve the reputation of his predecessor, particularly if that predecessor is a cardinal.

On January 6, 2002, the holy faithful in the Boston Archdiocese were led by Cardinal Bernard Francis Law, who had no idea what was about to befall his see that day, but had every idea what it was about. The *Globe* bombshell, about a local Boston Archdiocese priest, was called "Church Allowed Abuse by Priest for Years,"[8] but could have readily substituted "Cardinal Law" for the word "Church" in its title. The article revealed that in the early 1980's, when Cardinal Law reassigned Father John Geoghan to another parish in the Boston suburbs, he had done so knowing the priest had, in his previous parish, been accused of molesting seven boys from the same extended family. Cardinal Law and a score of Church officials learned through a series of failed reassignments and disturbing psychiatric evaluations that Father Geoghan was an uncontrollable child molester, amassing over 130 allegations of abuse spanning 30 years. Yet the troubled priest found extraordinary comfort in the Archdiocese elders who offered him their prayers, never their reprobation. Even in 1996 as prosecutors prepared the case against the by then defrocked priest, Cardinal Law soothed, "Yours has been an effective life of ministry, sadly impaired by illness.... God bless you, Jack."[10] Once considered untouchable by the clerics and religious he governed in Boston, Cardinal Bernard Law's tenure in the city was over before Bostonians set out on their commute that frigid January morning.

Born of Irish descent on November 4, 1931, Bernard Francis Law was destined for Boston. The son of a United States flier who would attain the rank of Colonel and move to Torreon, Mexico, to run an airline, Law lived a nomadic childhood. He graduated from the racially diverse Charlotte Amalie High School in St. Thomas, Virgin Islands, where he was elected president of the senior class. A Harvard graduate, he soon discerned a vocation to the priesthood and was ordained in 1961. Law became so involved in civil rights work in Mississippi that his name appeared on a hit list assembled by segregationists. His rise to national prominence began in 1968, when he was appointed to a staff position at the ecumenical office of the United States Conference of Catholic Bishops, allowing him to establish numerous influential contacts with Church leaders throughout the country. He became Bishop in Missouri's Springfield-Cape Girardeau Diocese in 1973, and in 1984 was installed as the Archbishop of Boston. The following year, Law was created Cardinal, a "Prince of the Church," by his Holiness, Pope John Paul II. Cardinal Law was on the "fast track."

Force of personality and the personal regard of the Pope contributed as much to Cardinal Law's influence as his new title, and

"His Eminence" reigned supreme at the top of the very Catholic, and thus very coveted, Boston Archdiocese. Cardinal Law once mused, "After Boston, there is only Heaven," a double entendre recognized readily by those who worked under him; while he undoubtedly loved the city, perhaps above all earthly places, the Cardinal truly acted if he, in governing the Boston Archdiocese, had been endowed with direct authority from "on high" to rule as he, and only he, saw fit. In the Cardinal's favor you were exalted; falling out of favor with Bernard Law was a career-ending tumble. There were no second chances for the latter group, in which Father Geoghan apparently did not belong.

The intrepid *Globe* "Spotlight" investigation team, which followed up with 40+ articles on the breaking scandal, would win the 2003 Pulitzer Prize for meritorious journalism for their work. The citation accompanying the honor read: "Awarded to **The Boston Globe** for its courageous, comprehensive coverage of sexual abuse by priests, an effort that pierced secrecy, stirred local, national and international reaction and produced changes in the Roman Catholic Church." [Emphasis supplied in original].[11] When the *Globe* aimed their sights on Cardinal Law, they had an outraged public on their side. Timing is everything, and for Cardinal Law, it couldn't have been worse; two weeks after the first *Globe* story ran, Father Geoghan was convicted of indecent assault and battery in the 1992 sexual abuse case of a young boy, in what was to be his lone conviction. Effectively, Cardinal Law was done.

By the summer 2002, that Cardinal Law would be removed from the Boston Archdiocese was a given; the only questions remaining for Cardinal Law were how far he would fall, and when? Moreover, could he avoid jail? In late November 2002, a court ordered the Archdiocese to release personnel files of credible accusations against priests and the Archdiocese's role in protecting these men. The Archdiocese's own spokesperson acknowledged that the materials were "horrendous." Dahlia Lithwick of *SLATE* magazine summarized the document production:

Law was not only aware of egregious sexual misconduct among his subordinates but was apparently engaged in elaborate efforts to cover up incident after incident of child rape. To be specific, the Cardinal admitted in a deposition that he knew that the Rev. John Geoghan had raped at least seven boys in 1984 before he approved Geoghan's transfer to another parish where other boys were at risk. Further disclosures revealed that the Rev. Paul Shanley, who at one point was facing trial for 10 counts of child rape and six counts of indecent assault and battery, had been moved from ministry to ministry in what amounted to an attempt to protect him. Law himself lied to a West Coast bishop about Shanley's history and certified in writing that another rapist priest, the Rev. Redmond Raux, had "nothing in his background" to make him "unsuitable to work with children." [12]

When 58 Boston clergy presented the Vatican and the United States Conference of Catholic Bishops a letter/vote of "no confidence," Cardinal Law's fate in the fourth largest diocese in the United States was sealed. The evidence against the Archdiocese was piled too high for him to survive and for the Archdiocese not to pay for it, effectively bankrupting the see with an $85 million dollar settlement. On December 13, 2002, a disgraced Cardinal Law submitted his resignation to Pope

John Paul II, but only after receiving a request signed by the Boston clergy, respectfully urging the same. Cardinal Law stated:

It is my fervent prayer that this action may help the Archdiocese of Boston to experience the healing, reconciliation and unity, which are so desperately needed. To all those who have suffered from my shortcomings and mistakes I both apologize and from them beg forgiveness. The particular circumstances of this time suggest a quiet departure. Please keep me in your prayers.[13]

    A quiet departure *and* a cushy landing. For Cardinal Law, after Boston it was not Heaven, but an enviable close second: Rome after a brief stopover in Maryland.

    Cardinal Law became chaplain to ironically, the Sisters of Mercy of Alma, in Clinton, Maryland, trading stewardship of an archdiocese of 2.1 million Catholics for the company of a few nuns. "I offered and he accepted," said Mother Mary Quentin Sheridan, the Superior General of the Sisters of Mercy of Alma, a 60-member, Michigan-based order devoted to service through teaching, health care and spiritual work. "As Sisters of Mercy, the nuns have taken a vow of service, often working as teachers or health professionals. The sisters living in Maryland include a medical student, a philosophy student, an employee of the Washington Archdiocese, one who works at the National Shrine, and one who is a coordinator for the Council of Mother Superiors." This was all that Mother Sheridan could offer, for it was all that was approved for her to share; the shots were now being called not by the Archdiocese of Boston but rather the Archdiocese of Washington, D.C., then under the rule of Theodore Cardinal McCarrick.

The obscure job seemed intended both to humble him and to remove him from the public eye; though the convent was located in a D.C. suburb, Cardinal Law was rarely seen in that city or Boston during the following year. He did not attend the installation of his successor, Archbishop Sean Patrick O'Malley, in July 2003. But the Cardinal was hardly in seclusion. During those same months, he made several trips to Rome, attending a historic Latin Mass at St. Mary Major as well as a Mass in St. Peter's Square. Then the other shoe dropped: In an act that further shocked the victims and a vast majority of those that comprised the Catholic community of over one billion world-wide, Pope John Paul II brought Cardinal Law to Rome and named him "Archpriest" of St. Mary Major, long considered the most choice and prestigious pastoral appointment within the shadows of Saint Peter's. The wounds were reopening yet again, and on his syndicated radio show, FOX commentator Bill O'Reilly railed:

You may remember that I was a driving force in bringing down the villainous Cardinal Law in Boston, a man who allowed child-molesting priests to run wild. When Law was forced to resign, I was happy. But then the late Pope John Paul II gave him a cushy job in Rome, where Law remains today. If it were up to me, the Cardinal would be in prison.[14]

Unfortunately it was not up to O'Reilly.

In Rome, Cardinal Law sat on a number of conclaves, including, disturbingly, the Pontifical Council for the Family, up until his retirement in November 2011 at the age of 80 after a spectacular fete in his honor. He kept his Cardinal appointment, led a life of Roman royalty, enjoyed a papal apartment, two (nun) staff members and a salary of $12,000 USD a month, spoils symbolic of the Church's failure to grasp the severity of the situation. He was an accepted member of Italian society and performed a Mass at the funeral of his protector, John Paul II, which drew sharp and immediate criticism from the United States media both liberal and conservative alike. At the time, I wrote in the *Asbury Park Press*:

[T]he church has been corrupted by weak, selfish leadership, and "enough" is long overdue. Cardinal Law oversaw the transfer of pedophile priest, Paul Shanley from New England to California. In fact, Shanley is a member of and was a speaker at North American Man-Boy Love Association, (NAMBLA) conferences. Cardinal Law and Church hierarchy members like him are the root cause, not of the sexual abuse acts but certainly the proliferation of the scandal. They are the guilty parties and not the fall guy as some uber-defenders of the Church have asserted. Bernard Law and seven of his Bishops stayed within the guidelines of the misguided and liberal Massachusetts laws and avoided jail. At best, they skirted the law; at worst they aided and abetted rape, kidnap and torture. [15]

When the Massachusetts Attorney General issued his report entitled *Child Sexual Abuse in the Archdiocese of Boston* (July 23, 2003),[16] he criticized Law but did not conclude that Law had tried to evade investigation or break any laws in existence during Law's tenure. Indeed, state child abuse reporting laws, enacted in 1973, were not applicable because they were not expanded to include priests and other church workers until 2002 (in that same year a reckless endangerment statute was also passed criminalizing the reckless failure to take reasonable steps to alleviate child sexual abuse when there is a duty to act). The Attorney General found "overwhelming evidence" that Cardinal Law and his senior management had firsthand knowledge that children had been abused, and determined that the abuse could have been prevented if the Archdiocese itself had adopted a policy of promptly disclosing allegations of child sex abuse to authorities instead of handling it internally and informally and thus, as ineptly, as it did. Even the Archdiocese's post-scandal efforts were deemed lacking, the report noting "no sense of urgency" in attacking the child sexual abuse problem that thrived in an environment of "institutional acceptance." That the Roman Catholic Archdiocese of Boston was a duly registered Massachusetts Corporation, making Archbishop Law essentially Chairman of the Board and Chief Executive Officer, was a fact highlighted by the Attorney General in his analysis; the report was spot-on in its conclusion that this CEO, with a nineteen-year tenure, bore the ultimate responsibility for the cover-up, as would any business CEO in the face of frank corporate mismanagement.

The Catholic Church is in good (or bad) company here. As I immersed myself in this project, my *Sports Illustrated* subscriptions were necessarily set aside for more relevant religious publications. How thrilled I was to have sports briefly back on my reading roster (albeit disgusted by Jo Pa's fall from grace) in David Gibson's *Religion News Service* article, "Is Penn State Like the Catholic Church?" a perspicuous look at how these mega-institutions deal with a scandal:

In whatever their bona fides as religions, Penn State and the Catholic Church are big, self-protective institutions. The cover-up is always as bad (or worse) as the crime, and Penn State leaders feared scandal --

and probably harm to their own reputations -- so much that they didn't think about the welfare of the children. Same with so many bishops....

"The sort of instinct to protect the institution is very similar. And of course, in both cases, it backfires horribly. If your idea was to avoid a scandal, you sure failed," Phil Lawler, a Catholic journalist in Boston, told The Associated Press.....

That is why the public blamed bishops more than the predatory priests, and why so much anger has focused on Paterno rather than on alleged abuser Jerry Sandusky.[17]

In the aftermath of Boston, the Church was forced to reevaluate its dysfunctional institutional culture and take a hard look at the climate that allowed the sexual abuse of children to flourish. In 2002, the United States Conference of Catholic Bishops met in Dallas and approved the *Charter for the Protection of Children and Young People*, affirming commitment to creating a safe environment within the Church for its youth and seeking to salve the badly damaged trust between the Church and its members. The *Charter* created a National Review Board, which was assigned the responsibility to commission a descriptive study, with the full cooperation of the dioceses, of the nature and scope of the problem of sexual abuse of minors by clergy. The National Review Board engaged the John Jay College of Criminal Justice of the City University of New York to conduct two studies analyzing allegations of sexual abuse in Catholic dioceses in the United States, and so the corporate introspection of the Church, with laity assistance, began.

The first study, *The Nature and Scope of Sexual Abuse of Minors by Catholic Priests and Deacons in the United States 1950-2002*,[18] was completed in 2004. While there was abuse prior to 1950, by and large, individual parish record keeping and dioceses records were too poorly maintained to be of value. Based on surveys completed by 97% of the Catholic dioceses in the United States, the study concluded that of 109,694 clergy in the 195 dioceses in the United States, 4392, or 4%, stood accused of sexual abuse against a minor. The number of accusations against these 4% clergymen totaled 6700. The John Jay report found that 81% of the victims were male and more than 75% of all of the victims were over the age of 10.

The findings are only as good as the data provided and in some instances dioceses were less than candid. The data on clerical sex abuse by priests, religious and deacons was self-reported by Catholic dioceses and religious orders. Moreover, only minors were included in the study; the report did not include the sexual abuse of dependent adults such as mentally retarded men and woman or the abuse of power involved when homosexual bishops and cardinals violated their vows and sexually seduced seminarians. Female religious orders were also not surveyed. Despite its flaws, the study did proffer some theories that were widely accepted in peer review, namely, that similar to the general population, child sexual abuse in the Church was committed by priests "close" to the children they abused.

The second, and by far more controversial John Jay study, *The Causes and Contexts of Sexual Abuse of Minors by Catholic Priests and Deacons in the United States 1950-2010*,[19] was released in May 2011. With causality at the heart of this study, it was bound to cause a stir.

Everyone waited with baited breath - was it a "gay" thing?

Researchers found absolutely no correlation between celibacy, homosexual identity and the sexual violation of a minor. Expanding on its 2004 findings, the criminologists concluded that sexual abuse is a crime of opportunity, not of sexual identity, period, and this is consistent with the overwhelming empirical data on the matter, scholarly studies too numerous to mention. Certainly there were homosexually oriented priests who were abusers, just as there were heterosexually oriented abusers. In fact, the John Jay report noted the rise in the number of gay priests from the late 1970's onward actually corresponded with a "decreased incidence of abuse - not an increased incidence of abuse."

This put to rest the "Gay Myth." Or it should have. There have been over 14,000 claims of abuse and the cost to the Church is approaching $3 billion in settlements since 1950. The Church needed someone (or a group of someone's) to hang this on and who better than the homosexuals, a group with whom no love was lost. Only their strategic planning went awry when the professional laity conclusively found that their accusations were proved false by their own $1 million dollar study. The problem is that no matter how laity researchers analyze the data, the church hierarchy will play the "gay card," arguing that if 81% of abuse accusations came from boys, then this must be "a homosexual issue" pervading the walls of the Church. Say this about the Church hierarchy in America: When pinned to a wall they do not fold into the fetal position – they attack. The gay community saw it coming and at first took a wait-and-see approach. Radical websites such as massresistance.com took up the cause of the Church and rallied that this was an indictment on all homosexual activities and the purge of its existence must be holocaustic in execution. Thankfully, it was not.

The Holy Father, who has called homosexuality a threat to the very future of humanity and who in 1986, then known as Cardinal Joseph Ratzinger, coined the infamous phrases "*intrinsically disordered*" and "*an intrinsic moral evil*" to describe homosexuals, knows full well that homosexuality and pedophilia do not go hand in hand. En route to the United States for his 2008 visit, Pope Benedict XVI responded in this enlightened way to a question about the crisis: "I do not wish to talk about homosexuality, but about pedophilia, which is a different thing."

But the Church paid for this study, and at least one finding needed to come out in its favor. The hallmark of pedophilia in the clinical psychiatry world is sexual interest in prepubescent children. One of the more suspicious findings was the report's conclusion that fewer than 5% of the abusive priests were pedophiles; the study inexplicably used the victims' age of *10 or under* as defining prepubescence, finding that 22% of the priests' victims fell in this category. Yet, the *American Psychiatric Association's Diagnostic and Statistical Manual of Mental Disorders* (DSM-IV-TR) classifies a prepubescent child as generally *age 13 or younger*. If the John Jay researchers had used that standard instead of the artificially low standard, the vast majority - 73% - of the abusers' victims *would have been considered prepubescent*. But it sounded good for the Church that they really didn't have that nasty *pedophile* problem!

In any event, there were plenty of teen victims as well, and this data, based on a skewed and seemingly arbitrary 10 years of age standard, minimized them, although I have to acknowledge, so by that token would have the American Psychiatric Association's 13 years of age standard, *the* recognized diagnostic standard. Considering that law enforcement uses the word pedophile generally to describe anyone preying on the *legally underage* (under the age of consent), this, in itself sets the standard, not the Catholic Church.

The John Jay criminologists introduced "ephebophilia," the sexual attraction to *postpubescent* males, as distinct from pedophilia (as if the former is okay). This also worked in the Church's favor in another way; the Catholic League argued that since the boys were post-pubescent, and "most were *only* touched inappropriately" it wasn't pedophilia: "Let's get it straight, they weren't children and they weren't raped."[20] This nuance permitted them to bring it full circle back to, you betcha - it's not pedophilia if the boys are post-pubescent, its homosexuality.

The DSM-IV-TR also doesn't include ephebophilia as a diagnostic category, even though sexual contact with children is explicitly illegal in all jurisdictions in the United States. It's splitting hairs between what shrinks consider psychiatric illness and what cops consider illegal, but I'm getting to my point, I promise. I'm not arguing that an offender's predilection for attraction isn't often ordered on the maturation level of the child (some preferring prepubescent versus post-pubescent victims), but in my mind, its not really clear why abusing a 13 or 14 year-old is *any* different from abusing a 10 or 11 year-old. I am not alone:

Blogger: A reader sends along a link about the [John Jay] report and remarks:

"Forgive me, though, for thinking that the author's objecting to the term 'pedophilia' as "malicious" where 'ephebophilia' is the correct term seems a laugh[t]er. As a daddy to two boys that are 11 and 13, they still seem like children to me if technically they are no longer 'pre-

pubescent.' Get a grip".

Blogger: Yeah. The whole "it's wasn't pedophilia, but ephebophilia" thing seems like the sort of pettifogging distinction without a difference that butt-saving bureaucrats like to make. Let me put it this way: if some priest laid a hand on my 15 year kid, I wouldn't stand there parsing distinctions about pedophile vs. ephebophile. I'd call the cops. I'd also engage in intense interior debate about the morality of beating the living daylights out of the priest who harmed my kid.[21]

I'm not arguing there isn't a sliding scale of disgustingness here, with the barometer measuring from the downright vile (infants, who will appear in chapter 11) to the questionable (how about the day before a child reaches the age of consent?), but, whatever the age, if the child *is underage*, is it not a crime in any case? In the context of our issue, if the religious member has a consensual sexual relationship with an appropriate aged male, then, and only then, can it be called a homosexual relationship or encounter? If the religious member is with an *underage* child, male or female, it is child molestation, the act of a predator violating a child, and that priest is a pedophile.

Pedophilia is not the exclusive domain of priests. If we look at the study's more useful *overall* numbers and not their parsing out of ages, 4% of priests stood accused of sexual abuse against a legally underage minor, a standard that makes absolute sense to me. The significance of this statistic is that the occurrence of child sexual abuse in the Church was found to be no more prevalent in the Church than in other secular institutions, and other studies have come to this same conclusion. This is a critical point; in the public's (mis)perception, pedophilia is rampant in the Catholic Church. That's inaccurate and I will be the first one to stand up for the Church in this regard. This is not exclusively or even mainly a Catholic Church problem. The sexual abuse of children is epidemic in all classes, professions, faiths, ethnic communities and homes around the world. When we refer to the Church's sexual abuse *crisis,* it's not about the numbers, but about the Church's shameful mishandling of the same.

What is abundantly clear is that pedophilia is a question of stunted sexuality, of power, and disordered attraction, *not* of sexual orientation. A related finding of the John Jay study, and one that has been remained virtually unimpeached, is that sexual abuse of a minor is primarily a case of opportunity and that most abusing priests would abuse either gender or any age of child depending on victim availability. Above all, proximity dictates the victim.

In my experience, priests mainly have access to two categories of males. First is the child under 16. This is the youth that is "forced" to go to church with the family on Sundays and holidays. They are the most vulnerable. They are the altar servers and those who are doing CCD service works. The second group is the fatherless male age 15 to 17. These are the boys that are starting to "sleep-in" and not as motivated for participation in Mass or holy days of obligation unless forced by a single mother with that priest's intervention at the home or at the rectory office. The third is the adult male; the "dad" factor. The predator focuses on the first group, the under 16 male, because that is what is most available to him; he is not, by definition, a homosexual. He is attracted to the child's status, not male gender. When the child grows and ages, as with Jack Banko, the attraction is lost and the predator moves on.

Try as they may, the bishops were not going to be able to pin this on "the homosexuals." They needed a blame shift, and quick. Rejecting the conflation of homosexuality with pedophilia and any cause and effect relationship, the report posited that sexual abuse occurred because emotionally immature priests were entering seminaries poorly prepared and unmonitored, and under stress, landed amid the social and sexual upheaval of the 1960's and 1970's, causing a spike of abuse cases during that time period; media criticism of the report dubbed it the "Woodstock" defense. The timing of events in my Prologue, set smack dab in the early 70's, would seem to support it, but *no one* was buying the "decade made me do it"; no, it wasn't the culture *outside* that was the problem, but the culture *inside*. Arthur Jones hit the nail squarely on the head in his NCR (National Catholic Reporter) column on May 18, 2011, when he named arrogant clericalism as the culture that in many ways created the offending clerics and allowed the abuse to flourish:

The time lag in reporting is not to be explained by sociological data and its interpretation but by the emotional and psychological impact of sexual violation on a young victim. Most take a decade or more to find the security and courage to come forward.

....

Those who see the main conclusions from the Executive Summary as support for the bishops' blame shifting tactics are probably right. Yet these conclusions are only a part of the whole story and in some ways they are of minor relevance. The finding that the majority of cases occurred in the 1960's and 1970's can be quickly challenged. It is more accurate to say that the majority of cases reported in the post 2002 period involved abuse that took place in the period from the sixties to the eighties. Its way off base to assume that the majority of incidents of abuse happened during this period. Fr. Gerard Fitzgerald founded the

Paraclete community in 1947 to provide help to priests with problems. From the beginning he was treating priests with psycho-sexual issues and in a letter to a bishop he said that 3 out of every 10 priests admitted were there because they had sexually molested minors.

Fr. Gerald wrote that letter in 1964. Unfortunately, it is difficult if not impossible to do a study of abuse victims between the 30's and the 50's but Fr. Gerald's information leaves no doubt that sexual abuse by priests was a significant phenomenon long before the free-wheeling 60's and 70's. The one constant that was present throughout the entire period from before the 60's to the turn of the millennium has been the cover-up by the bishops and the disgraceful treatment of victims. The John Jay researchers were commissioned by the bishops to look into the reasons why priests molested and violated minors. They were not asked to figure out why this molestation was allowed to happen. That would have been deadly for the bishops and they knew it.

Nevertheless the researchers could not avoid the blatant role played by the hierarchy. In this regard, the report should not be written off as largely either irrelevant or enabling of the bishops' never-ending campaign to avoid facing their responsibility square on.

....

Rather than go to such great lengths to try to exonerate themselves the bishops could have done what they should have done....try, at least, to begin to understand the profound depth of the spiritual wounds inflicted on these many men and women, once innocent and trusting boys and girls. [22]

"Secrecy, non-accountability, and the arrogance of exclusivity"[23] have long been the hallmarks of the Catholic Church, so why would anyone think they would so readily offer a sincere and public *mea culpa* in the wake of the crisis? They wouldn't and didn't. Cardinal Mahoney of Los Angeles, in a statement of mind-boggling ignorance or deep denial, or both, said to the press that he "thought that the cause of pedophilia could be cured by transferring a priest to a new environment where the temptation would be less." Cardinal Law alternately blamed the bishops in his see that managed priest personnel and at the same time insisted that he was "*doing what was in the best interest of the Church*" (which he repeated 11 times in his 2002 deposition). How can they apologize to victims and their families when they do not consider themselves at fault?

For this reason, bishops, by and large, have been rehearsing the lines and edicts from Rome in both letter form and public statements to tow the company line and stay out of trouble with the public. It is rare nowadays that a clergy member giving a statement speaks in anything but "talking points" replete with the buzz words "zero tolerance" and "accountability" and polite expressions of sympathy for the victims.

But old habits diehard. As recently as April 2010, the Vatican's second-highest authority said the sex scandals haunting the Roman Catholic Church were linked to homosexuality and not celibacy among priests. Tarcisio Cardinal Bertone, the Vatican's Secretary of State, made these comments during a news conference in Chile, where one of the Church's highest-profile pedophile cases involved a priest having sex with young *girls*: "Many psychologists and psychiatrists have demonstrated that there is no relation between celibacy and pedophilia. But many others have demonstrated, I have been told recently, that there is a relation between homosexuality and pedophilia. That is true. That is the problem."

The rebuke was swift. Rolando Jimenez, president of the Movement for Homosexual Integration and Liberation in Chile, released a press statement that read in part: "Neither Bertone nor the Vatican has the moral authority to give lessons on sexuality." On its face it would appear that the Vatican Secretary of State did not receive his pre-visit brief on the exact nature of the scandal in Chile when he made his extraneous and embarrassing comments there.

The Chilean church scandal involved a pedophile priest who victimized young girls, including a teenager who became pregnant. At the time, the Archbishop of the Chilean capital in Santiago received multiple complaints about Father Jose Andres Aguirre from families concerned for their daughters. But the priest - known to his parishioners as Father Tato - continued serving at a number of Catholic girls' schools in the city. Later the Church sent Aguirre out of Chile twice amid abuse allegations. He was eventually sentenced to 12 years in prison for abusing 10 teenage girls.

One of the girls, identified as "Paula," said that she and the priest started to have sex when she was 16 and that it lasted until she was 20. She told the Chilean newspaper *La Nacion*: "I thought it wasn't that bad to have sex with him because when I told priests about it at confession they just told me to pray and that was it. They knew, and some of them guessed that it was Father Tato. But everyone looked the other way. No one corrected or helped me."

She said one of the priests she confessed to about her sex with Aguirre was Bishop Francisco Jose Cox, who himself was facing allegations of pedophilia. Cox had been bishop in La Serena, in northern

Chile, for seven years when he was removed in 1997 amid rumors that he was a pedophile. In true Church fashion, he was transferred to Santiago, then Rome, then Colombia, and finally Germany. Cox volunteered to be confined to a convent in Colombia to continue "praying to God for his pardon for the errors he has made."

Closer to home "trainee" priests are being grilled about their sexual experiences under tough procedures designed to stamp out child abuse in the Roman Catholic Church: "Every job interview has its awkward moments, but in recent years, the standard interview for men seeking a life in the Roman Catholic priesthood has made the awkward moment a requirement."[24] They are being confronted with a list of shockingly intimate questions from psychologists paid by Church officials in the United States to try to weed out men who they think could go on to commit sexual assaults. The questions include: "When did you last have sex?;" "What kind of sexual experiences have you had?;" "Do you like pornography?;" "Do you like children?;" and, "Do you like children more than you like people your own age?" Men training to be priests are also asked detailed questions about their sexual fantasies, the reasons why any earlier romantic relationships failed and the nature of their relationships with their parents. They are being routinely tested for HIV/AIDS and made to sit for exams to test for such conditions as depression, paranoia and "gender confusion'" in an attempt to search for clues about possible deficiencies in their character.

But why? The John Jay researchers had concluded that it was *not possible* for the Church, or for anyone, to identify abusive priests in advance. Priests who abused minors have no particular psychological characteristics, developmental histories, or mood disorders that distinguished them from priests who had not abused, they found.

The questions form part of a grueling screening process introduced by the U.S. bishops following the 2002 revelations. Vatican guidance indicated that men who actively "practice homosexuality" should be barred. But seminary rectors were left to interpret the meaning of less obvious instructions to reject candidates who showed "profoundly deep-rooted homosexual tendencies, or support the so-called gay culture." Though some Catholics still saw room in that language for admitting celibate gay men, in 2008, the Vatican instructed the bishops that they had to go even further than simply establishing that the candidate was capable of living a chaste life. The Vatican insisted that the sexual orientation of the candidate must be determined as well - a demand that was interpreted as a witch-hunt for trainees who were homosexuals. Critics said the orders - which apply solely to American dioceses and which were detailed in the *New York Times*, disqualify gay men from entering the vocation.

Whether he is celibate or not, the person who views himself as a 'homosexual person,' rather than as a person called to be a spiritual father — that person should not be a priest," said Father Toups, of the [U.S.] bishops' conference.

Beyond his assertion that "I know it when I see it," no one interviewed for this article was able to describe exactly how screeners or seminary directors determine whether someone's sexual orientation defines him. Some Catholics have expressed fear that such vagueness leads to bias and arbitrariness. Others call it a distraction from the more important objective of finding good, emotionally healthy priests.

"A criterion like this may not ensure that you are getting the best candidates," said Mark D. Jordan, the R. R. Niebuhr professor at Harvard Divinity School, who has studied homosexuality in the Catholic priesthood. "Though it might get you people who lie or who are so confused they do not really know who they are."

"And not the least irony here," he added, "is that these new regulations are being enforced in many cases by seminary directors who are themselves gay."

It is difficult to gauge reaction to the recent guidelines among seminary students and gay priests. Priests who once defended the work of gay men in the priesthood have become reluctant to speak publicly.

"It is impossible for them to come forward in this atmosphere," said Marianne Duddy-Burke, the executive director of DIGNITY USA, an advocacy group for gay, lesbian, bisexual and transgender Catholics. "The bishops have scapegoated gay priests because gays are still an acceptable scapegoat in this society, particularly among weekly churchgoers."[25]

Seminary rectors had previously estimated that nearly half of U.S. seminarians were homosexuals by orientation. Some had reported flourishing gay subcultures among trainees and claimed the priesthood had become a largely "gay profession." By the admission and estimation of its own clerics, to purge the Church of gay priests and seminarians would be to put an end to the priesthood today.

This is why the destructive stereotype of the "homosexual priest pedophile" lives on. There are almost no "public" models of healthy, mature, loving, celibate homosexual priests to rebut that misperception because they are rightfully worried about how their parishioners would react, fearful of reprisals and punishment within the Church, and mostly, of being painted a pedophile. Certainly a lot of obstacles to overcome, but maybe the power to change perceptions lies within their court? "Not long ago an experienced priest with many years in a parish ministry told me that the only way that things will change is when all the homosexual priests decide one Sunday to 'come out' to their parishes.... [S]omething of that nature could serve as a significant 'teaching moment' for the entire church."[26] With the Church still unapologetically unaccepting of homosexuality and still trying to link the same with the child sexual abuse scandal, sadly, a triumphant Mass revelation by proud, chaste homosexual priests remains the stuff of PG-13 feel good movies with a happy end.

Depending on the order or diocese a religious order is associated with, there are two to three vows professed: celibacy, poverty and obedience. Most dioceses and orders do not require the vow of poverty and there are many that are liberal with the amount of money that can be made by a member through speaking engagements, book writing and professional services such as teaching or administration of educational institutions. (Then) Father David M. O'Connell, as president of The Catholic University of America, in Washington, D.C., had an annual salary of $370,000, of which he kept a modest sum for living expenses and donated the vast percentage (some 80%) back to his order. O'Connell is now the Bishop of the Diocese of Trenton.

Celibacy is the key. A *heterosexual* male entering the seminary can (and will) explore his sexuality. In most cases it's encouraged by to do so in order to have the candidate comfortable with his vocational calling. Once final vows are professed and ordination has taken place, the expectation for the new priest is celibacy. If he is a good priest, and celibate, he conforms to his vocation and remains obedient.

I'll now repeat the same paragraph and substitute a single word.

Celibacy is the key. A *homosexual* male entering the seminary can (and will) explore his sexuality. In most cases it's encouraged to do so in order to have the candidate comfortable with his vocational calling. Once final vows are professed and ordination has taken place, the expectation for the new priest is celibacy. If he is a good priest, and celibate, he conforms to his vocation and remains obedient.

Married priests will not be introduced in this lifetime; Pope John Paul II saw to that with his elevation of cardinals in his own image and theology. But that's not at issue here. Heterosexuality does not a good priest make and pedophiles are not looking for a relationship. What the Church and its seminaries need to do is to employ a pre-screening and ongoing screening process for its potential candidates putting aside the gay-factor. The same premise holds true that no one wants a flamboyantly gay priest in their midst anymore than anyone wants Father leering at their mom, sister, wife or daughter – it's called "boundaries" and if those guidelines cannot be followed in the seminary, an evaluation needs to be made as to the candidate's suitability for the Vow of Holy Orders.

Keying in on the celibacy or "married clergy" arguments is both a centuries old theological argument; it's a contemporary discussion as well, and a discussion that the hierarchy will not have. Should a priest marry and have children, a diocese would be forced to pay insurances it does not have today on top of increased salaries and living expenses (a family would not be expected to reside in a rectory that doubles as an office). Extended health insurances as well as absorbing educational costs and post-mortem benefits to a spouse are not practical nor is it even open to debate. Dioceses and parishes simply do not have the resources needed to increase the overhead to support thousands of dependents that would result if clergy married.

This begs the case to come full-circle, what can be done to "weed out" undesirable candidates from the priesthood and who actually will dictate what constitutes "undesirable?" A caring, loving man of faith and compassion that enters the priesthood, who happens to be homosexual does not equate into sexual deviant, no more than a man who is being ordained in Nevada, where prostitution is legal, that visits a brothel the night before his ordination. The vow is celibacy; it's what is done *after* ordination that the candidate must answer to. If a vow is broken, *this* is where the bishop must intervene. If no civil law is broken, it should be handled internally. Simply put, if a law is broke, the Church is not suited for, or capable of, carrying out civil justice. They've proven this, time and time again.

The rigorous vetting process for seminary candidates is not all that rigorous. It's relaxed due to the empty seminaries. The candidates must be screened and monitored. The seminary is a school and a probationary juncture in the life and times of a man considering the priesthood. That said, the same man being ordained in Nevada that habitually visits a brothel needs to be observed in order to determine if he is capable of "breaking the habit" or if his internal vow is likely to be broken. The same applies to the caring, loving man of faith and compassion that enters the priesthood, who happens to be homosexual. The question is not whether his social leanings are rebellious and contradictory to the established Church teaching (be it right or wrong), but whether he is capable of simply shutting off his sexual urges with men to keep his internal vow. The bishops need not concern themselves with numbers and be more cognizant of each individual's traits and talents to the service of Christ to which they are called.

4
"No Honey, Just Bad People"

"Mr. Novozinsky, are you writing a book about bad priests?"
"No honey, just bad people."

-Fifth-grader Audrey Cook and me on my 50th birthday

Between 1974 and 1978 I attended the Divine Word Seminary in Bordentown, New Jersey. I left there after my junior year. I was dismissed because of what was deemed a "lack of vocation."

I agreed.

Shockingly enough, my mother and stepfather agreed as well. I felt a sense of sadness because Divine Word was not a hardcore seminary. The academics were not rigorous, the school dress code was not enforced and torn jeans would often be the uniform of the day at this former estate of Napoleon Bonaparte's brother. Divine Word Seminary was also a haven for underprivileged, inner-city boys from the west side of Philadelphia. It became a word-of-mouth, affordable, Catholic education and no one was turned away for admission. I forged many friendships there and grew a strong sense of faith, though I never suspected that there was an overall sexual abuse crisis looming in the sacristies of the Churches. No one talked about it and I don't think anyone realized that such a thing ever occurred.

I studied for a diocese post. Upon admission to Divine Word Seminary you declared a vocation of missionary to the Society of Divine Word, the Montfort Missionaries or the Diocese of Trenton (Marist came later in my junior year). Before I left Saint Mary Academy for my freshmen year, Monsignor George Everitt advised me to declare for the Diocese because "we look out for each other." He was right. We had about a dozen "diocese boys" at Divine Word at any given time. We were a small and close-knit group that did watch out for each other. I am still looking out for them today.

The Bishop of the Trenton Diocese at the time was His Excellency, George W Ahr. Having been named to the post by Pope Pius XII in 1950, he visited Divine Word from time-to-time and he was quite engaging. Bishop Ahr was a student of pomp and enjoyed all of the perks of office, and he impressed upon his seminarians the significance of regalia and rolling out the red carpet for him; acts of fealty were encouraged. Not a particularly tall man of stature, he was rarely seen without full garb, e.g., robes and cape, which only added to his bulk. Festooned in black and purple, he was an imposing figure to a 13 year-old boy. One other thing that struck me about Bishop Ahr - of all his seminarians, His Excellency knew my name from the first time I saw him on the Bordentown campus in September 1974. What I didn't know was why.

At our first chance meeting, the Bishop was coming out of the Main House where the religious lived opposite of our dorm, with Divine Word's Father Paul Conner trailing behind him. A former college football player, Father Conner turned down his draft call from the Green Bay Packers for a life of service to Christ as a Divine Word missionary. He was principal of the Divine Word Seminary from 1969 to 1976 and was quickly becoming a father figure to me and I wanted to be noticed by him. Strong, tall, and built like he could still take a three-point stance on a gridiron – he was the first priest that heard me say "fuck" and let me get away with it and he was about to hear me say it again.

I had served Mass for Bishop Ahr at Saint Mary of the Lake and was certainly no stranger to him or rendered speechless in awe of his presence. Still the same, he was my bishop. "Mister Novozinsky," the Bishop said, stopping me and my newfound friends in our tracks, "How's Lakewood?" Puzzled and taking his extended hand to kiss his ring, I replied, "Jackson. You mean Jackson." Bishop Ahr knew his seminarians and his diocese. "You live in Jackson and for some reason, your mother belonged to Saint Mary which is Lakewood." Now it was my turn to cock my head in a confused way. "We belong there, Bishop Ahr. Still do." The Bishop then proceeded to set me straight as he, unbeknownst to me, did to my mother and my stepfather some two months earlier: "Son, your stepfather is a divorced man." With this said, the Bishop turned and ducked into his car. My face saving reply to my friends within earshot was, "Fuck him. He doesn't know me." As Father Connor closed the car door for the Bishop, in the same motion he laid his arm around me and gave me a knowing and supportive look.

In the summer of 1974, his Excellency was made aware of Father Jack Banko. This was not the first time that "Father Jack" had come to his attention. As far back as 1972, the prefect for Saint Mary Seminary and University in Baltimore had warned the Trenton Diocese of Banko's the sexual tendencies. The problem was that those tendencies were difficult to pin down.

Jack Banko was popular with women and men alike. Every time a complaint or suspicion was brought to the attention of the rector of the school he attended as a seminarian, it seemed that Banko would counter the same-sex allegations with a "normal" relationship. Apparently in the late 1960's to early 1970's, "bisexual" was not deemed a logical explanation.

The Bishop became aware first-hand of Jack Banko's exploits not long after Banko arrived at Saint Mary of the Lake. The proper chain of command from parent to pastor to bishop was followed, but as expected in the pre-email days, replies were not forthcoming for weeks or even a few months. However, frustration began to show when five and six and then seven months passed and not a word came out of the Bishop's mansion in Trenton, all the while the boys were still being subjected to Banko and his sexually abusive advances. As much as he tried, Father Everitt could not be in all places at all times and his associate pastor, Father Jerry Brown, was not a suitable caretaker for the slippery Banko. At the end of the 1974 school year, the parents of Saint Mary Academy had their fill and went directly to Sister Harold Phelan, who, having harbored concerns about Banko for a while, placed a phone call without hesitation to the rectory of Saint Mary of the Lake. Sister made it perfectly clear to the pastor that Jack Banko was no longer to be on the grounds of the school and was no longer to ask for early dismissal for any boy because such permission would not be granted. Not only that, but no child would be released at normal dismissal time to Jack Banko, and if necessary, the police would be called. Sister's network extended to the Lakewood Police Department, and in this circumstance she would not be reluctant to call them - they would respond to her instantly. Every story needs a hero.

Father Everitt, however, did not know how to respond to Sister Harold, who, according to someone in the room that day, was very adamant. She reduced arguably one of the most influential if not powerful priests in the state to a lectured seventh grade boy. The demands were non-negotiable and Father realized that, but he was not prepared for what came next.

Sister Harold had four families in her office that day and also a name of another family who she would be talking to later that day, and each with a "Banko story" to tell. Jack Banko was sexually assaulting her students and their sons and she was not at all satisfied with how this situation was being addressed. She demanded answers and expected those answers to come from Trenton. Sister insisted that Father set up a meeting with the Bishop and the parents of her school immediately.

In his journal, Father noted (this time in long hand which leads me to believe it was entered after the phone call ended and he had time to digest what had just happened): "Call from Sr Harold today was distressful and will require much time and influence with the bishop. Jack Banko needs help and guidance that is beyond my expert(ise). Sister finds him reckless and a homosexual. She didn't come out and say it, but it's implied. Trenton needs to be called soon and this issue resolved without bringing it to light." Father had easy to decipher handwriting (and even shorthand), but most journal entries were jotted notes. As he realized the gravity of the situation, his notes became more and more concise and the "jots" were now beginning to tell a story. The wise priest had been around long enough to realize that this was not going to end pleasantly. But it had to end.

In the pecking order of the local clerical chain-of-command, the bishops are at the top, then the monsignors, followed by the priests. The religious brothers are a step and a half to the rear of priests; they wear the same clerical garb but are without question the "worker-bees." A religious brother is a member of a Catholic religious institute who commits himself to following Christ in consecrated life of the Church, usually by the vows of poverty, celibacy and obedience. A layman (in the sense of not being ordained), he usually lives in a religious community and works in a ministry that suits his talents and gifts. A brother, for the most part, employs a trade; he might be a doctor, nurse, teacher, electrician, cook, lawyer, technician, parish minister or artist. He tries to live his faith by being a "brother" to others. Brothers are members of a variety of religious communities, such as the Divine Word ("SVD" translated *Societas Verbi Divini*), which may be contemplative, monastic, or apostolic in character. Some religious institutes are comprised only of brothers; others are so-called "mixed" communities that are made up of brothers and clerics (priests and seminarians). When a school of a religious order is in need of teachers, they look to within and place affiliated brothers and nuns in those positions. This way they are covered by existing insurance and salary, however paltry it may be. This was certainly the case at Divine Word Seminary.

When he came to the Divine Word Seminary in September of 1976, the nation's bi-centennial year, Tony Conti was a quiet and reserved young man. He was given to long walks and enjoyed the outside – he was most at home in the solitude that the acres upon acres of grounds that the Bordentown campus had to offer.

His was not a happy home. His intense parents had high expectations for their son, and had gone as far as they could with the raising of a young teen. It was time to have someone else get them through the formative years. Tony was just another of those boys that filtered in and would filter out no closer to the taking of vows in formal service to God or more aware of the Catholic faith then a local school girl at nearby Notre Dame High School.

Tony had friends, but mostly stood alone and certainly didn't stand out. He came to Bordentown as a freshman at age 13, weighing less than 100 pounds, and by June of that same school year, he was anally raped, drugged and threatened by Brother Deo Gratias, SVD. The worst part of this tragedy is that no one seemed to notice or care.

Tony was observant. He had street-smarts from the city of Trenton, where his father was a State Police forensic expert. He seemed to grasp, faster than most, where trouble was and where to stay away from, and he recognized trouble in Brother Gary Craanen, SVD:

Brother Gary, I believe he was some sort of dean and teacher. When he manned the main office at the end of the school building near the entrance to the dorms, when one on one in his office he was very touchy-feely with 13-16 year old boys, especially the younger 13 and 14 year olds, my self 13 at the time. When I was in full length jeans or shorts his hands would always manage to get to my legs and he would rub them up and down it what today I realize was fondling, it made me feel very uncomfortable. I did see other students leave his office after being in a closed door situation and a number of them had tears, or were on the verge of crying. I remember "Pete" as one of these kids who did not seem to enjoy being in Gary's presence. But as a dean when one is summoned to his office you had to go as a student, and many times a conversation could justify closed doors legitimately, but why were students crying when they left his office. As a young teen the last thing you wanted to let your peers see is you crying, after all this was high school.

True to his instinct, Tony avoided Brother Gary Craanen. But Divine Word Seminary wasn't very large and there weren't many places to hide when you were prey. Brother Gary Craanen might not have exerted himself upon Tony, but it was only a matter of time before another missionary did.

Brother Gary Craanen was a big bear of a man. He was born and raised in Wisconsin and had more than a slight resemblance to a Norwegian hunter. With red hair and full hanging beard, the voice he projected in song caused townspeople to stand still from walking outside the chapel just to listen. He was at the time no nonsense. He had his favorites and if you fell on his wayside you stayed there. There was little room for error with Brother Gary - he taught religion and he was the vice-principal and dean of discipline. I kept my distance. I'd only go to his office if absolutely necessary.

That was not the only reason I avoided Brother Gary. Brother Gary would not allow anyone in his inner-circle that was not invited. To garner this invitation one had to be loyal and this meant drinking with the brother on weekends when most others went home. This was largely a harmless activity in the 1970's but being under the "supervision" of a priest or a brother, it had to stay secret. One day the secret slipped.

I stayed one weekend and a drinking party ensued. I was not sure that I was "invited" and I didn't press the issue. I was a freshman and part of my desire to be at a boarding school was to escape the daily alcohol-infused routine that was my home. The dorms at Divine Word featured a long row of military barrack-like formations where the freshmen and sophomores slept on the top floor and cubical formation for the upper classman, downstairs. The vice-principals (Brother Gary and Father Walter Miller) had rooms in the dorm with the students, but were separated by doors. On this night, Father Miller was away on parish duty leaving Brother Gary on weekend dorm duty. All this meant is that he would be responsible for making sure that no one broke in or out of the dorms and little else.

With less than six freshmen and sophomores staying over the weekend, the dorms were essentially vacant. My bed was outside Brother Gary's room, separated that night by three vacant beds, those of my friends Jay Lee, Henry Link and Bill Sellnow, who were all gone for the weekend. I won't pretend to know what time I heard the stirring and to be honest, I don't think it was all that late but the lights were out and the dorm was still. Brother Gary's keys arrived before he did. The ominous jingle of that endless ring of keys reminded me of Marley's ghost visiting Scrooge on Christmas Eve. Obviously drunk and accompanied by the eternal cloud that follows a chain smoker, Brother Gary, who was puffing away, was not alone. Interestingly enough, this was what earned him the nickname (used by him to this day) of "Puff." He had a sophomore student with him, and they were heading towards the vice-principal's room. Once inside, the lock clicked and the student and the brother were alone. From the vantage point of the door jam, the light in the room never went on but the stereo played classical music. My curiosity gave way to fear. I was not naïve and I knew that the combination of alcohol and late night opportunity were combustible. I wasn't alone though. Tom, one of the juniors, came up to the floor because he smelled cigarettes; smoking for the underclassmen was forbidden and one of the rare rules enforced. When he came up to me I told him what had just transpired and he gave me a knowing and disgusted look. He had seen it before and told me to get my stuff; I was going to stay in the upperclassman dorm that night. Now fully awake at this point, I asked Tom if Brother Gary was gay and he replied that he "was something" and that it's best not to be in the vicinity when he was drunk. Though never spoken of, my suspicions concerning Brother Gary were confirmed. He was gay and he was interested in the boys that he was in charge of at the seminary. I told my mother and stepfather who didn't seem to have any interest in pursuing it once they were satisfied I was not harmed. My stepfather muttered in disgust, "Banko." He left it at that and walked away.

My mother was the person that Sister Harold had to call the day she spoke with Father Everitt. To one of the parents in the office, when the call was made, it was assumed that I, too, was a victim of Father Jack's as well. I wasn't, of course, having been saved that October morning by JR. I was a favorite of Sister and she called me to her office from my classroom. "Bruce, I want to ask you something and I want you to know that there are no 'special secrets' and you need to be open and honest with me." I loved Sister and it was made even easier that I also respected her. She didn't mince words: "Did Father Banko ever say anything sexual to you, touch you, try to touch you or anyone you know?" I confessed to the events of October 18, 1973, but made it clear that JR stood in the way of us. She asked if he hurt me that day or made any attempt to persuade me to be alone with him since that October morning and I told her that he hadn't. She asked me if I knew of anyone that had and I told her that they were all rumors, yet she still wanted the names. I was able to give her two names and she said to another adult in the room at the time that those parents were in her office when she called Father at Saint Mary of the Lake.

Father Everitt made an appointment to see Bishop Ahr and all the parents who were present in Sister Harold's office that day. It was the summer, and Father made it clear that there would be no second meeting. If the parents had a story to tell the Bishop, this was the only day and this would be the only opportunity.

Father's journal picks it up from there: "… [F]amilies (names withheld) came to the meeting. All four from SMA and Lake Church. Three boys are altar boys. Novozin name given but did not attend under the bishop's order (mother widowed and stepfather divorced)."

Each family was to wait to be seen individually by the Bishop in the foyer and Father Everitt was the first in his Excellency's massive office. The Bishop was setting the tone for the meeting; Father's journal read: "Bishop in full garb, not to be confused with a parish priest." It was his meeting, his home, his diocese, and his priest. When it was time to see the first family, Father was instructed to remain outside the office with the other waiting families and pray with the boys; a brilliant defusal strategy since it was natural that the parents would join in prayer, thus disarming the anger that would naturally be directed towards the Bishop that summer morning. He also instructed Father that no conversation was to ensue after each meeting. Prayer was to be constant and small talk used to keep the subject of what was being discussed at bay. Father Everitt did as he was told.

Family by family was ushered into the Bishop's office. A journal entry expressed Father Everitt's relief that each family was dressed "to the occasion" in suits, ties and appropriate dresses. The parents sat and the boys were instructed to remain standing. The Bishop listened to each boy as they "told on" Father Jack. Parents were asked to allow their boys to speak without interruption. There was to be no coaching or leading. If their son left out any important detail of his story, it must not have been relevant. This made each boy nervous. They were speaking to a powerful man about being molested by a priest in front of their parents.

All the boys cried and the mothers did as well as they recounted in confessional-like detail the opportunities Father Jack gave them with trips to the shore, beer and rum with RC cola, money and other gifts. Each was told that he had plans for them and they could always depend on him for spending money and company anywhere they wanted to go. Some told of touching and fondling. No one pressed them for more information than what they offered; to do so would open the door from the touching and fondling to the actual rape by a priest of a schoolboy. Indeed, each boy was told by Father Jack that they were special to him and that no one would understand their love if they found out so it was best to keep it to themselves. As each child finished, they received the Bishop's blessing and were told that they were not to repeat this conversation to the others or to Father and "the sisters at the school." There were no ultimatums and no threats, just the Bishop, their Bishop, instructing them how this was going to work.

According to the journal entries from Father Everitt, no family left once they were done with the individual meetings. They remained until each family finished with the Bishop. Father grew increasingly "concerned" with any "meeting comparison" that may go on after explicit instructions were given to each family and to him to remain silent. He didn't have to wait long for his fears to be realized. Outside of the Bishop's mansion in the Berkley Hills section of Trenton, the boys went one way, as the parents remained talking. One parent was asked about the Novozinsky's and was told by another that "Connie (my mother) is not considered the Bishop's problem" because she was married to a divorced man. *This* is how Bishop Ahr knew my name on the grounds of Divine Word Seminary.

Peter (last name withheld) was a year behind me at Divine Word Seminary. His father was a single parent that raised Peter and put him in the local seminary. Peter was outgoing, boyish in looks and made fast friends with just about anyone he came in contact with. In the limited extra-curricular activities that Divine Word had to offer, Peter was a mainstay in them all. He played basketball, showered and then went to choir rehearsal. He dressed like most of us, but had an ever-present bandana hanging out of his rear pocket and a taste for corduroy pants twelve months out of the year. His likable persona made him a mark for homosexual advances and solicitation at Divine Word. Peter was solicited twice during his time there, once by a student and once by Brother Gary. Both instances were off-campus, both in the middle of the night. The very act of soliciting a minor is a crime, and Gary Craanen committed it not once, but at least twice, as would be confirmed years later.

John "Jay" Lee was my best friend at Divine Word. We drank together, hung out together, took virtually the same classes together, and looked out for each other all the time. Whereas it took the administration a full three years to figure out I didn't have the wherewithal for a commitment to the priesthood, it took them about twenty minutes to have Jay figured out. But they let us stay, amongst others, because we were classified as "Payers" to the administration office at Divine Word.

"Payers" is faculty lounge slang for someone whose family pays the full tuition at Divine Word. It was policy at the time that no one with the inability to pay could be turned down for admission or dismissed from school once in. This is where the inner-city families played the system for a free (or next to nothing) Catholic education that was a world away from the streets of Philadelphia or Brooklyn. Payers made up for those who couldn't or simply wouldn't. The Lee family and the Novozinsky family were Payers. If a discipline or academic issue came up, the first thing identified was the status of tuition. If the student was a Payer, generally they would be afforded the maximum rope allowed and then some before they were hung. It was truly rare when a Payer was dismissed from the school.

Case-in-point. The summer between my freshman and sophomore years, I developed my body by free-lifting heavy weights and on testosterone overload, an attitude that included being a racist, a bully and a thief. When I came back to Divine Word for my sophomore year, I was a cocky asshole. I had a favorite target and his name was Albert Livingston, who was a year junior to me. Albert was black and had a demeanor that rubbed me the wrong way. He was a city boy but which city, I can't recall. To me, he was "nigger" or "boy." One day, Albert struck back – he had his fill and he let me have it square on the cheekbone with a closed fist. I'd like to say that this had a made-for-TV ending and I got up, brushed it off and made a friend for life, but that was not the case. I went after Albert, tackled him and before I knew it, was being torn away by Father David Striet. Father pulled me off Albert and in one fell-motion, I punched Father flush to the ear. In two years, I had gone from altar boy to assaulting a priest. There was no fall out, no punishment and no (justified) excommunication. I went on my way and things didn't change in my attitude or my ways. I was drinking more and more and stealing. As long as I stayed on the grounds of Divine Word, I was virtually untouchable, and I had no idea why.

    Bruce Springsteen has a song on his *Greetings from Asbury Park* album called "Lost in the Flood." Leaving chapel one day, I sang an inappropriate verse from the song that blatantly smears our Blessed Mother. A teacher heard it and reported it. Nothing. In what should have been the final straw, I went into Bordentown on a Friday night and stole beer with three of the inner-city students from Philadelphia and one from New York. We were caught by the police and returned to the Seminary grounds. Not taking any chances, I got the names of each priest that sat on the Dismissal Board and went to their confessional to negate any opportunity that they could "vote" at my dismissal hearing at the end of the year when those with discipline issues faced the potential of being asked not to return to the Seminary the following school year. When each abstained as the vote call was made, they knew the "fix was in." The Sacrament of Reconciliation worked to my advantage and I was able to return for my junior year by a skin-of your-teeth vote of three (stay), two (dismiss) and three (abstain). Within ten minutes of my reprieve, I learned that I was nowhere clear of the woods and a tree was about to fall on my head. This smart ass punk was about to meet one bad ass priest.

In my freshman year, we took a bus trip to the Bronx, New York, to attend the ordination of Eric Vargas. Eric was a former seminarian at Bordentown and he asked that we all attend. Father Paul Connor was at the driver seat of the bus and as we left we stalled causing a car to bang into us. The three occupants sprang from the car and aggressively came towards the bus as Father left his seat telling everyone not to move. As he exited the bus, the three noticed he was a priest and told him he was "lucky;" without missing a beat, Father Connor tore his roman collar from his shirt and continued moving purposefully towards the trio as they fled back to their damaged car and sped off.

The dormitory door opened with such rage and force that it kicked back and hit Father Paul Connor in the face, cutting his lower lip. According to those who witnessed it, he didn't even flinch. This time he continued purposefully towards me, yelling my name, his footsteps coming closer and closer to my bed area. Before I could react, Father had what was left of my shirt-sleeve in his hand and me hanging in an awkward position, the collar of my shirt (or what was left of it) tearing into my neck. "Want to punch a priest? Punch me you little asshole. Call me a nigger. You think we're a bunch of fucking idiots. Come on tough guy; call me a nigger – now. Hit me. Walk into my confessional. You got away with it this time, but if you spit on the sidewalk, I'll rub your face in it and kick your ass all the way back to Jackson and I don't care much fucking tuition your parents pay."

Father Connor dropped me to the ground and I didn't move until he left the building. The last thing Father Paul Connor said was "real tough man." When I finally started to slowly get up, I realized that the blood on my face was not mine, but from Father's cut lip. My shirt was torn, my neck red, my eyes streaming tears, and my ego bruised. No one made any effort to help me and I didn't want to face anyone. It was the last day of school and I was going home. It was ironic but as I sat on my bed waiting to be picked up I realized that I did everything to stay in a place where I didn't want to be and the only guy I wanted to be like just beat me up.

Jay Lee was also a minor when Brother Gary Craanen solicited him for oral sex – twice by his telling. Some 35 years earlier, he told me about it and in January of 2011, I remembered the details. My research was ongoing and the memories of Divine Word flooded back to me. I contacted Jay and Peter the next day through a social network site that both were on. Peter told me that if not for Gary Craanen he would have been a priest today – he said it and I truly believed that he meant it. Today with a wife and children, he still felt a loss for the vocation that went unfulfilled. If a man can look at his wife and children and say to another person that he still feels a vocation, there stands a true man of God.

Peter said that Craanen tried to come into his bed the night before they drove to a seaside cookout and that he told him, "No." Peter had enough and abandoned Divine Word that year. He finished up his high school years at McCorristin High School in Trenton, but his past stayed lockstep with him; on his first day of school at McCorristin, as he turned the corner in the main hallway, Peter came face-to-face with the new religion/music teacher – former Brother, now Mister Gary Craanen. They never spoke. Gary Craanen left the Society of the Divine Word, taught at McCorristin for a short stay, and then distanced himself from his East Coast victims; he was moving back to Wisconsin.

I set out to find and confront the predator once known as Brother Gary. The Internet allowed me to do this without much effort. What I found out shook me to the core.

Not at Divine Word for even a month, Tony was introduced to Brother Deo Gratias, a timid, foreign religious Brother. Gratias was not a teacher. He was more of a helper, a gofer at the Seminary. No one fully realized his role. He didn't seem to possess any direct skill-sets, no ambition, and carried little to no personality that set him apart. He was an enigma to most, an annoyance to some, especially the faculty, for not observing the rules about faculty/student interactions.

Gratias and Tony were brought together at the Thursday night faculty dinners when the staff mingled in with the students and ate one meal a week with them. The friendship formed over the shared interest of coins. Gratias would invite Tony to his room in an isolated part of the Main House that housed the religious staff. It was also here that Tony took his first drink, offered by Gratias. Drugs would be next and then fondling. It took less than one month for Brother Deo Gratias to rape Tony from behind by forcing his penis into the boy who had passed out on the bed, in a house filled with priests and other religious. Tony said to me, almost as a validation for his memory serving him correctly, that he remembers the wine, St. Michael's Special, made in the Divine Word house in Conesus, New York.

The wine shortly turned to Jack Daniels, then to drugs, to numb him to whatever may happen to him in that room with the brother. As Gratias felt the boy succumbing to his advances and satisfying his vulgar sickness, his timid demeanor turned threatening, and he warned Tony never to tell anyone. He said he would spread rumors to the staff and students that Tony was supplying drugs from Trenton to students and that he, Tony, came onto him. Although Tony was given a generous scholarship, his parents still had to scrape and save and live bare bones to allow him to attend Divine Word, so the guilt was enormous not to disappoint them and the brother's threat, albeit based on lies, would destroy them. Their son was an addict and it was not even Christmas of his freshman year.

The abuse lasted three years – the scars remained with Tony a lifetime. This is why he reached out to me in October 2011. Tony was weak in the mid-1970's; I was weaker. Tony was being abused and violated; I was merely a bully that would have had no sympathy for him. Ironic how 40 years later we could be stronger together.

Tony told me that the Divine Word order moved Gratias out of Bordentown and sent him to places without schools. He kept tabs on Gratias as the anger and the alcohol brewed inside of him. The missionary order sent him around the country and then for some reason he was exiled to Mexico City. Tony, for reasons known only to him, visited him a couple of times at other Divine Word locations, making the excuse that he was visiting other clergy he knew from his seminary days; he had a burning curiosity to keep tabs on this vile person. Regardless of not being associated with schools, Deo Gratias always seemed to have young boys around him. Whenever Tony showed up, he knew he would be certain to find boys around Deo, and each and every time this was the case.

The last time Tony saw Gratias was in 1990 when he traveled to a suburb of Mexico City called Coyacoan. There he confronted his tormentor to no avail - denial runs deep in a predator and this foreigner was a hardcore child molester who had erected a strong wall against anyone that accused him. While in Mexico, Tony saw that Deo Gratias had an entourage of boys ranging from ages 12 to 18; as rector of the Divine Word missionary house, he had full control of everything. These boys were constantly running in and out of the rector's bed room at all times of the day, and one night Tony concluded that those in the Divine Word had to know what Gratias was doing to some extent, as they were on top of moving him from location to location.

Finally, after 20 years had passed since being raped by Gratias, Tony decided to inform some priests that were still at Divine Word since the 1970's - Father Raymond Lennon and Father Martin Padovani. Tony's choice of confidants were not random; Ray Lennon was Principal when Tony was there in 1977, and Martin Padovani is a well-known marriage counselor and author of many books on relationships. Both would have been aware if any formal charges had been levied against Deo Gratias while in Bordentown. Both assured Tony on that September day in 2001 that they would personally deal with this situation. According to Tony, Father Lennon broke down in tears.

Ten years later, and after the death of Deo Gratias in 2009, nothing had been done. No one called Tony to express any remorse, only Martin Padovani offered any professional help. In a letter to me, Tony wrote, "they never did anything for him (Deo) they just conveniently hid the problems."

Still, to this day, Tony remains hopeful in Father Raymond Lennon and rightfully so. Father Lennon is a good and sincere man. In the years since I have seen him, his fatherly embrace has transformed into a grandfatherly love for his former students and Tony said that he seemed genuine when he claimed to not be aware of what was going on at his school. Tony has been sober for three years now. He is successful in business but has never been able to reconcile his sexuality and has never had a single relationship with a woman or man. He considers himself gay and attributes this to the rape and violations he endured from 1976 to 1978 – during his formative years of puberty, he never had anything else to compare that physical contact to. He said to me in closing that the more he got sober the more memories he recalled from his teen years. He said he almost wants to (but won't) drink again to stop this pain, his life having been devastated by alcohol for over 28 years after that first drink in a secluded room in the rector's house on the campus of Divine Word Seminary in Bordentown, New Jersey.

Bishop Ahr gave Father Everitt explicit instructions: "Never allow this to happen again." Street smart and a true veteran of diocese politics, Father assumed that the meeting had touched the Bishop, even appalled him, and it was left to him as the pastor, to remedy the issue. Father John Banko had to go. But go where? As was the standard operating procedure for the Diocese then and for decades to come, Father Jack, like other "misguided" priests, was headed to a rehabilitation facility or for a transfer. He was young and energetic and it was believed that a predator priest could be rehabilitated. Father Everitt began his inquiries and did not tell Father Banko about the meeting with the Bishop. Unbeknownst to the pastor, Banko was vacationing at the New Jersey shore with an altar boy as the meeting with their Bishop was taking place. When Bishop Ahr found out a week later that Father Everitt's plan was to transfer or rehabilitate Jack Banko, he immediately called the pastor asking what business it was of his to make such a bold move. Father didn't back down to his boss and told him that he was "taking care of the issue so that it never happened again." A week later, he was advised in a letter from the Bishop that the "it" he "never" wanted to happen again was referring to "attention starved" parents coming to meet with him; Bishop Ahr didn't want Father George Everitt to allow parents from his parish to speak to him about Jack Banko ever again.

From: Bruce Novozinsky January 9, 2011 at 7:28 p.m. to Gary Craanen
I think we need to talk.

***

From: Gary Craanen January 9, 2011 at 8:39 p.m. to Bruce Novozinsky
Hi Bruce,
It has been a long time since we've last seen each other. What do we need to talk about? What made you get in touch with me? I'm glad that you did. I really have not heard from anyone. Gary

***

From: Bruce Novozinsky January 9, 2011 at 9:11 p.m. to Gary Craanen

Gary,

I have spent the last several years researching a book I am writing on sexual abuse within the Diocese of Trenton and the cover-up of abusers by Bishops Ahr thru Smith.

Recently while looking into issues in our seminaries I have started to receive emails and stories from people from DWS. Allegations against staff in Bordentown have been made and I find them credible. I am reaching out to anyone from that time frame for comment. I am putting my book on hold for the time being to substantiate these claims or refute them because of the people involved.

Do you care to comment?

***

From: Gary Craanen January 9, 2011 at 9:29 p.m. to Bruce Novozinsky
I really think I would need more information. This is a very difficult area and people lives are at stake. I don't think I can break these that may have been told to me in confidence.
Garu [sic]

From: Bruce Novozinsky January 10, 2011 at 1:17 p.m. to Gary Craanen
Gary,
I'm afraid that it's not a question of who confided in you. You are among the names that are being mentioned.
BN

***

From: Gary Craanen January 10 at 6:23 p.m. to Bruce Novozinsky
Bruce,
It's difficult to respond at all because you have placed me in a catch-22. No matter how I answer, I'll be found guilty. If I say yes then you can have a field day. If I say no, you'll call me a liar and it is just a cover-up. You already mentioned in your last e-mail that you find the allegations credible. So, there is no answer that I can give.

***

So began my 24-hour exchange of emails through Facebook with Gary Craanen. It had been almost 35 years since we last saw each other, but suddenly he was keeping me up nights. Things were not adding up about Craanen. I certainly believed Jay Lee and Peter. Jay was now a Detective in Annapolis, Maryland, with the juvenile sex crimes division. My first obstacle was convincing Jay to come forward and, at first, that was not easy. Jay had never told his family or his wife about Craanen, and it took a few months of emails between myself and Jay to convince the detective that personally and professionally, he needed to come forward.

"Racine, Wisconsin is a city with a diverse population of 80,000 people that value family, hard work, education, the arts, and the Green Bay Packers, although not necessarily in that order," quips the city's website. With quaint farmlands and villages clustered minutes outside the city, Racine hits the sweet spot between city life and "Smalltown, USA," attracting residents for life. It's a town embracing all the simple best of the Midwest, where catching a really big fish will make the evening news, where your morning cup of coffee is accompanied by a Danish "Kringle" instead of a Dunkin Donut, and where once and a while matchmaking still happens the sweet old-fashioned way.

As it apparently did in 1981. The community of Saint Catherine's High School in Racine, sure liked a good love story:

"... In August, 1981, S. Carol Wester, principal, asked Sue to mentor a new faculty member, Gary Craanen, a former SVD who had been employed by Green Bay Premontre (now Notre Dame), to "take care of him." Very soon, seeing the complementary nature of their personalities, matchmakers began emerging from the wood-work. S. Agnes Schaaf (Dominica) asked Sue if she would mind if she prayed that they "find each other." Fr. Slosar laid odds on a romantic attachment for Sue and Gary. After working on several school projects together, their relationship blossomed and by Christmas of that year, they were engaged. In the fall of 1982, their SCHS "family" actively participated in their very joyful wedding. The Art Department teachers contributed to the wedding with Betty Sargent "Sarge", serving as matron of honor, Dave Hietpas, designing their chalice and Carol Preston, making their rings. Joe Grauwels served as best man. At the wedding, S. Carol Wester said, "When I asked you to take care of Gary, I didn't expect that it would be for the rest of your lives!"[27]

To say I was floored was an understatement. The former Divine Word missionary, Brother Gary Craanen was married. But I found out more; the former Divine Word missionary Gary Craanan was teaching at a Catholic high school and involved in Big Brothers and Big Sisters. Then I found out much more; the former Divine Word missionary was now a "daddy," having adopted children since his marriage.

What I have learned since researching this book is that there are three types of claims; 1) the crackpot; 2) the credible; and 3) the claim that mentions names but remains unsigned. For claims 1 and 3, I simply refer the letter/email writer or phone caller to their local prosecutor's office. For the claimant that I find credible, I assist as I did in this matter. I contacted the Diocese of Trenton and Monsignor Joseph Rosie on January 9, 2011:

From: bruce novozinsky <bnovozinsky@me.com>
Date: January 9, 2011 7:38:15 PM EST
To: jrosie@dioceseoftrenton.org
Subject: URGENT: Credible claim of sexual abuse within the Diocese of Trenton

Monsignor Rosie,
It is no secret that I am well into the research and writing on a book that traces the history of the sexual abuse crisis within the Diocese of Trenton from Bishop's Ahr through Bishop Smith. The progress of this project that is over six years in the making is documented on my website www.novozinsky.org.

My research has brought many, many letters and emails on a daily basis into me; most I look into and some are just too outrageous that I dismiss or send an email back to the individual pointing them in the direction to their local Diocese.

I attended Divine Word Seminary in Bordentown from 1975 thru 1978. I have now received claims of abuse from students that were there during that time involving a religious there. I looked into it of course because of my relationship with the accusers and my association with the accused and affiliation Society of the Divine Word. I find these claims credible and what you need to explore is the fact that the accused is still in an active ministry (and I believe in a school) within the Trenton Diocese.

One of the accusers is a detective in Maryland for a juvenile sexual abuse division.

Bruce Novozinsky

    I was sitting in the conference room at the Diocese of Trenton 23 hours later and laid out my case against Gary Craanen. The Diocese took the claims seriously and Monsignor Rosie notified the Burlington County Prosecutor's Office who contacted me and opened a file as an active investigation with the help of Peter and Detective John Lee.

    The next step was to inform the Society of Divine Word administration. I did so by email to Father Raymond Lennon, the same priest that Tony Conti poured out his soul to but who apparently never did anything to forward the allegations. I needed to emphasize the significance to him; these were credible accusations and he needed to be diligent in cooperating with the investigation and retrieving the records that were about to be asked for by the Burlington County Assistant Prosecutor in charge of the case, Michael Sperry, and the assigned detective, Michael Troso.

The Divine Word missionaries have been relatively unscathed by the abuse crisis though there have been some claims and convictions against members of the order. It was now time for the student to become the teacher and advise my former principal that if he were asked for information, he needed to be candid. On February 13, 2011, I wrote:

From: bruce novozinsky <bnovozinsky@me.com>
Date: February 13, 2011 11:21:38 AM EST
To: Ray Lennon
Subject: [Blank]

Father,

I assume that you have been advised not to meet with me and that's okay. I am sending you the email I sent to Gary Craanen. I have also spoke to John Shuster who is opening a file on him with the Wisconsin SNAP. I spoke at length with Father Don Ehr as well.

I am pursuing this to the legal limits that I am able to. If other names come up (and I expect one other one will) I will be doing the same there as well.

Father, I say this out of respect for you for the guidance you gave me years ago. I have been doing my research for 4 solid years now and have been a student of the abuse crisis for ten years; those following up on these claims are the real-deal and do not play around. If the Society has anything to share concerning any individual, get out in front of it.

I hope one day to see you again.

By this time, Father Lennon had been in contact with his superiors, who advised him in no uncertain terms that he was not to speak with me on this matter. Prosecutors and even dioceses are more and more relaxing statutes of limitation but religious orders are still holding onto these until every avenue is exhausted. Divine Word had further instructed anyone involved in any questioning about Gary Craanen to refer to him as "Mister" and not "Brother" or "former Brother."

Since January 10, 2011, at 6:23 p.m., I have not heard from Craanen. He blocked me from viewing his Facebook site, so I reached out to him one more time, this time using his school email address, through which I advised him:

From: bruce novozinsky <bnovozinsky@me.com>
Date: February 10, 2011 9:26:03 PM EST
To: gary craanen
Subject: [Blank]

Gary,

By now you are undoubtedly concerned - I noticed that you shut down your FB profile. The last time we exchanged Facebook messages *you gave a very unconvincing non-denial, denial to accusations made against you by three former DWS students. I can assure you that I am looking into each and every one thoroughly. Each accusation is (e)signed and as I am obligated to notify my diocesan representative as well as the local prosecutors office. I believe in due process and fully knowing hat you never have to answer to me, if there is anything you care to say, I'll listen.*

I have received a great deal of accusations across my desk. Some are credible, most are not. When I discovered the three accusations levied against you it struck a cord that I could not shake. Those coming forward were friends from a long time ago and had no reason to trust or confide in me; they looked at the research I am doing, the book I am writing and they were detailed in their encounters.

As I started looking into your life since Divine Word (my wife had you as a teacher in McCorristin) the more concerned I got. I won't sugar-coat this; I believe those that have come forward. I know you have adopted children and I know that you are (were) involved with Big Brothers / Big Sisters and that you open your home to foreign students. If these allegations are true, this is very alarming to me.

You do not have to answer to me - I'm nobody. You may also never have to answer to the allegations that have come forward, but I do believe that one of two things will occur first, you will one day be discovered or 2) you will answer to God.

To date, I have not received a reply from Craanen, nor do I expect to. I continued corresponding with Peter and with Detective Jay Lee of the Annapolis Police Department, the latter who dedicated his life to vigorously defending those that suffer abuse, as he did at the hands of Gary Craanen.

From: bruce novozinsky [mailto:bnovozinsky@me.com]
Date: Sunday, March 20, 2011 4:24 PM
To: P; John Lee
Subject: Craanen

I have been doggedly pursuing Gary Craanen. He has blocked me from emails and Facebook, but I am not letting up. I don't know the details from each of your incidents, but I can tell you this: I am confident that you have a civil case against him (and Divine Word) - let me explain. The statutes of limitations are three years. However, if the individual being accused of solicitation or physical abuse moves out of the state of New Jersey the statutes of limitations are suspended. It's as if time freezes. Men, I can't tell anyone what to do; I can't advise or encourage but in my research it would be remiss of me if I didn't pass this on to you. You have a case and you have the right. Bruce

Here is the reply I received from Detective John Lee:

Bruce, Thanks for the idea. We each will handle our days at DWS in our own way. As you know I am an "in your face" relentless child abuse detective and FBI Task Force Officer. I fight for kids every day. Perhaps that's my way of making right my past, who knows? I have given countless hours of thought and prayer to Gary Craanen and my experiences with him. My choice is to do nothing that hurts the good name of DWS. I credit DWS with making me the man I am today. Gary Craanen didn't fit into the SVD lifestyle and left the society. Bruce, I know there are lots of reasons to do just what you are suggesting but my choice is not to. Please let me deal with this in my own way. You have helped me to talk about it and open up about it. My choice now is to do nothing that hurts DWS in any way. I Love ya brother and respect the path you have chosen, please respect mine. Jay Lee

I was furious.

My communication with Jay Lee ended. But who was I to force the issue? Was it my story or his story to tell? Did I own the haunting memories, or did he? Months went by and my draft of this chapter was well underway. Then, on December 29, 2011, I received the following email from Detective John Lee on his departmental email:

From: John Lee
Subject: [Blank]
Date: December 29, 2011 12:48:56 PM EST
To: Bruce Novozinsky

Here is what I came up with. If you need more let me know. This is what happened to me. Feel free to use it of publish it or put it on your blog or whatever you like. Feel free to use my name.

Here are my recollections of Brother Gary Craanen at Divine Word Seminary in Bordentown. I am terrible with dates and even years.

I know I attended DWS for three years starting with 9th grade. So I attended DWS 1975-76, 1976-77 and 1977-78. I chose to not return to DWS my senior year. Brother Gary Craanen became the Vice Principal/Dean of the school I believe my sophomore year. He was the center of student life and activity at DWS. He had an office on the first floor of the school building at the end closest to the dormitory. Brother Gary appeared to be a happy guy. He had a loud laugh, which could often be heard, down the hall. Gary was a touchy feely guy who liked to violate your space when talking to him. He liked to put his hand on you when he talked. When he got close, the odor of cigarette breath was often evident. He was grossly obese and clearly never exercised.

    I never respected Brother Gary as an authority figure, mentor and teacher. He was one who wanted to listen to my concerns and always made time to talk with me or other students. I found it odd he would often shut the door when talking to students. He would often shut the door when we spoke. His desk chair was positioned so it was easy for his to lean over and get close when talking. He would often put his hand on my leg when we talked. He hand was in a position on my upper leg that was clearly uncomfortable. I found this a bit odd, yet the thought never crossed my mind it could be anything sinister. After all he was Brother Gary. If something similar happened today I would call it assault. He was clergy and this was the 1970's. They could do no wrong. There came a time when Gary Craanen was invited to my home in Cranford, NJ, for dinner. I am sure he was invited by my mother, a devoutly religious woman who felt it her duty to feed the good Brother Gary and any other man of the cloth. He enjoyed a good dinner with the family. We sat around the table and talked for a long time after dinner.

As the night wore on it became obvious Brother Gary was in no hurry to leave. It got later and later and he didn't leave. At some point my mother suggested he spend the night and return to Bordentown in the morning.

My bedroom was on the second floor of the small cape cod home. It had two twin beds. At some point Brother Gary and I went upstairs and went to bed. As I was lying in my bed turned with my head toward the wall and away from Brother Gary. I heard him say "Jay are you awake?" I ignored the voice and then heard "I want to suck you." I ignored Brother Gary again. I heard him say one more time "let me suck you." I remained still and didn't say anything I was so scared. I heard Brother Gary move around a bit and eventually go into the bathroom. I fell off to sleep. I woke up in the morning feeling terrible. Did this really happen? Why would Brother Gary say such a thing? Did I dream what he said? If I did dream what he said then what kind of sicko dreams of oral sex with a man of the cloth? I knew deep down I didn't dream any of this!

There came a time when Brother Gary moved out of the DWS main house and moved to an apartment in Bordentown. We were told he was "just taking a little bit of time off." At some point (I know it was cold out), Gary invited me over to his apartment. I remember we went out for dinner (I don't remember where). After dinner he offered to go to the liquor store and buy some beer for us to have back at his apartment. I thought to myself, how cool is this? Brother Gary is buying me beer. I remember going back to the apartment, which was somewhere very near DWS. I remember it being a long set of steps when you walk in the front door and at the top of the steps was the kitchen. The home had little furniture. I remember having beers and talking for hours. Eventually it was time for bed. I remember sleeping on the floor in the room near the kitchen. Once again in my sleep I hear Brother Gary say "Jay are you awake?" Was this a dream again? No it was not. I was wide-awake in an instant. He repeated "Jay, are you awake" he then said "come on, suck me off. I will suck you off." He said a bit louder "Jay wake up." I made believe I was asleep. I didn't know what else to do. I opened my eyes slightly to see the obese Brother Gary standing over me naked and masturbating. He had his eyes closed and was saying over and over "come on suck me." I was paralyzed with fear. Brother Gary stopped a short time later and disappeared into another room. I stayed away from him since that day. I no longer have trust in the clergy or the church. I often sit in Mass and wonder if the priest who is on the altar is like Brother Gary. I am learning later in life through best DWS friend Bruce that I was not the only one and others had it much worse than I did! Feel free to use this story any way you like. It is the truth.

Signed,
JOHN R LEE JR (JAY)
Det. John R. Lee
Criminal Investigations Section
Major Crimes Unit

Within hours, this entire chapter was turned over to the Archdiocese of Milwaukee and the President of Saint Catherine's High School, Christopher Olley.

The Reverend Jerry Brown came to Saint Mary of the Lake in the mid-1970's a priest with a history of untreated mental illness, refusal of medications and psychiatric assistance, and sexual abuse with minors. He was an alcoholic and a gambler who frequented Monmouth Park with a hefty bankroll from his two aunts, Helen and Ruth, who lived in the shore town of Point Pleasant. He had a tendency for attracting the wrong type of attention. Once at a breakfast hosted by a local retirement community he referred to the possibility of a black bishop as "another nigger in Trenton." The story made the *Asbury Park Press* and Monsignor Everitt knew that his problems were large.

Brown was effeminate and vivacious. He had the trust of elderly women within the parish, knew how to work the "coffee clutch," would bring lavish gifts to parishioner's homes when invited for dinner, and insisted on picking up the check if dining out with others. According to my research, Brown never made what is commonly known as "the house call," where a priest gains the trust of the family and offers to say prayers or "tuck in" their child for bed without the parents nearby. Jerry Brown was too smart for that. He had the financial resources to distance the abuse he inflicted on his victims and would take them on group camping trips and excursions to the seminaries of Connecticut and Montreal. Parents never had to worry about paying for their sons when Father Brown was around; his standard response was, "Helen and Ruth are paying."

His aunts' beach house served as a "safe house" for Brown's overnight abuse excursions, which he generally reserved for his youngest victims. After gaining the trust of the parents and the child, Brown would propose a day at the shore, adding that he had to get back at a certain time to conduct Mass on Sunday. He would suggest that in order to beat the summer shore traffic, they leave the night before and stay over, go to the beach the next day, and then arrive home by nightfall. The home was a one-floor beach house just like the other 50,000 or so that dotted the Jersey Shore from Sandy Hook to Cape May. It was an efficiency unit with two small bedrooms. When he stayed there, one of his aunts' bedrooms was vacated for the use and enjoyment of Brown and his guest.

Those that found themselves at the beach house were brought there at about 9:00 p.m., usually after a movie and dinner, as per multiple sources. A stop at a local liquor store was made because the aunts didn't allow alcohol to be stored at the house. The drinking would start in the car, the bottle hidden and brought into the house.

A young and trusting body that is suddenly absorbed in alcohol, a full stomach and a late hour, reacts with fatigue, and the priest knew full well this to be the case. On the order that "tomorrow was a busy day" the young man would go to the bed followed by the priest in a long nightshirt. As the boy started to doze, the priest would lift his shirt, exposing women's underwear and his erect penis, while rubbing his penis on his victim.

Jerry Brown was not looking for any type of interactive sex from his victims. He was a man that was content in pleasuring himself on a lifeless and non-participating, young boy.

In March of 2011, I received this email that shed another light on the pathology that was Jerry Brown. This was more in line with my experience with the priest, and laid the groundwork for the validity I was seeking.

From: <name withheld>
Date: Mon, March 07, 2011 9:07 am
Subject: Hi Bruce
To: bruce@novozinsky.org

    Bruce, For several years now, I google the name "Father Gerald Brown" just to see if anyone had reported an act by him and this is the first time I've seen anything. I have been in contact with the site "Bishop accountability.org," but they had nothing on Brown as of several years ago.

    My name is <withheld.> There were seven children in my family growing up. We attended St Mary of the Lake church and occasionally Holy Family. It wasn't until 20 years after my daughter was baptized at St. Mary of the Lake that I found out my brother was molested by Brown. Brown baptized my daughter in 1981 and my brother was her "God" father. It almost sounds like a sick joke now. I had taken out pictures around ten years ago and my brother said "Mare, put them away I don't want to look at them." I asked him why as he looked so happy. He said he was happy to be holding my daughter and he loved her very much, but he couldn't stomach looking at Brown for another minute. He told me what happened on a "camping trip" with Brown. The first place Brown stopped on his way to the camping site was, of course, the liquor store for booze. That night all of the other boys on the trip took single beds or bunk beds and left my brother, a first timer on one of these trips, to share a double bed with Brown. My brother told me all of the other boys laughed at him as it was his turn this time. I believe they looked at it like hazing. Anyway, you can imagine the rest. I must say, I was in a folk *singing group at Holy Family and didn't have any problem what so ever with Father Jack Banko, but maybe it wasn't females he was interested in. All I remember of MSGR Everitt is an old man with cloudy eyes. He seemed very kind to me.*

I'm writing, just to let you know there are more out there than you can even fathom. Most have bottled it up and refuse to talk about it. If there is nothing at this point that can be done about it, why the hell even bring it up and humiliate yourself. I think that's the way my brother sees it. Out of all seven children, the ones who do go to church, I don't believe any go to the Catholic church. Thank you for bringing things out in the open. It will help to deter the future pedophiles if thy [sic] think someone will "out" them.

Sincerely, <name withheld>

I know all about the camping trips. I know because I was a victim of Father Jerry Brown.

In the summer of 1977, I was preparing to enter my third year of seminary at Divine Word. Father Brown asked me to accompany him on a trip to Boston, Massachusetts. The plan was to stop off at a local seminary in Connecticut, say Mass, and proceed onto our destination. There were two other boys with us; Jim, one year older than me, and Glen, one year younger, and all three of us were altar boys at Saint Mary of the Lake at one time or another.

Lakewood to Boston is a six-hour drive. It took us two days and I never made it to Boston.

We left on a Thursday afternoon and drove directly to the Panda Inn (a local Chinese food/packaged goods place) and picked up hard liquor. I was in the backseat of the priest's car and pornography was under the seat in front of me, by my feet. I took it out and nudged my back seat companion. Not only was the porn "hardcore," but it was "vintage" as well. The porn was in book format and published in the 1940's and it was packaged in a shopping bag with *The Joy of Sex: A Gourmet Guide to Lovemaking*.[28] I laughed and asked the priest what he had in this bag and he replied "bed time reading." Without hesitation Brown instructed everyone in the car that sex was a natural impulse that each and every boy in the seminary (I was the only one actually in the seminary) experiences and needs to be aware of. We were 15, 16 and 17; it was porn and we had an abundance of it to go along with liquor – what could go wrong? Plenty.

We pulled into the Howard Johnson's right off of Interstate 95 in Connecticut. This is where we were going to spend the night before going to the seminary that Brown was going to celebrate Mass at the next day.

My mother had packed me a suit and we were all under the impression that this was a celebratory Mass of Father Brown's anniversary of becoming a priest. We checked into the HoJo's and the priest paid, in cash, for a single room with two double beds and a rollaway. The money didn't come from his wallet but from a worn letter envelope with what I found to be an odd inscription of "+JMJ." It was only years later that I learned this to be a designation for "Jesus, Mary, Joseph."

We went to the room, left for dinner and a movie. It was during the movie that Father Brown touched Glen's arm in a fit of laughter at the comedy and did not remove his hand for the rest of the showing. Glen told Jim and me about this afterwards when the priest stopped at the liquor store. I remember Jim (the oldest of the three of us) saying, "He's queer." Nothing else was said.

When we came back to the room, I immediately called out "I have the rollaway bed" and no one argued with me, as it was protocol back in those days "to call" something in order to make an indisputable claim; I had "called" the rollaway and, therefore, the rollaway was mine. Jim and Glen were big for their age but agreed that they would share a double bed. Jim actually made a bed on the floor. We watched some pre-cable TV and fell off to sleep after the priest did but not before Glen went into Father Brown's suitcase and made the discovery of women's underwear and a plastic baggie of what appeared to be human hair - human pubic hair to be more specific. Creeped out, we agreed to look out after each other from that point on.

The next morning we attended Mass. The celebration turned out to be the three boys and Jerry Brown on a side altar. It was during Mass that I realized that something was not quite right about this situation. The prior night weighed on me and the three of us were questioning the disturbing findings in the priest's suitcase. When Father Brown delivered a homily despite the fact that there were only us three boys in attendance, I sensed he had an agenda. In it he criticized the "women's lib movement" and stressed that men are the "keepers of the key." It was a rambling diatribe of how we were to keep secrets as sacred trusts between us. As he turned his head to consecrate the Blessed Sacrament, we all shared a knowing glance; Father Jerry Brown knew that we had ransacked his luggage and was now doing what he could to make sure that this would not become public knowledge. Confronting us outside the Mass would lead to confrontation and he knew that. On the altar and with God looking down on us, he had his stage and our undivided, captive attention and he knew we were listening and would not dare interrupt. He was right. He was smart, manipulating and evil, but he was right.

We checked out of the Howard Johnson's by noon. Mass was over and I wanted to go back and change out of my suit before leaving for Boston. Actually, I just wanted to go home. My mother and stepfather were in the Poconos for the weekend so I had no one to call to let them know I was alive and doing fine, but Jim and Glen did want to make the pay-phone call home. As they went to the restaurant to call, I went back to the room. Father Jerry Brown followed.

What happened next has not been told in detail in 34 years and never in its entirety, until now. Each and every word is true. Not a hint of embellishment because there's no need for it.

I kept the outside access door to the room open expecting Jim and Glen to enter at anytime. With my back to the priest, I took my suit pants off and opened my suitcase, which was on the rollaway bed. I was hit with a force that catapulted me across the bed and onto the floor. Father Jerry Brown, penis exposed from the fly of his pants, was on top of me fully erect and rubbing against my hip as his hand dug for my inner thigh. Before I could react, his fingers twisted my pubic hair and pulled – at that instant, I struck the priest with an elbow force that did not just strike his head - it literally went through it. Not a word passed between us. Not a violent outburst from me and not a grunt of obvious pain from him. In a single fluid motion the priest got up, fled to the bathroom and without closing the door entered the shower and masturbated. I left the room in my shorts I had just put on, my dress shoes and a white tee shirt. I left my luggage, suit and forty-dollars behind. I ran for Interstate 95, a distance that seemed like forever. I remember thinking of my options - the police station or a rest stop. I decided for the latter. Keep in mind that this was the late 1970's and as we say to our children ad nauseam, "times were different." I was not six years old, I was 16 and in great physical condition. I didn't look like the typical candidate for a kidnapping, or a sexual assault for that matter, and yet less than an hour before I had a priest on top of me. I decided to use the awkward outfit I fled the hotel room in to my advantage under the guise of a teen runaway, when panting, I arrived at the truck stop just off of the interstate highway.

From: <name withheld>
Date: Mon, May 9, 2011 14:12 pm
Subject: Did you find Jerry Brown?
To: bnovozinsky@me.com
Bruce,

If I used my name, you'd now me from our days over 30 years ago. I don't think that I'm comfortable enough to share that with you. I had so many bottled up dreams and memories through the years about Jerry Brown that exposing my self to you would conjure up things I have long ago locked away.

I don't know if I should thank you or hate you for the book that my sister tells me you're writing. I've looked on your website and what I read horrifies me because it's so close in line with what I went through. A part of me besgs [sic] you to stop and a part of me wants more and more to read because it validates my experiences that I told my parents about and they denied ever happened. I don't know if it was the faith they had in the church or the embarrassment of having their son abused by a priest. Either way, I went through it alone when it happened and years afterwards.

My sister told me that she spoke to you. At first I was angry with her but now I understand. I'm in the business of forgiving. She was the only person I confided in and that was only in the past 10 years. She sees your mission as a gift (her words) but I still have the jury out on you. You do give me hope that there will be justice done. I once heard you say "if the justice is escaped here, that's just a flicker of time; you'll get it in spades when the time comes." I also used that to a CCD class. I believe that and wish you the best. One day I hope we can sit and discuss. I know it's agony for you to write of your own experiences and I'll pray for you but in an awkward way, I look forward to your closure as I still hope for my own because sometimes faith is not enough.

If an email comes into me without a signature, I usually ignore it. I've received a lot of mail and email over the past three years that make accusations against someone, but if not "owned," to me, they are unverifiable claims.

But I know who wrote me this email to me back in May 2011. It became obvious to me because of one sentence. This was from a man that had a great family foundation back in the 1970's and more friends than one person should be allowed. His fear of this being public is that he was not going to allow himself to be labeled a "fag" or "queer." For telling his story, he does not want to be labeled a "whistleblower." He is an ordained Catholic priest in the Diocese of Trenton.

My adrenaline was rushing, but I knew I wasn't invincible. As has been abundantly demonstrated, you can't always predict the actions or intentions of others. I was already getting a few "looks" as I ventured in and out of parked trucks. I had decisions to make. I decided that I was not going to approach those trucks with no known company brand. I thought approaching a company truck would afford me the best chance of making it back to New Jersey without being attacked twice in one day. With God's hand on my shoulder, I made my way to a trucker that was getting inside his oil truck.

Disheveled and out of breath, I asked the man for a ride. The story I concocted was that of a runaway, without money or food, and no place to go, my parents were worried sick and I needed to get back to New Jersey. As I spoke with my head cocked up to the cab of the truck, a voice came out of the unmarked truck next to his that I stood between, "Hey, I'm going as far as Bordentown, I can take you." I had a would-be ride on the hook but I decided to take the chance at the direct ride that would put me 20 minutes from home or at the very least in the same town as the Seminary. I jumped in the unmarked truck and we were I-95 south bound in minutes.

Five minutes into the ride, I regretted getting into that truck.

To: bnovozinsky@me.com (via email)
Bruce,

I always wondered what ever happened to Father Brown. I was a parishioner at Saint Mary of the Lake when he was there. One night he came up to my parents at a restaurant in Lakewood behind the church and asked for money. It seemed a little funny to me that a priest would ask for money when he was in walking distance from his church and the way my parents acted towards him was very unlike them to a priest. My father all but ignored him but when he reached over to tweak my nose, my mother almost jumped across the table and demanded my father give him the money so "father can get to where he is going."

In the last years of his life, Monsignor George Everitt had been ill. He had the heart ailments of a man his age and the stress of a parish; also being a community leader and vicar of Ocean County had taken its toll on him. Under the direct order of newly appointed Bishop John Reiss, George Everitt was taking a much needed and well-deserved vacation.

As Father Everitt was planning his respite, Jerry Brown was planning a sleepover party at the rectory.

The exact night of the party is in question. I asked this information of two of the four boys that were there that night and yet the timeframes remain sketchy. And while they could supply certain information - pertaining to the third and fourth boys involved - they would not offer those names to me.

This much is clear. The priest served the four boys alcohol. One of the boys was a 13 year-old from nearby Brick, and the younger brother of one of the older boys present. At around 10:00 p.m. Jerry Brown was forced to rush the boy to nearby Paul Kimble Hospital for what would be diagnosed in the Emergency Room as a case of acute alcohol poisoning. While in the ER, Brown conspired with the other boys to lie about alcohol being served, coaching that they were to say they came to the rectory for help because they had nowhere else to go when the 13 year-old got sick. When the boys' parents arrived, Brown tried to sell them the story but the parents were not easily fooled and could tell the truth was not being told. They called the police and when Monsignor Everitt came home from his vacation, the Chief of Police came to see him at the rectory.

The truck driver that was taking me to New Jersey told me to "relax and take it easy." He had a knowing look on his face, as if this were not so random. My instincts told me I was safe, but I was still guarded. He was tired but said that the rest at the stop we'd met at did him a world of good and he appreciated the company. He said he was gassed up and ready to go. He warned that the traffic may be a problem, but I was to just let him know if I was tired or hungry "or anything." He knew who I was, but I had no idea who he was.

He asked me where in Bordentown I was going. He said he lived there and that he could take me anywhere. "Anywhere" included home if I wanted. Now I knew that he had me pegged because how did he know I didn't live in Bordentown? I told him (and insisted, though he didn't challenge me) that I was "from Bordentown." He made eye contact with me and said, "from Bordentown ain't Divine Word." A sickening feeling came across me – this driver knew me, but I had no idea who he was.

His brother, Tim, went to Divine Word and was in my class. There were no more lies I could spin; I was caught, but safe, and the driver reassured me that my secret was as good as kept as long as I went home, because "I don't need to be the last guy seen with you." I more than understood. At that point I made up my mind to get to Bordentown and call my sister for a ride home.

Some 150 miles later, we arrived in Bordentown. The trucker said I could go to his house, or Divine Word, or make a call from a pay phone while he waited for me. I chose the latter. I didn't want to explain to a classmate what had happened (we were not close to being friends) or the priests and brothers at Divine Word. We went to Anthony's Pizza on Route 206 where I was a regular customer during the school year. There really was an "Anthony." The owner saw I was tired, hungry, and "not right." He fed me and allowed me use of his phone and my sister was on her way.

I returned for my junior year at Divine Word in the fall of 1977 – it was to be my last year. I don't know if the trucker and very Good Samaritan ever told his family because no one ever mentioned a word about it, but my parents certainly did when I got home. I was candid, up to a point. I told them about the liquor and the underwear and the baggie of what seemed to be (and was) pubic hair. I didn't tell them about the attack in the hotel room. I decided not to, because I was afraid that they would not believe it and if they did, they wouldn't do anything about it. It was that simple. I didn't have the faith in my parents to do what needed to be done. I remember my sister telling me that if it was a plumber or a janitor who did this, she knew they would have called the police. In the end, my stepfather did come back to me in a rare demonstration of parental concern. He said to me one night in our backyard that he'd never allow me to be in that situation again and he was sorry.

I never asked Glen or Jim about the situation and how Father Brown explained my disappearance to them that Saturday morning. When my sister went to retrieve the items I left in Brown's car she was told by Father Brown that he said to the boys that I was ill and was taking the bus home. I had a sense of guilt about not telling them of the attack but I was 16, in a seminary, and didn't want to be labeled. Not an excuse, just the way it was back then.

The next week I was no longer serving Mass or taking part in the Sunday liturgy at Saint Mary of the Lake. After the 11:00 a.m. Mass my stepfather had my mother take us kids right to the car and he met Monsignor Everitt in the pathway between the church and rectory. His gestures were more than animated and his finger was inches from the Monsignor's nose. All Monsignor could do was listen. He didn't get a word in edgewise and my stepfather left without allowing the aging cleric a moment of remorse or rebuttal.

Monsignor listened as the Police Chief informed him of the events that took place in the rectory in his absence. Jerry Brown was upstairs and according to the cleaning lady at the time, was not coming out to eat or say Mass. The Mass schedule was in complete disarray and some Masses were canceled as a result that week. This didn't matter to

Monsignor as he climbed the steps and entered the room of an unshaven and unkempt Jerry Brown.

According to Monsignor's journal, Brown was in his black suit pants and tank-tee shirt and the odor of alcohol and perspiration filled the stale and confined room. The rectory was air-conditioned but the monsignor opened the window anyway to circulate the air.

Monsignor told the priest to get himself together. He directed him to clean up, put fresh clothes on and come down for a meal. The priest complied and afterwards he joined the monsignor in the main living space in the rectory. He was fully refreshed and actually jovial as he entered the room. Monsignor wrote that his charge "seemed in good spirits and in complete contrast to the person I saw upstairs 2 hours ago." Jerry Brown knew he was in trouble but had been in front of his direct superiors in the past and survived unscathed. He figured this would be another in a long line of mea culpa in his past.

He was wrong. Mercy was not in the mind of the Monsignor.

That night in that study, Monsignor George Everitt ordered Father Jerry Brown off of the premises of Saint Mary of the Lake. He was told to collect his personal artifacts and leave within one hour. He was to take only items from his room and not the church (his personal challis) and he was to leave any credit cards for which the parish was responsible. He was given $100 by the Monsignor and told not to return, the remainder of his items would be forwarded to him once he informed the rectory of his new location.

In his journal, Monsignor observed: "... Father requires help beyond Lakewood and the diocese and certainly beyond me. He is not in denial but rather seems to be suffering from a sxual [sic] disease or homosexuality that has taken over his mind as well as body. He has a perverse affection for boys according to the complaints received and claims made."

George Everitt had just fired Jerry Brown.

Jerry Brown was not going quietly.

There are two consequences when a priest has been credibly accused of sexual abuse. The priest can be directed to lead a life of "prayer and penance" or the Vatican can remove him permanently from the priesthood. The penalty of "prayer and penance" is usually employed for those of advanced age and infirmity; critics see it as an "easy out" for a repeat sexual offender. Under this directive, the priest may not celebrate Mass publicly or administer the sacraments. He may not wear clerical garb or present himself publicly as a priest, and he is directed not to have any unsupervised contact with minors. But who monitors all of this?

In early 2011, I posed the question of "prayer and penance" to Monsignor Joseph Rosie of the Diocese of Trenton. His answer was "corporate" and contrived, but to listen to Rosie, he really believed it to be the best approach.

"Where is Jerry Brown today?" I asked the Monsignor. After a nervous blink, Rosie replied that he was living a life of "prayer and penance." I subscribed to the oldest lawyer trick in the book, never to ask a question you don't already know the answer to. Monsignor answered exactly how I anticipated. I said, "I know what he's doing, I'd like to know exactly where he's doing it." Each and every priest I spoke to of Brown reacted the same way – nervous. "Bruce, he is being carefully monitored. He's an old man." Monsignor knows as we all do that the Diocese and Church itself doesn't have the resources to carefully monitor the priests they have in "prayer and penance" especially one with the refractory tendencies of Jerry Brown.

Brown is a two-time loser with the tribunal council of the Catholic Church. Once Monsignor threw him from the rectory at Saint Mary of the Lake, he was welcomed back by then Bishop John Reiss, given a new assignment in Willingboro, New Jersey, and once again he sexually abused and assaulted young boys. He is a vile predator that still remains "at large" as far as the victims are concerned.

———————

In August of 1989, many years after the trip to Massachusetts that ended in Connecticut, my mother and stepfather invited Father Brown to a barbeque in honor of my mother's birthday. His final words to me that day when I asked him about wearing a roman collar were, "all that's in the past, let's just move on – see everyone's happy today."

Jerry Brown then tweaked my nose.

5

Trenton and Metuchen Split;
The Cardinal McCarrick Syndrome

"The greatest persecution of the church doesn't come from enemies on the outside but is born from the sins within the church."

-Pope Benedict XVI on predator clergy

When Bishop George Ahr retired after twenty-nine years on June 23, 1979, he was the longest-serving bishop of Trenton, his legacy regarded as "leading a growing diocese that found itself in a significantly changed world."[29] It was a generic legacy as far as bishops go, certainly long in tenure and prolific in parish growth, but no more meaningful or standout than the rest the U.S. episcopate at time, falling woefully short of what it could have been had he had the courage to face off squarely and openly against the sexual abuse crisis in the Diocese of Trenton that he was aware of first-hand.

Indeed, things, good and bad, flourished under Bishop Ahr. He was a builder, and new parishes were complimented by a spike in priestly vocations, making God Inc. of Trenton a most desirable place to live and work if you were in the business of the Church. The problem was that the 1970's had brought a rush of sexual accusations against parish priests in the Trenton Diocese. On April 22, 1980, John C. Reiss, who had been Auxiliary Bishop of the Diocese since 1967 and thus was also well aware of what was going on, succeeded Bishop Ahr. Bishop Reiss, a forward thinker and decisive man, knew just what to do.

Catholic ministry in New Jersey owes its origins to stalwart Jesuit priests who traversed the state in the 1700's visiting scattered Catholic families. The Catholic Church hierarchical structure as we now know it began in 1853, with the formation of the Diocese of Newark, out of which the Diocese of Trenton was carved to serve Catholics in the southern part of the state. In 1937, the Trenton Diocese itself was split to form the Diocese of Camden. In 1980, the newly appointed Bishop Reiss led the Trenton Diocese into its 1981 centennial founding celebration, and into another historical diocesan divide. On November 24, 1980, the Trenton Diocese split to form the Metuchen Diocese, which was to encompass the four northern counties of Middlesex, Somerset, Hunterdon and Warren.

The Diocese of Trenton split into Trenton/Metuchen was impulsive, but necessary due to over-population of the growing Catholic community. The Trenton Diocese, while large, was certainly not unmanageable. When the split was made, perhaps prematurely, most of the priests that stood accused at the time were taken out of Trenton and moved to the north, in the new Metuchen territory, and literally under the sheltering care of Bishop Theodore McCarrick, who preferred that a select few call him "uncle." His is a legacy that leaves much to be desired.

Theodore Edgar McCarrick was born in New York City on July 7, 1930, to Theodore Egan McCarrick and Margaret McLaughlin. The young McCarrick attended catholic elementary school and Fordham Preparatory School, continuing onto Fordham University after a brief study abroad, his goal upon return to study for the priesthood. He entered St. Joseph's Seminary, in Yonkers, New York, where he earned his bachelor's degree in philosophy in 1954 and a master's degree in history in 1958. Ordained a priest on May 31, 1958, in New York City, he went on to earn a second master's degree in social sciences and a doctorate in sociology from The Catholic University of America, Washington, D.C.

In 1977, Pope Paul VI named then Monsignor McCarrick as Auxiliary Bishop of New York, where he served as Vicar of East Manhattan and the Harlems. In 1981, McCarrick was selected by Pope John Paul II to be the first Bishop of Metuchen where he served for five years until his 1986 assignment to the Archdiocese of Newark, and then almost five years after that, in 2000, he garnered a most prestigious appointment to the Archdiocese of Washington, D.C.

Dr. Richard Sipe is devoted full-time to researching the sexual and celibate practices of Roman Catholic bishops and priests. He has spent his life searching for the origins, meanings, and dynamics of religious celibacy. His six books, including the seminal works *A Secret World* and *Celibacy in Crisis*, explore the evolution of the celibacy concept. Dr. Sipe, a former Benedictine monk who was laicized and married, has, as a certified psychologist, treated numerous priests with sexual problems.

Dr. Sipe makes some pretty bold statements about celibacy and pedophilia, not all that I necessarily agree with. Dr. Sipe theorizes that mandatory celibacy is intimately bound up with pedophilia in that sexual deprivation can be instrumental in predisposing a person to have sex with a minor. Look, if I'm a priest and pushed to the point that I'm breaking my vow, it's going to be with a grown woman, period. However, to the extent that Dr. Sipe suggests that in combination with the other factors that comprise the clerical culture, required celibacy predisposes, promotes, retains, hides and defends clergy who are sexually active in their ranks, we see eye to eye. While by no means isolated to Cardinal McCarrick, his culpable conduct so personified this principal that Dr. Sipe named it after him: "The Cardinal McCarrick Syndrome."

In the course of his research, Dr. Sipe discovered documentation substantiating not only McCarrick's cover-up of the child sexual abuse scandal, but also evidence that McCarrick was same-sex active, neither fact hindering his career. Dr. Sipe shared with me:

The facts are clear, simple, and typical of the heritage of tolerance of abuse and cover-up inculcated by Theodore E. McCarrick, Archbishop of Newark (1986-2000) and perpetuated by his successors. There is documentation that records McCarrick's sexual activity and sleeping arrangements with seminarians and young priests even when he served as the first bishop of Metuchen after serving as an auxiliary bishop in New York.

On file are the unsealed "MEDIATION DOCUMENTATION FOR FR. G." that involved McCarrick, the Dioceses of Metuchen and Newark, NJ. (2006). A financial settlement was reached. The case was sent to the Congregation for the Doctrine of the Faith in Rome, but it has not yet responded. Documents include the history of McCarrick's initial sexual gesture and approach to the victim then a seminarian, in the bishop's Metuchen residence in 1986. Documentation includes hand written correspondence (letters and cards) from McCarrick postmarked between 1987 and 2005. Many of the letters are signed "Uncle Ted." The names of other priests who were either seen having sex with McCarrick or witnessed McCarrick having sex with another priest are also included in the file. One of the priests is still in active ministry another left the ministry and was assisted by the church and McCarrick to re-educate for another profession. The names of other sexually active priests are also in the reports. Records of McCarrick's activities with these priests are also included in medical evaluations and records all reviewed by Bishop Hughes of Metuchen already in 1995.

Excerpts from the legal settlement documents include firsthand accounts that are also in the Newark Archdiocese records of an incident on a trip with McCarrick, then Archbishop of Newark, New Jersey, with a seminarian and two young priests when they shared a room with two double beds, it reads:

[McCarrick, only wearing underwear, gets in bed with one of the priests]:

"*Bishop McCarrick was sitting on the crotch of Fr. RC. As I was watching TV with Fr BL [full names appear in the documents], Bishop McCarrick was smiling and laughing and moving his hands all over Fr. RC's body. Bishop McCarrick was touching Fr. C's body, rubbing his hands from head to toe and having a good time, occasionally placing his hands underneath Fr. C's underwear. [I was] feeling very uncomfortable while trying to focus on television, and Fr. B.L., started smiling. As I looked at the bed next to me, Bishop McCarrick was excitedly caressing the full body of Fr. R.C. At that moment, I made eye contact [with] Bishop McCarrick. He smiled at me saying, "Don't worry, you're next." At that moment, I felt the hand of Fr. B.L. rubbing my back and shoulders. I felt sick to my stomach and went under the covers and pretended to sleep.*"[30]

The linchpin of "The Cardinal McCarrick Syndrome" is that the power position of a bishop or cardinal places him above suspicion and makes him immune from criticism. Here's where I stand on it. It's certainly not fair to criticize Cardinal McCarrick for being a homosexual; a man is what a man is. It is, however, certainly fair to criticize McCarrick for engaging in homosexual conduct in flagrant disregard of his vow of celibacy and leading other priests to break their own vows with him. Realistically, we will never get to a precise number of just how many priests break their vows, but the stories are out there and the breaches range from the one-time encounter, to fathering children, to being with children. Humans are sexual beings. Celibacy - forbidding sexual expression with others and even with one's self - is not a natural way of life and can't be easy, but it is a way of life McCarrick chose. No one twisted his arm; he vowed to live a chaste life with integrity. Had he not risen to such lofty esteem in the highest echelons of the Catholic Church, his breach could be viewed as a lack of willpower in grappling with one's innate sexual urges. It's in going back again and again and again for the forbidden fruit that the hypocrisy of McCarrick's venerated position, the Church's teachings on celibacy and homosexuality, and his conduct, wholly inconsistent with all the above, ripen together rather sickeningly. Dr. Sipe continued:

On another occasion McCarrick summoned the young man to drive him from the Newark Cathedral to New York City. He took him to dinner; and after, rather than returning to Newark as anticipated McCarrick went to a one-room apartment that housed one bed and a recliner chair. McCarrick said that he would take the chair, but after showering he turned off the lights and clad in his underwear he climbed into bed with his guest. Here is the account from the documents:

"He put his arms around me and wrapped his legs around mine. Then he started to tell me what a nice young man I was and what a good priest I would make someday. He also told me about the hard work and stress he was facing in his new role as Archbishop of Newark. He told me how everyone knows him and how powerful he was. The Archbishop kept saying, "Pray for your poor uncle." All of a sudden, I felt paralyzed. I didn't have my own car and there was nowhere to go. The Archbishop started to kiss me and move his hands and legs around me. I remained frozen, curled up like a ball. I felt his penis inside his underwear leaning against my buttocks as he was rubbing my legs up and down. His hands were moving up and down my chest and back, while tightening his legs around mine. I tried to scream but could not...I was paralyzed with fear. As he continued touching me, I felt more afraid. He even tried several times to force his hands under my shorts. He tried to roll me over so that he could get on top of me, but I resisted. I felt sick and disgusted and finally was able to jump out of bed. I went into the bathroom where I vomited several times and started to cry. After twenty minutes in the bathroom, the Archbishop told me to come back to bed. Instead I went to the recliner and pretended to fall asleep.

In a letter dated four days after this incident McCarrick wrote a note signed "Uncle Ted" that said in part: "I just wanted to say thanks for coming on Friday evening. I really enjoyed our visit. You're a great kid and I know the Lord will continue to bless you...Your uncle has great spots to take you to! [31]

"Uncle Ted's" relationship with his "nephews" took two forms; there were those upon whom he pressed his homosexual advances, and those that pressed their pedophilic advances on others and he protected.

All of McCarrick's protégés enjoyed McCarrick's benevolence whether they acquired the status by choice or by circumstance. But McCarrick's obliteration of his celibacy vows (homosexual or heterosexual, no difference to me) pales in comparison to his most spectacular breach, the use of his power to protect pedophile priests. Admittedly, nothing in the allegations point to pedophilia on the part of McCarrick, but to the extent that he cosseted the child molesters in his charge, using his position in the hierarchy to not only shield them, but promote and favor them, "Uncle Ted" might as well have engaged in the behavior. Debating which is worse - the act or the tacit approval of the act - is like asking which blade of the scissors was more responsible for cutting the piece of paper; in the end, they worked in unison towards the same result.

McCarrick also made sure his tracks were covered.

Around Thanksgiving 2010, I received the first of two blocked phone calls from a man in New Jersey. He asked me what I was looking into as part of the past of Cardinal McCarrick. I replied that what I had to go on was information from Dr. Richard Sipe, the story of a priest that resisted the advances of the then Bishop in the mid 1980's, newspaper articles, and related Internet chatter. The caller warned me once at that time and again in late December to "be careful. Others have spoken out against the Cardinal and were ruined – he has a large network of friends who intimidate and are good at it."

If the Cardinal's henchmen are out, I would be at the bottom of the list. In 2008, Dr. Sipe wrote an open letter to Pope Benedict XVI detailing the dimensions of the sexual abuse crisis in the United States, prominently featuring McCarrick as representative of the "top down" systemic sexual aberration. A current web search on His Eminence also produces many allegations about McCarrick, pointing back to the days he spent in New Jersey. In 2008, conservative religion columnist Rob Dreber backed Dr. Sipe's online thesis by writing:

Sipe has here written about an open secret among many Catholic priests and secular journalists who have covered the scandal. I will only say that what Sipe reports here is entirely credible, based on numerous interviews and conversations I've had with priests and a few laymen. I can tell you too that none of this is news to the Vatican. None of this has been in the mainstream media for the reason Sipe identifies.

I personally believe the allegations against Cardinal McCarrick are true, for these and another reason I am not at liberty to discuss. But can I prove it? Absolutely not. These remain only allegations, and hearsay. And I have never heard from a single accuser of Cardinal McCarrick that he ever did anything in violation of the criminal law.

I am thinking right now of a former priest I once interviewed -- not a priest who served under McCarrick's authority -- who left the priesthood in deep discouragement. There was a lot of gay sex going on among the priests in his Diocese, and allegations of sexual harassment of seminarians by priests at the seminary. The bishop (who had a reputation of his own for a lack of integrity on sexual matters) swept in, did a sham investigation, said there was no problem at all, case closed. It was a total cover-up. This is where the term "lavender mafia" comes from....[32]

So how did then Bishop McCarrick shield those in his charge? And more importantly, why?

McCarrick had full and complete knowledge of where the bodies were buried. The Bishop was the fox in the hen house and his superiors knew it. Records in the 1980's were sketchy at best, maintained mostly by volunteers and kept in manila folders with sticky notes. Six of the 10 known predators in the Trenton/Metuchen diocese tracked on *bishopaccountability.org* were active during the McCarrick years, shielded, transferred and protected. All the while, the loudest whispers were about the Bishop himself. The future Cardinal's secrets remained just that - secret.

In his book *Journalism is War*, George Archibald, a retired senior investigative reporter for the *Washington Times* and four-time nominee for the Pulitzer Prize in journalism, goes into graphic detail about McCarrick's exploits and his practice of advancing his "nephews" who acquiesced to his sexual advances.

McCarrick owned a Jersey shore home in Sea Girt, the coastal community of urban sophisticates. In this choice environment he carried on his trysts and extended promises of advancing the careers of those in the major (or college) seminary. None were underage but some could hardly be considered "consenting." On the record, two former seminarians have spoken publically about their encounters with the powerful Cardinal and the sexually charged weekends in both Manhattan and the Jersey Shore. Archibald names them as Robert Ciolek, now a New York pharmaceuticals attorney and one time ordained priest, and Father Carlos Miguel Viego of New York.[33]

In the late 1990's, McCarrick was ordered to sell his beach house by the papal nuncio in Washington, D.C. – he did so. He sold it to the Archdiocese of Newark, essentially to Archbishop John J. Myers of Newark, a man of similar ilk. Although in the wake of the Cardinal Law scandal Myers was instrumental in helping the nation's bishops craft a policy to cleanse the priesthood of pedophiles and restore trust among shaken American Catholics, a review of the Archbishop's record since 2002 revealed that, on at least four occasions, he has shielded priests accused of sexual abuse against minors and one adult. In the four instances, the priests had either admitted improper sexual contact, pleaded guilty to crimes stemming from accusations of sexual misconduct or been permanently barred from ministry by the Newark Archdiocese after allegations of sexual misconduct. The records review, conducted by Newark's *Star Ledger*,[34] revealed that the Archdiocese also wrote a letter of recommendation for one of its priests, a week after it learned that he was in fact accused of breaking into a woman's home in Florida and possibly assaulting her. In other cases cited by the *Star-Ledger*:

• In 2004, the Newark Archdiocese wrote letters to six dioceses in Florida on behalf of the Reverend Wladyslaw Gorak, one week after learning Gorak's ministry had been terminated in the Orlando Diocese — after he was accused of breaking into a woman's home;

• Also in 2004, the Archdiocese banned the Reverend Gerald Ruane from public ministry after investigating an allegation he molested a boy, but did not publicly notify lay people or other priests. Ruane continued to say Mass and wear his collar in public;

• In 2007, the Archdiocese failed to inform lay people that it found a molestation claim credible against the Reverend Daniel Medina, who had worked in parishes in Elizabeth and Jersey City. The case wasn't made public until a victims group uncovered an alert sent by the

Archdiocese in September 2008 to other bishops saying Medina was on administrative leave and could not be located.

In his retirement, the Cardinal is still a frequent visitor to the shore house according to neighbors. He is a known, albeit thinly veiled, advocate for gay rights.

6

Larry Becomes Lorenzo

"Is God willing to prevent evil, but not able?
Then he is not omnipotent.
Is he able, but not willing?
Then he is malevolent.
Is he both able and willing?
Then whence cometh evil?
Is he neither able nor willing?
Then why call him God?"

-Epicurus (Greek philosopher, BC 341-270)

My rapport with Larry is easy; the subject matter is not. Each call brings a new dark tunnel to shine a light in.

Larry explained to me that he legally changed his name to Lorenzo; this is his new identity going forward. Out of the utmost respect, I tread carefully when it comes to the D'Oria family. Like the parents of many sexually abused children, Larry's parents saw that "something" was not right with their son - but it was the 1970's and it was normal for parents to socialize their children into honoring priests by advocating respect and obedience without question.

Calling the son he named and baptized Larry, *"Lorenzo"* - sends a shive through the elder D'Oria's heart. He will tolerate others using it but you will "*never*" hear that name pass his lips when referring to his oldest son. By that same token, I have to respect that Larry/Lorenzo decided to legally change his name, and I will not insult him or disregard that choice by continuing to call him Larry when speaking with him, except herein when recounting his story as a young boy. From this point of the story forward, Larry has become Lorenzo.

Lorenzo claims that he changed his name in order to gain an identity that was free of "Big Larry" and "Larry Jr." When you read his writings it's obvious that the name change goes well beyond simply shedding the endearing nicknames families come up with when father and son share the same first name.

Lorenzo is what we would have called a "flamer" in the 1970's; stereotypically and flamboyantly gay through and through, Lorenzo's new fabulously international moniker suits this hairstylist well. Lorenzo is an extension of Larry, always on the move and the further from rural Jackson, the better, from the west coast to Europe to Florida. Anywhere and everywhere that he was comfortable and no one knew of his past he would establish shallow roots only to leave and start over again. Leaving "Larry" further behind with each relocation was the final puzzle piece that made him whole, or so he thought. Lorenzo remains true to his homegrown conservative roots in his political and social ideology, an incongruity which may not be readily apparent to him but which I observed by tracking for over a year his "likes" and "causes" on Facebook. Larry/Lorenzo's name change from the everyday vanilla to a more exotic version of the same name is indicative of his every move after his brutal assault; becoming his alter-ego "Lorenzo" allowed Larry to disassociate from the pain inflicted upon him so many years ago, but deep down, way down, Lorenzo is still at the core, Larry.

Father Brian Egan became Campus Minister at Georgian Court College in 1967 and stayed until 1978. Hailing from upstate New York, Father Egan was transferred from the college around 1978 because of alleged "inappropriate" acts with members of the same sex. As was sometimes the case, these transfers produced fortuity for the banished priest, an absurd result but one not entirely unexpected when the local diocese's only real concern was for the swift and stealthy removal of the thorn, and not for the action's impact on anyone else. A new beginning for Egan, as told, ironically, at his end. In January 2011, Alabama's *Birmingham News* obituarized:

Several years later, members of the student body of St. Bernard Prep and St. Bernard College saw his leadership shine forth as the school made a major transition from a two-year college to a fully-accredited four-year educational institution. Fr. Egan led the way and was named the new college's first president. His leadership of the newly-named Southern Benedictine College, and his charisma attracted students and supporters from the eastern half of the U.S. He presided over a thriving campus where many memorable visitors came to visit the college and seek his counsel. In 1979, Bishop Joseph Vath, first Bishop of the Diocese of Birmingham, invited Fr. Egan to become Education Secretary of the young diocese. Fr. Egan accepted this challenge and served in that role until 1985. During this period, in 1983, Bishop Vath also assigned Fr. Egan to leadership of Catholic Charities as well. He was the perfect selection for both these important tasks. His leadership both of the education and social mission of the local church was instructive to parishioners and immensely beneficial to students of Catholic Education, and to the many clients of Catholic Social Services, of the Centers of Concern, and of the associated ministries of the Charities network. Among Fr. Egan's significant achievements has been the entry of the diocese into housing for the elderly poor. He organized the activity that led to the formation of Catholic Housing of Birmingham which is the owner/operator of Villa Maria, the home for senior citizens located in East Birmingham. He served as an effective officer of the Catholic Housing Board from its inception until he retired where he trained numerous laymen and laywomen to participate in leadership of the housing effort. Fr. Egan celebrated his 50th anniversary in the priesthood in 2002, and was elevated to the position of Monsignor that same year. His priestly work was characterized by kindness, compassion and prayerful spirituality. He had a legacy of sanctity and humility that every priest strives for, and every layperson admires in a priest. Those who came in contact with him will recall a positive experience filled with his thoughtful concern and his ability to secure a resourceful outcome....[35]

An obituary is many things in one, a notice of a death, a story of a life, how a person, at his very end, can best be represented. Without a doubt, no one from Lakewood, New Jersey, and certainly not Lorenzo D'Oria, was consulted in writing Father Brian Egan's final tribute.

Larry continues (unedited)...

I stopped being a member of St Mary of the Lake Parish

sometime after entering High School (author note: 1975) I was still involved in altar service from time to time, but I got involved at my High School, St Joseph's High School in Toms River. As I moved myself away from the altar, I got more involved in music and music ministry, which I would participate in through college and beyond.

In my junior year of High School (author note: 1977) my Mother suggested that I go over to Georgian Court College to meet Fr. Brian Egan, a Benedictine priest assigned as the chaplain at the college. My parents had attended mass there and thought he was great, maybe he could be a good counselor to me. I obviously needed someone to talk to, a counselor, as it were. I had his card which they gave to me. I gave him a call and made an appointment.

I was greeted at the door by a man of 55, I was 16. I'd had a counseling appointment and I was prompt. Fr. Brian Egan met me at the door. We talked for a few minutes. I told him what was 'bothering me'. I was a moody teenager. I never mentioned Jack Banko specifically. However he did get my background, and he would have known I knew Banko. By this time I'm sure he was able to recognize me as gay from the start. It takes one to know one.

After some brief talking he asked me if I'd like to see the "spectacular architecture" of the Gate Keeper's House. He showed me around the ground floor and then proceeded to pounce on me on the steep stairwell up to the bedroom. I decided that counseling wasn't going to be too hard to deal with. We wound up playing right there on the stairwell. Best counseling session I'd ever had, or so I thought. I went home with a smile and a good attitude. After that I needed to see Fr. Brian Egan twice or three times a week at least. Brian was 55 at that time, but he was in great shape for a man his age. He played hand ball several times a week. It was also great because my parents thought I was getting counseling, so they didn't mind when I went over to see Egan frequently. I always felt better and had a smile on my face when I got home. Most men do after an orgasm.

I was entirely wrapped up in my music in those days, if I wasn't busy squeezing in more 'counseling'. Music was my real therapy. I was addicted to JS Bach, as well as Chopin. I didn't need therapy or counseling, all I needed was a piano and a couple of hours or serious playing to chase my demons away! My poor piano teacher! Fortunately for him, he liked Bach too! I only played and practiced when no one could watch me. I didn't care if you were listening from another room, but no one was allowed to watch me practice piano. I was much too nervous for that. One time Egan asked me to play for him at the chapel on the college campus. I did, and he offered me the position of Chapel Organist for weddings. I was able to do that because the organ was up in the choir loft. No one could look over my shoulder. I then made $100 every time someone got married in the chapel there. After offering me the job as organist for the weddings, He sat down on the rug on the altar, and patted the floor for me to join him. He put his arm around me and started to kiss me. I hesitated - we were on the altar! He was larger than I was, and stronger. He picked me up in his arms and placed me on the altar. He peeled my clothes off of me. We had sex on the altar. I can't believe that I've broken down and admitted this and actually written this on paper. But there's more....

That job kept me 'indebted' to Egan. I was making great money for doing what I loved to do anyhow. Back then "You Light Up My Life" by Debbie Boone was a popular song. Brian used to sing it to me constantly. To this day, when I hear that song, I want to puke! Brian Egan was a lot like Jack Banko. He was a skilled liar and manipulator of human beings, as well as a sexual predator. Just how much of a predator, I had yet to discover.

Most of the time I was in High School I worked for my father at his drug store in Jackson, NJ. I also went to school full time at St Joe's as well as worked on the farm and made music, when I wasn't busy being an "Altar Boy" for Brian Egan. One of my duties as an employee at the drug store was doing deliveries of prescriptions to customers. Georgian Court College was one of my father's customers. Brian Egan lived in the Gate Keeper's house on the campus there, across the garden from the glorious Convent they had there. It was an exact, scaled down reproduction of one of the great French Chateaus. The estate that became Georgian Court College had been built by J. Paul Getty during the roaring 20's. He was the person 'The Great Gatsby' was based on. His wife committed suicide in the Fountain of Apollo, when she found out he was having an affair.

I told you earlier, Brian Egan, was bigger and stronger than I was at that time of our 'relationship'. I made my scheduled visits to see him, two or three times a week. One night I was working at the drug store and I had to make a delivery to Georgian Court College. Nothing unusual, however, I decided to drop in on Brian Egan that night, just to say 'hello' and be a surprise, a nice surprise.

I knocked on the door, the same as usual. Brian came to the door and asked me to come in. I was on work time. I needed to not waste more than 5 minutes or so, or someone might get suspicious and think that I was wasting time while I was on the clock. I didn't need anyone getting suspicious. Brian insisted that I follow him to the kitchen. This was unusual. We didn't spend much time there. We didn't share food together much at all. I guess it wasn't on the menu. He made a fuss about showing me something on the back porch and proceeded to force me to have sex with him. I told him that I was working and didn't have time for that. Even I didn't have the cojones to even think about getting laid while on the payroll. I tried to tell him that my absence would be noted at work. He very forcefully, for the first time, pressed his mouth onto mine while grabbing my hair and pulling me to the ground. He then forced me to perform oral sex on him, forced being the operative word here. I was practically in tears. I was going to be late. He wouldn't take "No" for an answer. He raped me that night. My resistance was sure. I SAID "NO!" He didn't give a shit. He was bigger and stronger. He got what he wanted. This time, I did not.

I never forgave Brian Egan for having raped me. I didn't break up with him at first. The anger in me was seething under the surface. How humiliating...being forced. Now I was really pissed.

It was around that time that I heard from one of my classmates, another gay man in my class at St Joe's, that my 'boyfriend', Brian Egan, was carrying on like the Whore of Babylon. He knew this from having known another priest in Bricktown (author note: Brick Township, NJ is often referred to as "Bricktown" by local area residents) I do not recall any of the information about that. I didn't know the person he was talking about back then. I only got the connection to the gossip by my also abused schoolmate from Bricktown, had just unknowingly relayed to me about my rapist, my 'boyfriend'. He was old enough to have been my grandfather. And HE was fooling around on me and lying to me too! I was starting to be able to discern a pattern here. Turned out he knew of Banko, too.

I kept on with our abusive relationship for one reason. I was going to get out on my own terms. I was not going to skulk off silently. I waited. I watched. One day I stopped in unannounced again at Brian Egan's Gatehouse. I was working, and wouldn't have much time. I thought twice about it and I rang the bell. As usual, Brian Egan answered the door. I realized there was someone there and I introduced myself. Brian about froze. Now he had to invite me in.

He was as nervous as an illegal immigrant, about to cross a border. A sudden panic came over him like the proverbial cat caught with canary feathers popping out the sides of its mouth. He nervously went to the kitchen to refresh their drinks. I could smell the sex in the musky, stuffy air of his house. It smelled a bit like fresh locker room. I also noticed that this Man was extremely handsome. As far as I was concerned he was the next best thing to Tom Selek(maybe younger, but Tom Selek none the less). This was in March or April of 78'. I was still 17. I was a Senior in High School. I had about two months left at St Joe's. I was going to Trenton State College, now The College of New

Jersey, in September of 78. I was a hundred miles away from myself, staring at everything going on all around me. I was amazed and mildly amused. I was in a hurry, I'd better get to work quickly. I asked the guy, who had been introduced as John, what he did for a living. He told me he was a hairdresser. I asked where. He told me he worked at the Hombre in Bricktown, on Hooper Avenue. I asked him where he knew Brian from and he told me he'd met him at the gym. Racket ball. Right.

I committed the name of the hair salon to memory immediately. I didn't even write it down. I said "goodnight" to "Father Egan" and winked at John as I made my way to the front door. I never saw or spoke to Brian Egan again. The next day I called John when I got in from school. I went there that night.

That night, the rest of my life, in the future, came into view. I found out I had curly hair. I thought I'd had wavy hair. I was going to Trenton State in the fall and knew, that finally I was going somewhere that it was OK to be gay. I found out what sex with a normal guy felt like. It was worlds apart from the flattery and mental bondage of Banko, or the raw violence of Egan. It came with no strings attached.

It was John who would bridge the gap for me, between the gay world, and life as an altar boy party favor for wayward priests. It was John who would introduce me to his circle of friends, who took me under their wings, and into their beds too. None of them ever hurt me. As a matter of fact they even went out of their way to keep me out of harm's way. One of them slipped me 30 mg of valium, in a vodka and cranberry, to knock me out. They knocked me out because I was going to go move to Manhattan. I had been fighting with my father at home. They knew that if I had gone to Manhattan I would have wound up turning tricks and become a hustler. I guess I had told them that before they knocked me out. Not! They had been that route themselves, and knew I was headed to college. They wouldn't let me fall into Manhattan, as they had. Getting out of Manhattan had saved their lives. At least one in the circle did however die from AIDS. I'm not sure about the present whereabouts of any of the guys from that 1st circle of gay men who led me away from the clergy

Thank God! I would not be alive today if I had gone into Manhattan in 1978. One of my classmates from St Joe's, (name withheld by author) who was gay, went to NYC and Fire Island in the Summer of '78. I believe he died in 1981 or 1982. I would have been swallowed alive by the city in the rush of the late 70's gay life.

Banko and Egan had both trained me well in the art of cruelty. I walked away from Banko with what seemed like just a few emotional bruises. Egan, well...the second cut hurt me more deeply. However I didn't even notice until I was 38 or so that either of them had abused me. Before then I believed that I had been privileged, as Banko told me, to have been sexually precocious. Banko and Egan both treated me like a temple whore. The final straw that broke the camel's back for me was finding out that Egan and Banko had been having sex together. They knew each other all too well. Besides they may have had predator envy. Banko knew Egan before I got to know him. They were only located about a mile apart from each other. It takes one to know one. One was a sexy smooth talker who could charm the pants off a snake if he got it *drunk; the other a strong, rough hewn, sexual brute.*

At Georgian Court College, Father Egan was described as "arrogant" and "condescending" to the (then) all-female student body, although tolerated for his sermons and writings that were thought-provoking, topical and delivered with animation. Egan was seen as slightly rebellious, and for that reason, also tolerated by and large by the Sisters of Mercy, who were activists in these waning years of the 1960's. They openly protested the Vietnam War and the use of chemical weapons. It was no secret that the Mercies harbored conscientious objectors to the war and on more than one occasion arranged for transport for those avoiding the draft altogether. Some saw this as a social protest to the Johnson and Nixon administrations; others saw it as something much closer to home, a towing-of-the-line rebellion against the largely conservative Church hierarchy. The Church was not pro-war by any means, but it did not tolerate the behavior the 1960's dictated, and any order was order, even if it was being administered by nuns.

Complaints did come in to various offices about Brian Egan and it presented an administrative dilemma. Egan was Benedictine and not of the Diocese. He was for all intents and purposes an "employee" of the college. The calls to the Diocese of Trenton went unanswered and the calls to Saint Mary of the Lake Church were referred back to the Diocese and the vicious cycle continued.

Those calling Saint Mary of the Lake Church were simply not calling the right individual and that individual was Sister Muriel Lynch. Sister was of the old guard of the Sisters of Mercy, and had a very low tolerance for any sins against the flesh. She took a very strong stance on the behavior of Father Egan, but he would not back down. Very few could grasp the notion that a priest could "answer to" a woman and a nun, no less. Egan and the nun mistrusted each other from a distance. The D'Oria family, however, did trust Sister and their "claims" (as any offense against clergy were categorized as in that day and time) found credence with Sister Muriel. Time and time again, she brought to the administration the intolerable and disgraceful stories of the wayward college chaplain. Time and time again, Lynch was rebutted.

In the winter of 1977, the 61 year-old nun placed a call to Bishop Ahr. The phone call was put through to the Bishop himself who listened politely and promised to take "an active and personal approach" to the "priest issue" at Georgian Court. He did. He placed a call to Monsignor George Everitt who instructed Father John Banko to meet with Egan. They met and a sexual relationship subsequently ensued between the two clerics.

In 1978, Bishop George W. Ahr was nearing the end of his tenure at the helm of the Trenton Diocese and had by this time had it up to "here" with Lakewood. He was now aware that Jack Banko had engaged in pedophilic and now homosexual behavior. He left the Egan issue up to his Auxiliary Bishop at the time, John Reiss, who was poised to soon become Bishop. He took little time ridding the college of its Campus Minister in the fall of 1978. Egan was shipped south. Named President of Southern Benedictine College, in Cullman, Alabama, Egan lasted only a year because of his questionable behavior with students and then moved into a largely administrative role as Education Secretary, Diocese of Birmingham and Executive Secretary, Diocesan Board of Education. His obituary dialed to mention this.

George W. Ahr retired on June 23, 1979; he was the longest-serving bishop of Trenton. He later died at Morris Hall Home of the Aged in Lawrenceville, aged 88. In 1980, Reiss took over for Ahr and started to flex his muscle. Reiss was made keenly aware of abuse issues within his diocese yet didn't consider Egan too much of a threat; because he was assigned to a college, he was not within the diocese realm. To Bishop Reiss' credit, though, he took swift and aggressive action to rid the campus of this sexual abuser.

Bishop Reiss was born May 13, 1922, in Red Bank, New Jersey. He studied at Immaculate Conception Seminary, Darlington, and at the Catholic University of America. Ordained May 31, 1947, he received a doctorate in canon law from Catholic University in 1954. Reiss was the first (and to date only) man that has grown up in the Trenton Diocese that has gone on to be the vicar of the see. A simple man of few words, Reiss was a tremendous fundraiser. Among his accomplishments as Bishop of Trenton that resonate today include Faith-In-Service, a $32 million diocesan capital and endowment fund campaign from 1992 to 1995 that raised $38 million to provide financial stability for diocesan services; a new Morris Hall nursing facility, with St. Joseph Hall Skilled Nursing Center and St. Mary Hall Residence, dedicated Oct. 28, 1994; Villa Vianney, a residence for retired priests, dedicated Oct. 18, 1995; and a new Diocesan Pastoral Center, tripling the size of the diocesan office building, completed in 1997. He was aptly nicknamed "the Builder" in diocesan circles because of his construction initiatives and building expansions.

Brian Egan had a degree in education, so it was natural for him to wind up in the academic field; to date, there have been no other transgressions that are known or posted about him, yet that does little to diminish what he did to Larry D'Oria.

Larry D'Oria went to Father Brian Egan for help. Larry had shown signs of a priestly vocation and in a devout Roman Catholic family, this was the ultimate blessing that a parent could ask for. But now Larry's mother and father were desperate; their son was falling into depths that they could not comprehend. They looked at Brian Egan as their son's trusted confessor, counselor, advocate – they certainly did not see him as an overpowering rapist. Larry was the classic "young and impressionable," and they had their suspicions about Jack Banko. Rumors of the priest's behavior reached across Ocean County from the Church to the lake to the rest areas on the Garden State Parkway. Why didn't the D'Oria family step in and intervene? This was how I posed the question to them, in May 2011:

Mr. and Mrs. D'Oria,
Hope all is well. The book is coming along very well and I am in full throttle mode to complete in December, editing in January and release in February. I am hoping to have a "release dinner" on Saturday, February 4 in NJ. I will be renting the restaurant now owned by Pete Mazzella (of the St Mary Academy Mazzella's) to bring about 100 copies for signing. I want you there. Larry will hopefully be there as well. What I need from you now is closure on your piece. I'd like for you to look at the following as a lead and tell me your impressions:

1) *When did you first learn about Banko and your son?*
2) *Did you ever meet with the Bishop (Ahr)?*
3) *Who do you hold personally responsible for what happened to Larry?*
4) *Was there anyone that supported you from within the church? A nun? Priest? Anyone?*

5) Why didn't you go public with your proof?
6) Your relationship with Larry today.
7) Where is your faith today? What denomination?

On June 1, 2011, I received this reply from Mr. D'Oria:

Hi Bruce,

I'm pleased to know things are going well. We found out when Larry told us. He was 18. We never saw the Bishop but we saw a Fr. Procassini and reported the crime to him. Of course Jack Banko, Mons. Everett and all those who aided in the cover up. Only Sr. Muriel Lynch from GCU was our only support. We never went public but we expressed our pain in our Bible classes. Our relationship is normal but fearful. Larry was never the same child after the loss of innocence. Our faith is actually much stronger as we were led to a Full Gospel Assembly of God. Thank you for all your tireless work to repair a church gross error. Truly, Larry D'Oria

The answers of the parents are vague. The father places the blame at the doorstep of the Church and leaves it there. They do not take any action and do not shoulder any blame. But that was the wont of the times.

Brian Egan's guestbook canonized the man as a living Saint and touted him as a "priest above priests." Egan is a man that raped a boy on an altar, pressing his face on the relics embedded in its marble. This is a man that drove his penis and fingers into the boy's rear end and ignored his pleas to stop, the boy crumbled to the floor in humiliation and exhaustion. Egan was hailed in the guestbook as a "great uncle" and a pillar of the community and an educator. I was sickened by the entries and how a life could be led so duplicitously. It was at this moment that I decided to release a second "lead-in" to this book on the my website centering around the sacrilege the altar at Georgian Court College, coupled with Egan's obituary, as a shocking study in contrast.

The men of the cloth were not done with Larry. Almost 18, Larry was entering his adulthood involved with yet another priest from the near-by parish of Saint Veronica in Howell. Larry carried on a homosexual relationship with this man that spanned almost three years. Larry would spend the evenings at the rectory at Saint Veronica and Rob Deker would get up in the morning and consecrate the Holy Eucharist during Mass, as the nuns served Larry breakfast in the bed he just shared the night before with this man of God.

It was not long after he was raped that Larry became "Lorenzo" and sought to release his pain and detail his journey on the Internet under the manifesto of "Confessions of a Safe Sex Slut."[36] I found it in late 2009 and that was when I emailed Lorenzo. Lorenzo told me that he was surprised that I came across this. He was encouraged to write these things down by the purveyor of the website (I won't give the site the credence of mentioning it here), and I believe Lorenzo was duped into doing so. This was Lorenzo's world after being the rape victim of three abusive, predator priests of the Diocese of Trenton - priests John Banko, Brian Egan, and Rob Deker.

Lorenzo continues (unedited):

I came out in New York City at the Mine Shaft in 1978, just in time to experience the crescendo of Gay Liberation before the beginning of the epidemic. Life was wild! We did whatever the hell we wanted to, and as an 18-year-old, the world really was my oyster. I was already into some kinky stuff before I came out into the world of Leather. I wasn't always kinky; back then I had a lot of true 50/50 relationships.

I'll never forget sitting in front of the TV one night with my whole family, and though I can't remember the exact date, the news broadcaster announced that there was a strange disease killing gay men. He said that they didn't know much about it except that it was killing people rapidly. I remember thinking to myself, "Oh shit! How is this going to affect my life?" My family apparently didn't even hear what was said, or chose to not hear it. The story was also in the New York Times that day (For more in depth info read " And the Band Played On " by Randy Shilts.)

Around that time I met and fell in love with my first "husband" Ronald. He was outrageous and fun. We were two Geminis gone wild with spontaneity and enthusiasm. I might arrive at his house in Central Jersey on a Friday afternoon, and we'd have planned a quiet weekend. I'd arrive and he'd say, "Let's go to the city for the weekend!" And off we went, to the St. Marks Baths, or the Christopher Street bars. Christopher Street was the center of the universe to us back then, on the east coast anyway. Of course San Francisco was Mecca, hailing to all gay men and lesbians to come and be free! We were still experiencing the freedoms that came out of the 60's and the sexual revolution.

Ronald and I were both fucking each other and others as well. It was no problem, we were just dating and having a good time. But I fell in love in spite of him and his admonitions to just be cool. Then he fell in love too. That was in April of '82. He was always getting sick. It didn't seem strange to me. Some people are just sick a lot, I told myself. Merrily we continued on. Ronald was in the Air Force, and on my 22nd birthday he told me that he was being transferred to Germany. Great present! He was scheduled to leave in September. "Well, at least I have three months to love him," I told myself. The summer was a blur of fun activities, running around all over the country, and every moment I fell deeper in love with him. His illnesses didn't seem so strange, plus you can rationalize anything if you really don't want to face the truth. Love comes with a set of blinders, and lust comes with two sets!

Ronald had decided that we would do a cross-country trip to visit his family in San Diego before he left for Europe. I was his co-pilot. We left on July 3rd and arrived in Dallas the morning of the 4th. His friends, the one we were going to visit, were still up partying from the night before. So, we joined them! Eventually we got to San Diego and had a spat.

We broke up, and he told me to go to San Francisco by myself. I had a friend who had migrated to Mecca (SF) from Jersey in 1980. I would stay with him.

Back in NY there were rumors on the street that something was going on, and that we needed to be careful. It was suggested that we use condoms: a completely novel idea to a bunch of 70's gay men. We did as we pleased; how dare they tell us to wear fucking condoms! They were for heterosexuals! The rumors continued, and I did change my habits when tricking anyway, but not with Ronald. I was relieved because I really hated cum up my ass. It was "messy" and uncomfortable. I started to tell guys how much I got off on them cumming on my chest so I could rub it in instead. That helped, but it wasn't enough for some.

Meanwhile, I went to SF a single, free man. "Young, dumb and full of cum." On my first night there my friend Mark took me to the Eagle and out on Polk Street. I was quite charmed but my friend, who was much older than me, was being very protective. The streets had signs posted on telephone poles that read: "Do you have gay cancer?" The poster showed pictures of different types of Kaposi's Sarcoma lesions.

OH NO! Cancer? From being gay? Couldn't be so. Already AIDS was all over the streets of SF, but only just a rumor in NYC.

The second night I went out, alone this time, to the Castro. At the time Castro was not the leather area; that's where the regular queens hung out. People were friendly and we chatted but all of them asked me where I had been in SF, and when I told them that I was out on Polk they'd run as if looked like Quasimodo! I couldn't figure this one out. In NY I could get picked up in 5 minutes. In SF I couldn't get laid! I just scratched my head and said, I must not be trying hard enough. But it became clear to me they were afraid of the guys from the Leather

Community in the Castro area. Those were the "bad boys." They did terrible stuff and all this epidemic of gay cancer must surely be their fault, or so they thought.

Later the next day I was walking down Castro St. and someone came up to me, handed me a card, and walked away. The card said: "I want to be a pig with you. I want you to sit on my face and stick your cock up my ass." Then it had his address. I ran down the street yelling after him, "Hey, wait! I'm coming with you!" Finally I'd found some action! When we got to his apartment there was an opium party going on. It was his birthday, and I was to be his special trick for an exhibition at the party - I was going to fist him. He left to get cleaned and meanwhile I got cozy with one really hot guy. The guy came back and was incensed that I was playing with someone else. I told him to fuck off, I was still there for him and when he was ready it would be his turn. He didn't want to know about that. So the hunk and I left the party and went to his house, where we did have safe sex. He was informed. I was the bottom and I didn't care if he had to wear a rubber. I didn't like them, they were too straight!

I returned to San Diego a changed person. A scared person. Upon my arrival, Ronald told me he loved me and wanted me back. I'm still convinced that he broke up with me just so he could feel good about my going alone to SF, because he had gotten ill and was in the hospital with a mouth full of thrush and cold sores. He could hardly speak or eat. Needless to say I got back together with him.

Our return trip went through Denver, and we spent time at the now infamous "Ball Park" bath house. The one with the waterfall! They were famous for the waterfall in the pool, and what went on behind the waterfall as well. We made our way back to the East Coast and finished out our summer together, whenever we could and whenever he was feeling well enough. He was stubborn and resilient. We were each others inspirations. We were totally in love.

The day finally came when he had to be deployed to Germany. I drove him to the airport on McGuire AFB. I'm not sure how I held it together, but I was able to maintain my composure until he'd gotten out of the car and I drove away. My heart was crumbling into a million little pieces. Surely I would never recover! I had to pull the car off the road and park. I was hysterical with a tear-stained face and sobbing as if my mother had died. I finally got it together and went home. About 7 hours later my phone rang. It was Ronald calling from Germany. " I love you and I can't live without you! Come to Germany!" I didn't hesitate even a second. I said, "Sure." With that I burst into tears of joy! I was in beauty school at the time and I had to finish that first. I wrote him every single day before I went to bed.

One day I came home and he was on my front porch waiting for me! But, he looked a bit thin. This was not the musclebound Mexican I had fallen in love with. He was going to a doctor's appointment, to see some sort of specialist. The doctor told him he had a weak immune system, and asked was he a homosexual? This was in the days before "Don't Ask, Don't Tell." Much worse, it was the height of the witch hunt conducted by the military in the early 80's. After the Navy found out that the Village People were gay, and they were going to use "In the Navy" as their recruiting song, they never forgave us. The entire military during the Reagan era was completely homophobic and conducted witch hunts on a regular basis.

Ronald got better and went back to Germany. He visited me several more times before I was to move in with him there. We didn't practice safe sex, but we were in love, and we'd stopped fooling around with others. We were being good now. We spent two and a half wonderful years there in Germany. We traveled every weekend we could. Ron was frequently sick and in the hospital. AIDS had just begun. Ronald was one of the very first people with AIDS in the U.S. Air Force. The doctors were puzzled. He wouldn't admit to being gay; they would have thrown him out on his ass if he did, and with a dishonorable discharge to boot! How he stood up to their repeated grillings I'll never know. He was sent back to the US to see a specialist in Texas at Whitehall AFB. When he arrived they put him in isolation, and no one would come into the room without full protective coverings on: masks, gloves, the whole nine yards. His doctor arrived, dressed the same as the others who had come and gone.

"You have AIDS, you have 6 months to live, if you're lucky."

Ronald was not about to let anyone tell him what was up. He got back on a plane, wearing a mask and dragging his tired, sick self back to Germany to bring me back to the states. He was afraid that having to deal with the military would be too much for me to handle all the household goods and so on.

Besides, he had something to tell me.

We had been having some problems since he'd cut me off from sex, which was a few months before. We'd also started to use condoms. I can still remember every second of the last time we made love. I had a funny feeling. And I was about ready to head off on my own because I was young and horny, only 23 years old. I decided I really loved the man, and that I would stay with him. When he came home from Texas, he said that we needed to talk. I said that I had to go first. I told him that I loved him and that no matter what we'd stay together. He told me that the doctor told him he had AIDS. We cried each other to sleep wrapped in each other's arms. I couldn't be afraid. Everyone else was. How could I be afraid of Ronald? It wasn't possible. Besides, he'd already been dragged through the mud by the doctors and the authorities. I only knew that I loved him.

I called my mother to tell her Ronald had AIDS, and she said, "I assume you're coming home on the next plane and leaving him."

"No," I replied. "I'm not and if I want your opinion, I'll ask for it." I hung up on my mother for the first and only time in my life. She called back to apologize. Ronald got his orders to go stateside and was being medically retired. We were moving to San Diego.

When we passed through New Jersey on our way, my parents would not let him enter the house. This cut through me like a stiletto followed by a cinder block to the head. I told my family to go to hell. Ronald and I went to a hotel, and got our tickets to San Diego. We were headed to his father's trailer on Coronado Island, where we could see Tijuana from the roof. His dad was there when we arrived at the airport. "Who's that?" he said, referring to me. I had a feeling we were in for a bumpy ride.

We stayed with his dad until Ronald's pension came through and we were able to save for an apartment. I had learned barbering while in Germany and had a New Jersey cosmetology license. I needed to get a California license and a job. We needed to get away from his family. They were unprepared for his illness, or for my presence. I was this white boy on Chicano turf. Even though I spoke Spanish, I had no right to be there.

Once we moved into an apartment, we both did work for the manager while I awaited my license and testing date. Ronald would work and never complain, even though he started to look like a cadaver in motion. He still insisted on cooking for me, because I was out working more. His hospital stays got longer and longer, but the Navy Doctors were different than the Air Force Doctors. They were human and treated him with respect, even though they still wore much of the protective gear. I used to love to freak out the nurses by eating food off his plate or drinking from the same cup. I was still negative. Ronald made me go every month for an HIV test. The nurses at the health clinic finally said, "Listen, if he tells you to come down here again, you bring him with you and we'll tell him to leave you alone."

I was very young. Sometimes when he was in the hospital I would sneak out and get laid. I always made sure that I was home by the time the bars closed. Even when he was home sometimes I'd go out. But I had to work fast, and be safe too. It was grueling working all day and going to the hospital every night. The Navy sailors were mostly gay; they were a great comfort, and the doctors there treated me like I was his partner, which they didn't have to do. The witch hunts were still going on, but that's another story and another book, "Conduct Unbecoming," also by Randy Shilts. I know many of the people in that book, because I met them in San Diego, or had already met them in Germany. Some of them I even slept with.

Ronald held on to life with an iron grip. Eventually two years had passed since that Texas doctor told him he had six months to live. We drove to Texas and he marched into the hospital and found the doctor.

"You don't know anything!" Ronald said to him. "I'm still here, Mr. High and Mighty!" The doctor looked as if he'd seen a ghost. Ronald was ecstatic, He'd told that bastard what to do with it too!

Back in San Diego we had lots of heart-to-hearts. He wanted to die at home, and I promised him he could. He took me on a tour of the AIDS ward at the Naval Hospital. There was a strange shuddering sound that seemed to cut through me. "Listen carefully," Ronald told me. "That's the death rattle. You must promise me that if I ever get to that point you'll help me out of my misery. I don't want to die like that!"

Eventually, the time came, and Ronald told me he wanted to go home. I told the doctors that he was leaving and they made him sign *papers stating that he was doing so against medical advice. He knew that full well.*

At home he was able to walk for a few weeks, although he slept a lot and was rather fragile. We continued to sleep in the same bed and share our space, except I had to have my own bathroom, by his insistence. Because of his cold sores and stuff he ingested a lot of blood. One night in the middle of the night he got out of bed and was puking up blood in the bathroom. There was blood everywhere. He wouldn't let me near him to help him, even though we were both crying. I hated to watch him suffer. He worked so hard to protect me from his disease.

The next week he fell into a coma-like state. I was the only one who could communicate with him. By this time I had lots of help. There were the hospice nurses, as well as an entire cast of characters and friends who came and went. I had stopped working because I needed to be there for him. His family was even around, and treating me better. They finally realized that yes, I did love their brother and son. One afternoon, he began the death rattle. I called the priest and the family. Now was the time to show him how much I loved him and follow through on my promise.

I had stashed an arsenal of opium suppositories. He had planned this, and used them sparingly so I would have enough to do the job when the time came. The priest and family arrived; he was given last rites, and then I told everyone they had to leave.

I went took the suppositories from the fridge and went to his side, crying and telling him that I would do as I promised because I couldn't bear to watch him suffer. I rolled him over on his side, told him I loved him and as I got out the first suppository, he stopped the death rattle. I put down the box and kissed him. Then I got angry and asked him if this was just a test to see if I really loved him! I didn't care. I got to spend another night by his side with my arms wrapped around him. Finally I was the protector.

Ronald's state lingered. I was still the only one who could communicate with him. It was almost telepathic. He went on like this for two weeks, stubbornly clinging to life or some semblance of it. I was going crazy at home. One morning the nurses told me to go out to the salon and work for the day. I called my boss and said that I wanted to come in - I'd do walk in customers. After lunch at home and time spent with Ronald, it was time to go back to work. Unbeknownst to me, one of the nurses had figured out what was up with Ron. He was staying alive for me. He was afraid to leave me alone and uncared for. She told him that at this point in the game I was young and that I would survive, and also that he was making my life a living nightmare by staying alive in a coma at home.

Five minutes later, on December 4th 1986, Ron died.

I was in the middle of a hair cut when the phone rang. The guy was upset with me for turning him over to another stylist. I was consumed with guilt because I wanted to be there when he passed. I buried my first husband in the military cemetery on Point Loma in San Diego with a full military funeral. I even put his ashes in the ground myself. We had a good lawyer at the time and I had been adopted by him; that made me his legal next of kin so his family couldn't take anything away from me. They didn't.

Here I was: a widower at 26! I had never imagined that I could be living all that had happened. Then I started my rebound. About one week after I buried him I had guys calling me for dates. About three weeks later I started going out, but now I didn't have to be home before the bars closed. I hung more and more in only leather bars, mostly Wolf's and another bar in San Diego. Then I started to go to Los Angeles, where I really broke out and discovered myself, as well as discovering crystal meth. People called me the "Safe Sex Slut." Men were dropping dead like bottles at a shooting range, and they were pissed at me because even under the influence of heavy drugs I could not be coerced into unsafe sex. I remember one guy was positively indignant when I told him to get out because he didn't want to wear a condom. I told him that there were plenty of guys who were willing to wear them and that he could go fuck himself!

The party raged on, and I went to Europe again on the money from the insurance policy. Ronald had instructed me to go back and take care of some unfinished business, and like a good boy, I did. I also partied all over Germany, Holland, France and England. I went back to many of the places we'd been together, and I fucked my way from one destination to the next. There was always one way or another to cover the pain of losing him.

In England I met a man at Backstreets, a London leather bar.

This really hot guy with an attitude, who was also the bartender, was hitting on me. To make a long story short, he fell in love with me. I thought he was okay. My trip was to begin and end in London for the European branch of it. I left London and continued a few more weeks in Amsterdam, Berlin and Munich. Finally I went back to London and hooked up again with Michael the bartender. All of a sudden he told me that he loved me and that he'd been to see a psychic and that he's spoken to Ronald! Michael said that Ronald told him to make me a tape and that the first song should be "One Hello" by Randy Crawford. It was the same song Ronald had put on the first tape he ever made me. I fell apart on the spot and did not stop crying for three days, even with sedation.

As it turned out, my bartender was a nurse who moonlighted at the leather bar for extra cash - and a good position to speak to everyone.

I was once again in love, and with Ronald's permission. Michael and I partied up a storm. He immigrated to the U.S. to be with me. One small problem: he was HIV POZ. For a while he came on a tourist visa and made friends quickly. Eventually we contrived an elaborate ruse to get him legal status, involving switched blood samples and all sorts of machinations. Once he became legal we partied on, every weekend. Eventually all the crystal meth got to him and he started to get paranoid. Life in paradise was no longer the same, so we decided we'd move. I agreed but said that I had to choose the city. In 1989 I chose Miami Beach, at the height of it's growing momentum as the chic art deco capital of the universe.

Michael took some time to go to England before joining me in

Miami. Meanwhile, I discovered Fort Lauderdale: the place I would soon call paradise to live in. Miami was cool, but all the hot leathermen were in Ft Lauderdale! I was partying and tweaking, in no time at all. Things were rough when Michael finally joined me. I'd moved cross country for him so he wouldn't have to be paranoid, and it wasn't working. Eventually we split and I went back to Miami; he bought a house in Oakland Park where I stayed often on weekends. It was safer than driving fucked up back to Miami.

One night I attended a party where there were copious amounts of crystal and just about every other drug ever invented. I crashed, exhausted on a couch, naked. When I woke up a guy had his cock up my ass, shooting with no rubber.

I ran out and got tested. Negative.

The next month I got tested again. Negative.

I figured I was okay until I went to the dentist one day, and the guy gets all choked up while he's looking in my mouth. He had to leave the room. The nurse came in and told me that the dentist just buried his brother two weeks ago who'd died of AIDS. When the dentist came back he tried his hardest to tell me that I needed to get to a doctor ASAP. I did so, and wasn't surprised when the results came back.

The safe sex slut had been beaten at his own game.

The doctor couldn't believe that I was so calm about it. No hysteria, no drama. Actually I was relieved of survivor guilt. I had already buried my first husband and about 60 friends in San Diego. I didn't see the drama. The blood tests showed that I had 99 t-cells, but the day before I was HIV Negative! This was the second, even ruder awakening. I was barely alive.

I was working two jobs on South Beach and hardly surviving. Now I decided to go back to school and get my degree this time. My parents found out and offered me to live at their home without having to pay rent to help me get through school. I dropped the A-Bomb on them and explained that I would come home only on a predetermined set of rules. We worked it out. My dad came and helped me move back by driving a U-Haul with me back to Jersey. I had to unload the truck myself. No one thought I was particularly sick. Cruising in Egypt strikes again! Holy Denial Batman!!! I promptly came down with a case of shingles that covered my body: front, back and sides, from my knees to my face! I had to be carried to the car to get me to a doctor. Then they paid attention.

I wound up at a clinic for the indigent, which I basically was except that I had a crash pad. There I found myself surrounded by all strata of humanity. There were hot guys, women, junkies and some kids. The whole world was there. It was a great place to hunt for dates! Shit, why not? You don't need to ask the question about status! Truth be told I never did ask anyone about their status. I have always assumed that all men were poz. Let's face it guys, a stiff dick has no conscience and all men are dogs, especially the guy who shoved his cock up my ass while I was passed out. Today he's a necrophiliac.

Bottom line is it's your responsibility to protect your own ass, not to mention the rest of you. The only intelligent thing to do is assume that all people you have sex with are poz. Then you don't need to ask, and they don't have to lie. No condom, no sex. Not more than a hand job anyway. Every person you sleep with carries within them the sexual history of every other person they've ever had sex with. And you too can sleep with thousands of men and all it takes is one foul-up! Wham! Welcome to HIV. Today it's not a death sentence necessarily. But boys, it's no walk in the park either. I went through college with HIV. It took five years, and I got the shingles every time I had a paper to write. I graduated and I came back to use my teaching degree in Fort Lauderdale. I joined a leather family as the household bottom. That lasted for a year before one of the partners left; I remained with the other one for six more years.

Somewhere along the line there must have been an accident or maybe I did something stupid because during one of my visits to the doctor he told me that I have hepatitis C. It didn't seem like a big deal then, but I found out that it sure ruins your sex life. Today telling someone you have hep C is like telling someone you had HIV back in the mid 80's. Instant freeze! Your number, that they just begged for, is being deleted from their cell phone as fast as you can say "Shit!"

Is it worth the trouble to stay negative? Is it worth not having certain experiences that you've fantasized about in order to stay alive? Is HIV really "no big deal"? HIV is like a pair of handcuffs that cannot be removed. You can exist with them, but they're uncomfortable. It will dictate what you can and cannot do in your life, if you don't take charge and do it yourself! Frequently young guys tell me that they're jealous that I came out in the late 70's in New York and got to be a tramp and a safe sex slut. They're not looking at the fact that I no longer can work due to complications from HIV and hep C. I did a year and a half on interferon and ribovirin to quell my hepatitis, but it didn't work. The treatment failed. Fortunately my HIV is under control and undetectable, but I have to give myself 14 injections a week to stay that way. I am the national pin cushion. Fortunately I had lots of practice with needle scenes.

By the way: what are your safety and health worth to you? Do you think that 14 injections - sometimes extremely painful due to my reaction to the drug - are worth a good fuck? A bareback fuck just like in all the hot movies and videos? Guess what guys: the majority of those performers are poz. NEWS FLASH!!!! They may look good at the moment, but sooner or later it will catch up with most of us, especially if you like to have a good time and party. PNP is for the birds! You can't make a good decision on drugs. If I hadn't been partying I would never have passed out on that couch with my ass up in the first place. I'd do it all again for some survivor guilt! I'd trade my 14 injections a week and the year and a half spent on Interferon (which, incidentally, is used for chemotherapy!). I'd trade all those hot fucks to know that I might live long enough to see my nieces and nephews married. I don't have any guarantees. At the moment I'm off of the interferon but will soon be doing an experimental drug study. I figured I did enough experimental drugs in my 20's and 30's. In my 40's now it might just save my ass.

At what price? I'm not done paying the price yet, and I was the SAFE SEX SLUT!

You need to be aware of every moment and know what's going on, so you can make the decisions that will affect how you will live. One of these days a new disease will come down the pike, and I can assure you it will make AIDS look like child's play. I would do it all again if I could bring back all the lost friends and lovers. Michael died in 2001. I can't even count the total number of funerals I have not attended; I can't do them. They hurt too much. And frankly, I have spent 20 years running from the AIDS Quilt. The hospice nurses made a panel of the quilt with Ronald's name on it. "Ronald [last name withheld by author]" it says. I've never seen it. Perhaps one day I will be able to bear the pain that wells up inside me ever time I think about his loss and the loss of countless men and women and children who have died from AIDS on this planet. I will begin to wail when I see the panel of the quilt with Ronald's name on it. No doubt I'll fall to my knees with the weight of years of repressed loss gnawing at my insides.

I shall wail until there are no more tears left, and then I will wail some more. The second wailing will be for the young men who will make bad decisions and the loss to their families and friends, when it is absolutely not necessary! All they had to do was stay safe and play well with others. We were all taught that in kindergarten. It's your decision. Cover your ass! Don't forget to cover your cock too, with a condom! Unless you just don't care about yourself, your families or your friends, or your fuckbuddies either. I figure if a guy is worth having sex with, he's worth protecting, from both of us and our stiff cocks masquerading as brains. If you are both poz and have been honest with one another, that's your decision. Can you really trust a stiff dick to do your thinking for you?

Come on. You know the answer.

After reaching the mandatory retirement age of 75, as dictated by canon law, John Reiss resigned as Bishop of Trenton on June 30, 1997. He was succeeded by John Mortimer Smith. Smith would reign over the Diocese for the next 14 years. It will take the Diocese twice as long to recover and Lorenzo, like so many others, a lifetime.

7
Bishop John M. Smith –
The Great Communicator Goes Silent

"I think the whole issue of child sex abuse by priests has been a very painful experience for any of us who are involved in the church but particularly for the clergy. We were embarrassed; we were ashamed we were hurt that this was going on in our midst. I'm thankful to God that the church in the United States had the courage to address it very directly.

-Bishop John Mortimer Smith

    Although not a native Floridian, the Sunshine State was Bishop Joseph Keith Symons' career homestead. Symons served the Church in Florida for 40 years from his 1958 ordination through his appointments as the Auxiliary Bishop of the Diocese of St. Petersburg, and Bishop of the Dioceses of Pensacola-Tallahassee and later, Palm Beach. As a teen, Symons had moved from Michigan to Florida with his family, and as a priest, he intended to retire there.

    By 1995, Symons had long moved on from Pensacola-Tallahassee to Palm Beach, but returned for some unfinished business in the Diocese. His successor in the Pensacola-Tallahassee Diocese called a meeting with Symons and a man who claimed to have been abused as a child by Symons. During the meeting Symons admitted to the abuse, assured everyone present that there was only one victim and agreed that he would seek counseling.

When the perfunctory meeting concluded, Bishop Joseph Keith Symons returned to work as the Bishop of the Diocese of Palm Beach, unscathed. Having expended his due diligence slapping the wrist of the man who once led his see, the Bishop of Pensacola-Tallahassee also went back to work.

But not for long.

Unlike Symons, the Bishop of Pensacola-Tallahassee, a native of New Jersey, had no intention of retiring in Florida. John Mortimer Smith was going home to become the Ninth Bishop of the Diocese of Trenton.

Three years had passed since the meeting in Pensacola, and Symons' victim, having duly kept the secret that he told only those in attendance at the meeting, became increasingly unnerved by Church rhetoric that incidents of clergy abuse were "isolated." It was only then that the sham that was the 1995 meeting became apparent to him. He broke his silence, forcing Bishop Symons to belatedly admit that he had molested five boys during his career. The Church sought a resignation from Symons, who was "depressed and disappointed" by the action, and subsequently, "relieved." His resignation was hailed by the Church as a demonstration of its swift response to clergy abuse.

That summer, however, police records made it patently obvious that when he was the Bishop of the Diocese of Tallahassee-Pensacola, John Smith had failed to act on the first victim's allegations in 1995. The Bishop had little comment, other than to describe the meeting he had set up as one "to effect a spiritual reconciliation."

Prosecutors cited the statute of limitations as preventing charges against Bishop Symons. Although his Floridian retirement plan was foiled by the allegations, Symons didn't have to worry. There wasn't a commemorative gold watch moment in his immediate future. Instead of being forced to retire, he returned to ministry in his native Michigan with the permission of the local bishop and the Vatican. Upon Symons' Florida departure, the spokesman for the Diocese of Palm Beach told reporters that while "there's obviously a tinge of disappointment" in the Roman Catholic community in Symons, "there is also the recollection of a man that was very compassionate and very gentle and meant so much to so many people."

Pope John Paul II assigned Bishop Anthony J. O'Connell to replace Symons and lead the Palm Beach Diocese through the healing process.

In 2002, O'Connell resigned after admitting he abused a teenage seminary student in the 1970's, plunging the fraught Diocese of Palm Beach into greater upset.

By this time, the John Mortimer Smith excuse train had rolled into Trenton.

If you meet Bishop John M. Smith on the street in Trenton, you would be hard-pressed to come across a more engaging, self-deprecating, humorous man. Kids love him, flock to him, and listen to him. The Bishop presided at several Masses that I attended and at each and every celebration, the love he had for the kids of the choir, the altar servers, and his congregation, was tangible. After the legion of priests in his attendance left the Mass in the recessional, the Ninth Bishop of Trenton would stay behind and mock-conduct the choir, much to the delight of the kids. His embrace is fatherly, his handshake firm, and his demeanor, genuine.

In his home neighborhood in an affluent part of Trenton, he was a staple at the neighborhood block parties and social gatherings. Years later when the dilapidated home was put up for sale by the Diocese because of its condition, Smith's successor, David O'Connell, drew the ire of residents who could no longer point to the block home and brag, "That's the Bishop's house." John Smith was a great neighbor, kindred spirit and the "great communicator" – but only to a degree.

Because of Florida, Smith's leash in Trenton was short. He had royally miscalculated his role in the Symons affair and thought that the miles between New Jersey and Florida would absorb the after-shock. He was wrong. And he was about to extend his series of bad decisions, playing hardball with a chronically ill 8 year-old girl's sacramental journey.

In May 2004, 8 year-old Haley Waldman was preparing for her First Holy Communion. Excited about her dress, her party, and sharing the event with her friends and three siblings, Haley left concerns regarding her Celiac Disease and the risk posed by consuming the Eucharist up to her mom, Elizabeth Pelly-Waldman. Pelly-Waldman explained to her pastor that Haley needed to receive a gluten-free Communion wafer because her digestive disorder made it unsafe for her to consume unleavened wheat wafers. When consumed by Celiac sufferers, gluten damages the lining of the small intestines, blocking nutrient absorption and leading to vitamin deficiencies, bone-thinning and sometimes gastrointestinal cancer.

The Diocese of Trenton told Haley's mother that the girl could receive a low-gluten wafer, or just drink the wine at Communion, but that anything without gluten did not qualify as receiving the Eucharist. Pelly-Waldman rejected the offer, stressing that because of the severity of her daughter's condition, the child could be harmed by even a small amount of the substance, even if diluted. She was a mother putting her daughter's health first. Any percentage of risk to a child's health, regardless of how scientifically small, is too great a risk for a loving parent. The Bishop of Trenton didn't see it that way.

After Haley's pastor refused to allow a substitute, a priest at a nearby parish volunteered to offer one and in a separate ceremony apart from her Communion class, Haley received the sacrament alongside her mother, who had not taken Communion since she herself was diagnosed with the disease.

Not to be bested, the Diocese informed Haley's mother that her Communion was invalid; a distraught Pelly-Waldman wrote Pope John Paul II and then Cardinal Ratzinger: "This is a church rule, not God's will, and it can easily be adjusted to meet the needs of the people, while staying true to the traditions of our faith," she reasoned.

The plea went unanswered and Pelly-Waldman felt her only recourse would be to discuss this with Bishop Smith.

The Catholic media weighed in and attacked the Pelly-Waldman family as "bashers." The *Catholic World News* snarked:

...In order to celebrate a valid Mass, the priest must use bread made from wheat, and wine made from grapes. This is not an arbitrary rule

concocted by the Vatican, but the Church's response to a divine imperative. "Do this in memory of me," Jesus said at the Last Supper. And so the priest does as Jesus did, consecrating simple bread and wine. The priest could perform the same ritual with rice cakes and apple juice, but then he would not be doing what Jesus did; the ceremony would not be the Sacrifice of Calvary.[37]

Haley's mother asked the Diocese of Trenton to change Church rules in order to accommodate her daughter. No doubt diocesan officials would have been happy to oblige, if they had been dealing with a local regulation or a question of ordinary ecclesial discipline. But it is not. The question of what constitutes the Eucharist - of how the Body and Blood of Jesus Christ become present on the altar - involves the most essential elements of Catholic doctrine. As Trenton's Bishop John Smith told the media, "This is not an issue to be determined at the diocesan or parish level, but has already been decided for the Roman Catholic Church throughout the world by Vatican authority."

What Smith did not include in his "I'm just following orders" reasoning was that during World War II, several priests would consecrate bread that was made from rice due to shortages of wheat and bread and obvious battlefield conditions. Did this invalidate the consecration? Is the grape juice used in the consecration of the Holy Blood, invalid? Is it the required "fruit of the vine?" What makes bread, bread? Is it the gluten that forms the bread matter? Bishop Smith had the answer he was sticking to, but certainly not the explanations.

The position of the United Methodist Church offers a clinical and sensible approach when it comes to gluten-free wafers. "There is no (Methodist) church law or official rule that would invalidate the efficacy of the sacrament when served with gluten-free bread," reports Dan Benedict, worship services director of the General Board of Discipleship of the United Methodist Church. As awareness of wheat and gluten intolerances grows, more congregations are offering wheat alternatives for Communion. The United Methodist Church, unlike the Catholic Church, believes the "substance of the sign is in the signified, Jesus Christ, and not in the chemical make-up of the sign." Finally, a substance over form argument that is reasonable in practice and theory.

The applicable canon law (924) states that hosts must be made of wheat, and therefore, a rice wafer is not permissible. "Bread is traditionally made of wheat," explains Joanne Novarro, spokesperson for the Rockville Centre Diocese in New York, one of the largest Dioceses in the country, "a rice wafer would not be a valid sacrament. It must be unleavened bread made out of wheat. It's what Jesus ate at the Last Supper, and we're recreating that meal at Communion. Canon law permits priests to set aside a special wine chalice exclusively for worshippers following wheat or gluten-free diets, eliminating the possibility of the hosts accidentally contaminating the wine. The canon law also offers parishioners the alternative of drinking only wine.

In fairness to the Church and canon 924, every conceivable effort has been made to work with the nationally recognized Center for Celiac Research to come up with an acceptable alternative to wheat wafers. Leave it to the resourceful nuns of the Benedictine Sisters to come up with that solution.

According to their website www.benedictinesisters.org, the Sisters came up with a recipe that not only satisfied the Vatican (and then Cardinal Ratzinger) but the Center for Celiac Research as well. How? They prayed, of course:

> [W]e prayed for divine inspiration as we began to research how we could meet the requirements of both these groups we hoped to serve. Throughout the years of our research and development we stayed in touch with the Office of the Secretariat for the Liturgy of the U.S. Council of Catholic Bishops. Through their help we discovered a company that produced wheat starch, which is wheat that has had most of the gluten removed. We began experimenting with this new product. There were many failed attempts and much frustration — the resulting breads were either too thin, too hard, or inedible. Then one evening, as our sisters were working, Divine Providence intervened. When mixing the ingredients, the result was a sticky, messy batter that seemed hopeless. They plopped some of it onto the baking plate and then decided to throw out the rest and start over. When they opened the baker they discovered a round, crisp, light wafer that tasted delicious. God had blessed our efforts with success.[38]

But for many afflicted individuals, low-gluten wafers, said to contain less than 0.01% of gluten, are not an option because even a tiny amount of the protein can trigger immediate reactions. Such was the case in Boston in 2001, when the family of a 5 year-old girl with the disease left the Church after being denied permission to use a rice wafer, upon edict by then Bernard Cardinal Law. The Boston family decided they did not want to settle for a low-gluten wafer or no wafer at all. They switched to a different church entirely; a Methodist congregation that accepted wafers made without gluten.

Alas, the baking nuns' serendipitous science venture was also satisfying no one in Trenton. On the one hand Pelly-Waldman was still uneasy about the risks posed by a low-gluten wafer and Bishop Smith was standing by the invalidation of the little girl's sacrament, piqued as he was by the intervention of the insubordinate rice-wafer bearing pastor and hewing closely to strict interpretation of canon law. He was also not about to bump heads with a precedent set by the still powerful and influential Cardinal Law, now in Rome.

When Hayley's mother finally met with Smith to discuss her daughter's invalidated first Holy Communion, she presented him with a plate of cut up pieces of bread, some of which contained wheat, while others did not. She asked the Bishop if he could tell which bread contained wheat. The ninth Bishop of Trenton was taken aback by the challenge, but flashed a smile to accompany one of his famous "off the cuff" responses: "I cannot, but Christ does." Touché, game, set, match, Smith. It could have essentially ended at that juncture of the meeting. The Great Communicator could have listened graciously, comforted the mother, cited precedent, administered a pastoral blessing and moved on; even up to the point when Pelly-Waldman asked for his advocacy to Rome.

But the city-boy surfaced. The irritated Bishop flatly refused to help facilitate any communication between Pelly-Waldman and the Vatican in Rome in her campaign for the use of rice-based Communion hosts during Mass. With the parties at loggerheads, the meeting was understandably "tense" (as described by Pelly-Waldman), and insiders at that meeting related that the Bishop's level of frustration gave way to his famous temper not often seen in public, but well-known to those that crossed him. "Smith is very charming in short, one-on-one meetings, but if challenged, it's up to his in-house employees to reel him in," according to one highly placed Diocese official. "In his last months (of office) he was more and more limited to what he took on personally because of this. We were aware of this, considered it a risk to the transition (to Bishop O'Connell), and took measures."

According to one source at the meeting, the Bishop refused to acknowledge any possibility of changing the wafer to rice, and grew agitated when it was brought up by a theologian attending the meeting with Mrs. Pelly-Waldman that the wafer has already gone through changes in recent years to conform to the Benedictine Sisters' low-gluten alternative. The Bishop refused to take the issue to Rome.

Meeting over; but what about Haley?

According to Mrs. Pelly-Waldman, the meeting did make an impression on her daughter, who was not present but did make a card for Smith thanking him for meeting with her mother: "Haley said she's sad," her mother said. "Haley thought a priest was someone you go to for help."

We all thought that, Haley.

Because of his connection to the Symons case, Smith was concerned with the image of the Church and the rising sexual crisis that was about to explode in Boston. When this came to fruition in 2002, the Bishop sprung immediately into damage control, fostering the impression that the Bishop was a man of action.

Less than three months after the *Boston Globe* broke the story of the cover-up and the criminal activity of the Boston Archdiocese and its Vicar, Cardinal Law, Bishop Smith formed a taskforce with Monsignor Walter Nolan at the helm that claimed to have thoroughly investigated over 50 years of Trenton Diocese records. Upon its finding and recommendations document, then Mercer County Prosecutor Daniel G. Giaquinto announced a decision on June 17, 2002:

> *[T]he Mercer County Prosecutor's office will not file criminal charges against 12 priests from the Roman Catholic Diocese of Trenton accused of sexual misconduct. Based on the applicable law, the nature of the incidents, and the ages of the victims at the time of offense and time of reporting, all 20 cases reviewed by the prosecutor's office were determined to be beyond the statute of limitations." I can think of few, if any, sexual assaults that are as repugnant as those which use trust in the clergy to get at child victims," Prosecutor Giaquinto said. "As detestable as this is, we will not be able to prosecute because the statute of limitations has run."*
>
> *"It is extremely commendable that Bishop Smith made the decision to break with past practice and come forward with this information," he continued. "This new leadership in the Diocese has been extremely cooperative during this investigation."*
>
> *Based on a decision by Bishop John Smith of the Roman Catholic Diocese of Trenton, on or about April 2, 2002, the Diocese advised the Mercer County Prosecutor's Office of complaints involving sexual misconduct made against priests over the past 50 years. Eventually, the Diocese forwarded complaints involving 15 victims to the prosecutor's office. Subsequently, five additional victims contacted the office independently of Bishop Smith's announcement, for a total of 20 victims. The alleged incidents dated from the 1960s to the mid-1990s, with the*

victims ranging in age from approximately 11 to the mid-30s at the time of the occurrence. Twelve of the alleged victims are male; eight are female.

The complaints allege kissing, fondling, mutual masturbation, oral sex and sodomy. Some victims allege that alcohol, marijuana and pornography were used to seduce them. Most of the sexual abuse alleged was not a singular episode, but consisted of multiple incidents that occurred over a period of time.

Twelve priests have been named in the incidents. The Diocese provided the identities of eight of these priests and four were obtained by those victims who independently contacted this office. Three of the accused priests are deceased, five have left the priesthood, and two are still active. One priest was unable to be named by the victim and thus his current status is unknown. Of the two priests who are still active, the Diocese is aware of their identities and locations.

The twelfth priest, Jean Level Eliscard, was prosecuted by this office in 1995 for the sexual assault of a 13-year old girl. The assault occurred in September 1994 and was immediately reported by the Diocese. Eliscard pled guilty, was sentenced to three years' probation and returned to Haiti. If he ever returns to New Jersey, he is subject to registration requirements under Megan's Law...." [39]

The "agreement" between the Prosecutor's Office and the Diocese of Trenton contains fundamental flaws that border on negligence on behalf of the Prosecutor's Office and a panic cover-up on the part of

Bishop Smith, Monsignor Walter Nolan and the suits (clerical or otherwise) in the Pastoral Center of the Trenton Diocese.

The timeline reflected in the agreement is based on the findings and recommendations document that led to the Prosecutor's press release. These following facts, then, are undisputed:

- On June 17, 2002, the date of the press release, a total of twelve priests of the Diocese of Trenton had credible claims of varying degrees of sexual abuse, sexual misconduct or solicitation for the purpose of sex of a minor, against them. The Diocese of Trenton found these claims credible and had passed those findings onto the Mercer County Prosecutor's office two months earlier, in April of 2002;
- Time frame of records review: 1960 through the mid-1990's;
- Total victims: 20;
- Of the twelve priests accused, the Diocese named 8. The other 4 were named by victims that came forward directly to the Prosecutor's Office;
- Left priesthood prior to June 2002 (5); deceased (3); unable to name by victim (1) and two were known to the Diocese to be active in the Diocese as of June 2002. The twelfth returned to Haiti and was apparently killed in the earthquake.

The list of names submitted to the Mercer County Prosecutor was an incomplete list of accusations against the religious of the Trenton Diocese during that time frame.

First, the names submitted to Prosecutor Giaquinto did not include the list of names of those that were transferred to the Metuchen Diocese in the early 1980's. Some have stood trial for their crimes while in Metuchen, but none for their crimes in Trenton.

Next, Pre-Megan's Law, the Diocese of Trenton and the local authorities were never notified that those accused that had left the priesthood were living in their neighborhoods.

Finally, Trenton's review was in the direct wake of the Boston scandal - by mere months - the true scope of the problem had yet to be fully realized. Church records are byzantine; the Bishop did not conduct a thorough investigation of all records or accusations from those who mattered - the victims themselves - but merely scanned vaguely annotated, poorly kept Church records.

The April 2002 findings report by the Diocese of Trenton filed with the Mercer County Prosecutor's Office was a "rush job," a black mark to the Diocese, and an affront to the victims and their families. To undertake a truly "thorough analysis" of diocesan records for a 50-year period is a gargantuan task; to aver that it was implemented and completed comprehensively in a span of 72 days is laughable if not making short shrift of the lingering damage to the victims.

The Diocese knew full well that in the wake of Boston, a records review was eventual and necessary; and doing it before anyone calls you on it, looks that much better.

BishopAccountability.org is a watch-dog organization dedicated to posting complete public record of the clergy sex abuse crisis on their website in order to foster true accountability. Their philosophy is straightforward:

A.W Richard Sipe has said that "secrecy and accountability cannot coexist." In order to hold the bishops accountable for bringing abusers into the priesthood and for transferring known abusers into unsuspecting parishes, we need a comprehensive archive of the evidence. That evidence is vast but scattered. It is our goal to assemble on the internet a collection of every publicly available document and report on the crisis....

Our standards for inclusion are broad. We offer documents representing every conceivable perspective on the crisis, and we intend to include every relevant diocesan and Vatican document. We endorse no particular analysis of the root causes of the crisis, and we advocate no particular remedies.... [40]

The leaders of bishopaccountability.org, urge dioceses to fully embrace the transparency and openness called for in the *Charter for the Protection of Children and Young People*, approved by the U.S. bishops in Dallas in 2002. In keeping with their no nonsense approach -- expose it or we will expose you -- the group's appeal to the dioceses is plain and simple: *Release the lists.* The dioceses still have a long way to go, according to Terence McKiernan, founder of the organization, "both in terms of how many are not doing it yet, and in terms of the quality of the lists, which in most cases leaves a lot to be desired." And while only a fraction have in some way made public the names of accused priests, in the overwhelming number of cases the releases had to be coaxed through lawsuits. List making doesn't entirely resolve trustworthiness issues, but release, by whatever means, is a step in the right direction for these dioceses:

- Baltimore MD
- Chicago IL
- Davenport IA
- Detroit MI
- Dubuque IA
- Fairbanks AK
- Fort Worth TX
- Gallup NM
- Grand Rapids MI
- Joliet IL
- Los Angeles CA
- Madison WI
- Monterey CA
- Orange CA
- Peoria IL
- Philadelphia
- Portland ME
- Sand Diego CA
- Spokane WA
- St. Petersburg FL
- Toledo OH
- Tucson AZ
- Wilmington DE and MD

Conspicuous by their absence are the New Jersey dioceses of Camden, Patterson, Newark, Metuchen and of course, Trenton.

I strongly exhort the Dioceses of Trenton (and Metuchen, because of the early 1980's Diocese "split") to follow suit of these open dioceses. It is incumbent on the current leadership of both dioceses, the Most Reverend Bishop David M. O'Connell of Trenton and the Most Reverend Paul Gregory Bootkoski of Metuchen, to issue a joint statement that they will open a one-year no stone unturned internal investigation of the 1960's through the present of any and all claims that have come into their respective territories, and follow up with the publication of the names of those credibly accused, their current ministry status (active, prayer and penance, defrocked, alive or dead) and municipality with last known address. The list should contain not only those publicly accused, but those from religious orders, those now assigned to other dioceses, and those who left the priesthood before accusations were levied against them.

On a cold day in Trenton in March of 2011, the cause of releasing the names was brought to the doorstep of Trenton's tenth bishop, David M. O'Connell. Members of the Survivors Network of those Abused by Priests ("SNAP") gathered at the Lawrence office of the newly installed bishop to call for identification of all clergy members who were proven, admitted to, or credibly accused of sex abuse. To date, there are nine priests (former, active, living and dead) that have not been officially identified, but whose names are available on bishopaccountability.org (with the exception of Jerry Brown). Those are the names the Prosecutor's agreement sealed. The Diocese of Trenton removed them from their assignments, took away their priestly faculties within the Diocese of Trenton, and instructed them to return to their religious orders or native dioceses. The Diocese of Trenton also informed their superiors of the reasons for their removal from all ministries within the Diocese.

This is all well and good, but it misses the mark. What the Diocese has not done is list those that have been credibly accused and remain in service or placed in "prayer and penance." The Diocese, under Smith and Nolan leaked the "easy marks" that appear on bishopaccountability.org, the known predators from the 1970's, 1980's and 1990's, because of the statute of limitations in place to shield them from prosecution, yet hid the priests that remain "on the payroll." The latter includes priests such as Chapter 10's Terence McAlinden, who was relieved of his priestly duties, banned from saying Mass in public (though not in private residences), and on administrative leave, yet still receiving a stipend from the Diocese, car allowances (insurance) and healthcare.

When SNAP staged their public and peaceful vigil outside the Diocese offices in March 2011, they got more than just interview requests from the local media. Slightly after noon, Bishop David M. O'Connell donned his coat and made his way to the organizers, the former priest Robert Hoatson and SNAP founder Barbara Blaine. The Bishop had broken through the ecclesiastical red tape and forthrightly faced a group of victims and their assembled advocates.

Bishop David M. O'Connell was born April 21, 1955, in Philadelphia. Bishop O'Connell, a priest of the Eastern Province of the Congregation of the Mission, also known as the "Vincentians," grew up in Langhorne, Pennsylvania. The O'Connell family constitutes long-standing parishioners of Our Lady of Grace Parish in Penndel, and the Bishop attended the parish grammar school taught by the Immaculate Heart of Mary Sisters. Certain from an early age that he wished to pursue the priesthood; Bishop O'Connell attended the Vincentians' St. Joseph Preparatory High School in Princeton. He continued his Vincentian education in Niagara University, New York, where he obtained a bachelor's degree in philosophy in 1978. Bishop O'Connell prepared for the priesthood in Mary Immaculate Seminary, Northampton, Pennsylvania, where he received a master of divinity degree in 1981 and a master's degree in moral theology in 1983. On May 29, 1982, Bishop Joseph McShea of the Diocese of Allentown ordained him a priest of the Congregation of the Mission in Mary Immaculate Seminary.

Following ordination, Bishop O'Connell's first assignment was as director of student activities and faculty in Archbishop Wood High School, Warminster, Pennsylvania, where he served from 1982 to 1985. He then pursued studies in canon law at The Catholic University of America, Washington, D.C., obtaining a licentiate in 1987 and then a doctorate in canon law in 1990. He has since received numerous honorary academic degrees from various colleges and universities.

While working towards his canon law degrees, Bishop O'Connell also served as registrar and assistant professor of canon law, theology and philosophy at Mary Immaculate Seminary. In 1990, he joined St. John's University, New York, where he served as academic dean for the following eight years. During his time at St. John's, he held a variety of positions, including professor of theology and religious studies, associate dean of the College of Liberal Arts and Sciences, academic dean and dean of faculty of the College of Liberal Arts and Sciences, and assistant to legal counsel. He also spent one year simultaneously serving as interim academic vice president of Niagara University.

In 1998, O'Connell was named the 14th president of The Catholic University of America. Among the many highlights of his presidency was the opportunity to serve as a member of the planning committee for Pope Benedict XVI's pastoral visit to the United States in April 2008 and to host the Pope at the University, where he delivered an address to Catholic educators.

On June 4, 2010, Pope Benedict XVI appointed O'Connell as coadjutor bishop of the Diocese of Trenton. On December 1, 2010, Bishop O'Connell was appointed the 10th Bishop of the Diocese of Trenton.

David O'Connell is no stranger to the media and is a most savvy communicator. An adept small-talker and glad-hander, he appreciates a large audience and appears to be a compassionate and animated listener. Not one individual I interviewed for this book denied that the Bishop's concern for the victims seems genuine but when it comes to action on their behalf, O'Connell is stepping away from academia and into the rough and tumble world of New Jersey politics. The adjustment has not been easy.

In his first six months on the job, the Bishop was the priest presiding over the funeral mass over Christopher Matlosz, a Lakewood police officer shot execution style; chastised a schism of a parish, West Branch's Our Lady of Guadalupe, for separating from the Diocese and joining up with the independent American National Catholic Church, a rogue movement of "modern" Catholic churches; deftly handled the uproar of the Catholic community of Toms River's Saint Joseph; and confronted head on a new onslaught on sexual abuse charges largely ignored by his predecessor.

O'Connell is not an admitted conservative; preferring to be considered a moderate, he has told me personally that he is "less right than you may think," a statement that may not only apply to his political leanings. While his comfort zone could be on FOX News, he is regularly sought after by the more liberal news media. He is candid in his private conversations and on more than one occasion has been known to coolly say, "I do not react to demands."

SNAP had demands on March 7, 2011, and the Bishop listened with pain etched in his face. It's what he said at the end that solidified the belief that he was either ill-informed during his transition or flat-out lying:

SNAP President Barbara Blaine recited a checklist of demands and asked O'Connell to post the names of all Diocese of Trenton clergy and employees "credibly accused" of sex abuse on the Diocese website.

In a 2004 report, the Diocese acknowledged credible allegations against 25 priests dating back to the 1950s. Blaine said 16 of those priests have been identified, but another nine have never been named. "We want the identities of those other nine to be made public," said Blaine. She passed out information on Diocese of Trenton priest Michael M. Garry, who Blaine said molested a pre-teen girl in St. Mark's parish in Sea Girt from roughly 1960 to 1963, though his name had never been publicly tied to the priest sex abuse scandal until yesterday. Garry died in 1988.

Speaking calmly and cordially, O'Connell told the group he'd consider all their requests, but he said yesterday was the first time he was hearing about some of the alleged abuse cases. "As horrible as all this is, and I feel terrible about, I can't do anything to change the past...."[41]

How could he not have known? How could the spiritual leader of 800,000 faithful not know the handful of priests' names that served this Diocese who were accused of sexually abusing children? He most certainly knew that there were nine names that needed to be made public because I personally told him this in his office a month prior to SNAP's demonstration. I wrote to him, Bishop Bootkoski, and the Mercer County Prosecutor's Office three weeks prior to his meeting with SNAP and spelled out exactly what was in the 2002 sealed agreement; O'Connell was well briefed by me, during which he asked no questions and took no notes, but listened contemplatively, or so I thought. I basically told him that SNAP was coming to his front door and to get his house in order. Reading the *Trenton Times* story of the encounter at my breakfast table, The Most Reverend O'Connell's feigned ignorance repulsed me. He knew.

As of this writing, it's been over a year since SNAP made their demands. In that passage of time, several other dioceses in the United States and three in Europe have made the lists of credibly accused offenders public. The Church of Ireland is on the brink of collapse and the Prime Minister has condemned the Vatican. A monsignor in

Philadelphia and over 20 priests in that Archdiocese have been charged with varying degrees of sexual assault and obstruction of justice. The Cardinal of Philadelphia's Archdiocese has resigned and his predecessor could have faced the final years of his life in jail had he not died the night prior to his scheduled testimony in the subsequent cover-up cases. A vile criminal and rapist, Terence McAlinden was still listed as a pastor in a church in Bishop O'Connell's own diocese while selling houses as a realtor on the New Jersey shore the day SNAP spoke to his Excellency. But rest assured, over a year later, Bishop David M. O'Connell is still "considering all their requests."

Given all the Church's politicking and covert efforts to shield the guilty, one would think the Church would bend over backwards to defend those priests who stand wrongly accused.

In a small apartment in central New Jersey sits a priest from India who was falsely accused of touching a child by a racist parent. He stood before a Grand Jury and was cleared within an hour. He was free to return to his county, but refuses to do so until the diocese he served restores his good name.

Meet Father James Selvaraj.

8
The Priest That Refuses To Run

"All the church always brings us is Puerto Ricans, Blacks and Indians as priests."

-Parent-Accuser of Father James Selvaraj

"Lou, if I find out this guy is dirty, I'll fucking bury him."

So began my odyssey in the world of Father James Selvaraj. It was 2010 that I met Father Selvaraj for the first time. He and I both remained guarded at our meeting and that was to be expected. "Father James" is one of those rare breeds that has seen, touched and felt the fire of an emotional hell of one falsely accused; the depths of isolation and pain of which most of us on earth cannot even begin to fathom.

The meeting that night was social. It was at a restaurant in Manalapan, New Jersey, which was deliberately selected so that conversation could be candid and to minimize the chance that we would be recognized. At our table that night was Father Selvaraj, John and Janet Zito, my wife Maureen, and Lou and Kathy Monticchio. I had known John Zito and Lou Monticchio for some 20 years prior to our dinner meeting. Solid and active Catholics, and not known to be shy in the mix of Church politics, they were members of the merged parish of Saint Raphael/Holy Angels in Hamilton Township, New Jersey, at the time of the accusations against Father Selvaraj.

The Zito's and Monticchio's are friends and steadfast supporters of Father James. I had read the stories of the accusations and the plight that followed him thereafter in the mid-2000's. I followed the news accounts and inquired about him with the Mercer County Prosecutor's Office. What I saw comported with that intel; the man that sat directly across from me at the dinner table in an outdoor setting was every bit as unindicted as the Grand Jury found him to be. However, I had to be sure in my own cynical mind that this was true. By the time dessert was served, I had my answer: I knew with inner certitude that Father James Selvaraj had been wrongly accused and while set free by the laws that govern this State, he continued to be unfairly persecuted by his Bishop-in-transition in New Jersey and abandoned by his Bishop-of-record thousands of miles away.

This is the ode of an innocent man.

James Selvaraj was born in 1959 in India to Singarajan, a high-ranking State official in Tamil Nadu, and Niraiseeli, a Catholic schoolteacher. All told there are six Selvaraj children (4 boys and 2 girls) all who are well-educated and respected in their home communities.

Education, faith and hard work were paramount in the Selvaraj household. When James was of university age, he attended the Jesuit Saint Xavier College and became active in social causes and programs involving human rights, adult education and village adoption. He became heavily involved in the infrastructure development of villages, drainage systems, road pavement, building homes, and medical camps.

In his final year at Saint Xavier, he attended a retreat. James may have been small in stature but was abundant in calling, a gift from God he felt rising within him: "In the final day of the retreat, I felt something deep inside my heart, a calm peaceful (feeling) and I felt the urge to answer it spiritually. The thrust of my inner being was to respond to that beautiful moment. I have not the words to put it in; I decided to join the seminary and to be a priest."

James Selvaraj was ordained on May 9, 1989, and his career in India was on the fast track. At first Father Selvaraj was assigned to teach as an associate pastor. He taught phonetics to student teachers-in-training as well as pedagogical psychology. Two years later he was named a pastor of a church with sixteen outstations and it was here that the young priest began to build a spiritual community with social awareness, utilizing his construction skills to renovate churches and build schools. It was as pastor that Father Selvaraj established a high school for under-privileged girls that gave them a foundation of self-esteem and social graces that they would carry with them throughout their lives. This is what Father Selvaraj has said gave him the most joy in his life. His efforts and tireless work and love of his parish sustained him in the longest of workdays that extended seven days a week. Bishop Teresnathan Amalanathar noticed his remarkable calling as well and after eight years, he called him to be his personal secretary. He remained in that capacity for two more years when the Bishop asked him to leave India for a very different mission in Trenton, New Jersey.

In June of 1999, Reverend Father James Selvaraj enthusiastically started his first United States ministry at Blessed Sacrament in Trenton, and then a year later he was assigned to Saint Mary of New Monmouth where he remained for three years. Father Selvaraj embraced his exposure to different cultures within New Jersey as part of a plan to better acclimate himself to the growing diversity of demographics of his home parish back in India. Father was outgoing, soft-spoken and because of his close-knit family and the personal ministries he was used to in India, he was naturally warm and embracing. After gaining the desired experience that Bishop Amalanathar had hoped for him, Father Selvaraj was transferred to Saint Mary of the Lake in Lakewood. His life would never be the same.

In the course of my research, I went back to Saint Mary of the Lake. This was my home parish for over 30 years and I drew on some of the old-time parishioners for their opinion and "take" on Father Selvaraj during his stay at the church. They had read about him and asked about him with concern, still in a state of disbelief. When we met, it was after a weekday morning Mass in the parking lot in Lakewood.

The sky was dark and we actually moved into the sacristy of the church that I had not visited since my sister died. As we moved into the building, it was 40 years ago, all over again - the brick façade of the building, the portrait of Monsignor Everitt hanging on the wall - all summoned memories, and I was surprised that they were not all bad. As the scent of a hundred years of candle wax permeated my sense of smell, I had to reel myself back to 2011. I was about to interview six people, who, well into their twilight years, had raised their voices in unwavering support of James Selvaraj.

Without prompting, Mr. Robb, in ill-fitting khaki pants and a bright green jacket (not much unlike the one they award at the annual Masters Golf tournament) spoke up and said "Father is a good man. Talked too fast, but at least he had something to say." I wasn't there to agree or disagree. I was hoping to remain objective and that those who I invited that day would see that – clearly they didn't. At first they were defensive of Father James, thinking I was an adversary. When I assured them that I wasn't, they became more relaxed in giving their opinions. One man, a parishioner for "over 50 years" claiming to remember my family, said that he didn't "give a shit, this place has changed." I asked him what place he was referring to: The church in Lakewood? The Catholic Church as a whole? It was obvious to me that he was talking about the latter but the generational gap prompted me to make certain; he confirmed the same. The general consensus of our little group, without dissent, was that Father Selvaraj was railroaded. One woman described his ordeal as "too much of a coincidence between all that stuff in Boston and the timing of Father being arrested." (Note: Father Selvaraj was never arrested.) I was surprised that this group, given their age, was tuned in to the abuse crisis and the timeline as it related to Father Selvaraj's ruin.

As I was wrapping up our conversation I simply asked them if they would mind writing the new Bishop, David O'Connell, and praying for Father. None would commit to the letter writing but as I turned to leave one suggested that they should pray; without the feeling that I was invited to join their coterie, I left the church.

In 2005, the 46 year-old priest was assigned at Saint Raphael-Holy Angels Parish on the outskirts of Trenton. This assignment came after a troublesome year at Saint Mary of the Lake with Father Michael Lang. Father Lang was abusive in demeanor and difficult to work with according to those that worked him at previous assignments. As Father Selvaraj related to Bishop John Smith in October 2004, Father Lang treated him "like a slave" and denied him food and daily basic necessities while he was under his guidance in Lakewood. But it was at Saint Raphael-Holy Angels that the priest's ensuing nightmare took place, when he was charged with endangering the welfare of an 11-year-old child.

The charges stemmed from a day that parents were invited into the after-school program of their children. In a written statement to me, Father Selvaraj picked up the events that changed his life from that point on:

It happened during the after school care program at the all purpose room (big open hall). Lot of parents, children, teachers and aids were there. The religious education children were gathering at the Church and their parents were standing in the hallways. The girl asked me to help her writing her name in my language. I held her wrist and helped to write her name on the black board. It is a matter of few seconds. The girl's mother was standing nearby and looking at [us]. I left the hall saying bye to everyone there including her. Afterwards the girl's mother left the all purpose room leaving behind her daughter with her close friend, who was the eye witness standing close to me while I was writing on the black board, and went home.

The adult eyewitness, a close friend of the parent-accuser, swore in a deposition that she stood inches away and saw Father Selvaraj do nothing wrong. The girl's mother, she claimed, was "overprotective of the child, and disgusted that all the Church brings us is Puerto Ricans, Blacks and Indians as priests." If she was so overprotective, why then leave her daughter in a place where she just witnessed someone touch her inappropriately? The story from the parent-accuser varied from statement to statement and none of it made sense and as expected, unraveled fast, but the priest would never be the same. He was the victim of racism by a parent and he was about to be the victim of race and culture clashes within the Diocese of Trenton.

On October 26, 2005, Father Selvaraj received a call from then Father Joseph Rosie (now Monsignor) of the Pastoral Center within the Diocese offices. Rosie, a direct man, made it clear that Bishop Smith needed to see him at the Chancery office within 15 minutes. Father Selvaraj told Rosie that he could not make it there before within the stated timeframe due to travel proximity. The allowance was made and the meeting was set for 45 minutes from the time the call came in.

Bishop Smith entered his office without making any eye contact with Father Selvaraj. He went on the offensive immediately and in a blustery and intimidating manner, said: "James, do you know what is going on? Do you know that they (the Hamilton Township Police) wanted to arrest you in handcuffs? Did you know that if you are found guilty that you will be sent to prison for five to ten years and you will be placed in chains and anklets and appear in the newspapers and television? There will be shame and humiliation, James. If they find nothing, it does not mean you are innocent. It means you will go back to India and tell your people how badly the Americans treated you. I don't care." The Bishop was furious but he was not backing down; Father Selvaraj asked, "What have I done? This is my second home; I am loved by many here." Bishop Smith sneered, "Do you want to cry? Do you want a tissue? You didn't listen to Mike Lang."

Now it became Father Selvaraj's time to be angry: "What credibility do you give Mike Lang? He's vindictive and (Monsignor)

Tofani said to my face that I was a beggar." Unmoved, the Bishop stood and said, "That's it, you're out! I will make a deal with the Prosecutor's Office that you are to go back to India, you will not be arrested but you are not to leave the Mercer County area and you are not to return to Saint Raphael-Holy Angels Parish or represent yourself as a priest; I am removing your faculty and you are not to represent yourself as a priest. You are now under the care of Monsignor (Gregory) Vaughn." The Bishop left and Monsignor Vaughn, the pastoral Vicar of the Diocese came in and escorted Father Selvaraj to his office. Vaughn was a mentor and pastor to Father Selvaraj and a close and loving friend. They were joined by Monsignor Ronald Bacovin, and both men comforted the shattered and humiliated priest.

The Diocese provided Father James Selvaraj with the services of legal counsel, Scott Krasny. On November 7, 2005, Krasny met with the priest and Lou Monticchio. Krasny advised Father Selvaraj that he was accused by the mother of the 11-year old girl of rubbing the girl's back in the classroom while at the blackboard. As was scripted by Bishop Smith 11 days' prior, Krasny described the charge as a second-degree sexual assault on a minor if it could be proven that he did this to arouse himself or humiliate the child. If convicted, Father Selvaraj could be looking at a jail sentence of 5 to 10 years. If the charge was reduced to a third-degree assault (or endangering the welfare of a child), he would be looking at 3 to 5 years, probation and deportation. The girl's mother was now going full bore, indicating that she witnessed the assault and was going to press charges and act as a witness for the prosecution. However, the Mercer County Prosecutor's Office was willing to deal with the priest in what Krasny called a "win-win."

The Prosecutor had agreed to charge Father Selvaraj with third-degree assault, and Father Selvaraj would plead not guilty. But all the information would be made public, and he still faced the chance of arraignment. Father Selvaraj would be processed and fingerprinted into the legal system, but the charges would never make it to trial and would be dismissed after 12 months. Furthermore, the terms called for Father Selvaraj to leave the United States and never return; if he did he would be arrested. Krasny indicated that the priest would face no jail time, that he would have no admission of guilt, and that he could return to his county to continue his ministry. Krasny was candid when asked if he would represent Father Selvaraj in the criminal trial, to which he answered, "at some point the Diocese objectives and [your] objectives would most likely come into conflict," indicating the Diocese would no longer pay for the legal fees for his representation.

The meeting between Selvaraj, Krasny, and Monticchio to discuss the plea bargain lasted two hours, ending at 6:00 p.m. on November 7, 2005. As the attorney got up to leave, he told the group that he expected an answer within 72 hours.

To Krasny, the plea deal was a good one, and one that Father Selvaraj should seriously consider. Krasny repeatedly cautioned Father Selvaraj that if he wanted to pursue clearing his name through the court system, he would be on his own because the Trenton Diocese would not retain Krasny for that type of legal service. Monticchio mentioned to Krasny, however, that the community supporting the priest would step in to take up that cause. The attorney questioned whether that could ever really occur, but he obviously didn't know Lou Monticchio.

By reputation, faith and activism, Lou Monticchio was not a man to be crossed. It was Lou that co-led a group that was asking questions about financial processes and controls within the Saint Raphael/Holy Angels parish in the 1990's. Lou is quick to point out, however, that his group never made an accusation about legal "wrong doing;" the group remained focused on getting answers to some basic questions regarding the finances of the parish, which they eventually got, and new financial controls were eventually put in place to conform to diocesan policies along with a change in parish leadership. His political astuteness, sense of fairness, calming demeanor and social graces did not imply weakness, in fact, just the opposite. And it looked like he was about to step up to the plate on the side of right, again.

That afternoon, Monticchio identified three questionable moves on the Diocese of Trenton; the first was that the Diocese, without being requested by the Mercer County Prosecutor's Office had already provided the Office with Father Selvaraj's personnel records; second, the Diocese restricted Father Selvaraj's mobility to the Mercer County region and had no lawful reason (or authority) to do so; and third, the Diocese had already assured the Prosecutor's Office that regardless of the outcome, Father Selvaraj would be sent back to India.

By the time 5:00 p.m. had rolled around, Bishop Smith had already cut a deal with the Mercer County Prosecutor and it was up to Krasny to sell it to Team-Selvaraj. It would be the last bit of advice Krasny would offer to Father James Selvaraj. He was fired from the case within 72 hours.

Without question, the fix was in. Father Selvaraj was the scapegoat for all of Bishop John M. Smith's past transgressions and mishandling of the abuse crisis in Florida, and his suppression of information while the Vicar of Trenton. John Smith was going to flex his ecclesiastical muscles and send James Selvaraj on the first available

Air India flight out of JFK and be hailed as the Reformer. But by Thanksgiving 2005, Father James had a new attorney, Marc Fliedner, of the law firm Kamensky & Cohen. Father Selvaraj was going to take on Smith with a King David like ferocity. The standoff started and neither combatant was going to blink.

Team Selvaraj had a great deal of faith in the well-educated and experienced Marc Fliedner. His primary practice focused on criminal defense. His impressive academic resume from Washington D.C. schools included a law degree from the National Law Center at George Washington University. His prosecutorial background and experience as Director of the Criminal Child Abuse Unit of Monmouth County, i.e., being on the other side of these cases, rounded-out his expertise to lead the defense of the Father Selvaraj case.

On December 1, 2005, the Bishop met again with Father Selvaraj and his new attorney as well as Monsignor Rosie and Mr. Steven Goodell, the attorney representing the Diocese. Reading callously from what appeared to be a prepared statement, the Bishop outlined the proposed restrictions to be placed on Father James Selvaraj. It read:

- Selvaraj would be dismissed from priestly faculties within the Diocese of Trenton due to the allegation of endangerment to the welfare of a minor;
- Selvaraj would never be incardinated within the Diocese of Trenton due to the allegation of endangerment to the welfare of a minor;
- Selvaraj would never "work again" in the Diocese of Trenton due to the allegation of endangerment to the welfare of a minor "as long as I am Bishop;"

- Selvaraj would not be provided any living accommodations within any rectory within the Diocese of Trenton. But according to Bishop Smith, "out of charity" he would be allowed to reside at Villa Vianney (a residence for retired priests);
- Selvaraj would not receive any support of salary or stipend from the Diocese of Trenton and could not wear a clerical collar and represent himself as a priest within the Diocese of Trenton;
- Finally, Selvaraj would be responsible for his own legal fees.

The Bishop advised the priest that this information would be forwarded to his home Bishop, the Very Reverend Yvon Ambroise of Tuticorin, India. When attorney Fliedner asked the Bishop to allow Father Selvaraj the opportunity to prove his innocence, the reply was, "Even if he proves he is a white as snow, he will be out. He is going back to India."

Father Selvaraj was devastated and withdrawn; his good reputation was shattered and all the Diocese of Trenton lent for support was the misguided and negligent advice to have the priest make a deal with prosecutors and return to India. But the timid priest opted to reject the decision against conventional wisdom; he was not going back to India with his name and reputation tarnished. He would face the Grand Jury. He did not nothing wrong. Moreover, if he "made the deal" he would be subject to Megan's Law registration if he ever entered the United States again. When Smith told Father Selvaraj on December 1, 2005, that he would never again be a priest in the Diocese of Trenton, the priest thought, "My life was ruined."

True to his word, after the Grand Jury exonerated Father Selvaraj for insufficient evidence, Bishop Smith refused to take him back.

Instead, he wrote a letter telling parishioners at Saint Raphael-Holy Angels that Father Selvaraj would be sent back to India. According to Monticchio, more than 650 parishioners signed a petition asking Bishop Smith to reinstate Father Selvaraj. Again, the Bishop refused. Yet, Smith conceded in a letter to Father Selvaraj's canon lawyer, Father Michael Maginot, that the priest had done nothing to warrant "even the preliminary investigation." The decision to send Father Selvaraj back to India was not a penalty, Bishop Smith said, but a precaution. Smith predicated this decision largely on a letter to the Diocese by Father Lang back at Saint Mary of the Lake that supposedly contained an encrypted warning given to Father Selvaraj about his outward expressions of affection. The letter (if it existed at all) was unsigned and not dated. Team-Selvaraj asked for a copy of that letter and was refused leading many to question its existence.

"Because of his overly friendly personality he has been warned on several occasions to be cautious concerning outward signs of friendship and affection toward young people," the Bishop wrote to Father Selvaraj's former congregation. "Our contemporary national culture and particularly the present church situation demand such caution. Father James does not seem to fully understand these cautions and their implications." While Father Michael Lang claims he was approached with complaints about the priest, he has never been able to substantiate those allegations by witness or written documentation. Father Selvaraj insists that he was never warned about his conduct with young people; it's his nature to offer genuine affection and accept it in kind.

Asked for clarification about Bishop Smith's decision, diocesan spokesperson Rayanne Bennett said, "We are confident that the process undertaken in this matter was appropriate and handled in a just and responsible way toward all parties involved. We have nothing further to add."

In February 2012, I contacted Father Michael Lang. Lang, a longtime reader of my website www.novozinsky.com, was asked by me if he had any comment surrounding the circumstances of his involvement with the Father Selvaraj case; he certainly did.

From: Mike Lang
Date: February 29, 2012 3:34:04 PM EST
To: 'Bruce Novozinsky' <bnovozinsky@me.com>
Subject: RE: Father James Selvaraj :: Comment for Book

Mr. Novozinsky:

First, you write to me for any comment after already writing your book. I believe this speaks volumes about the validity of your story. You state on your website that your book was originally scheduled for publication this month and that it is written and now just going through the final revisions. This supports that you have already concluded your verification of facts. Obviously, what you consider investigation is really conjecture, speculation and blatant partiality on your part. After reading the chapter on The Priest Who Would Not Run from your website, I have little to say except that your information is incorrect, unsupported, and biased. I have little doubt that people will see your book for what it is. I believe some people have already questioned your motives on your website. Your investigation of James Selvaraj's time in Lakewood amounted to asking a few people after a daily Mass six or more years after he served there. If this is "investigation" then I would never want a defense that depended on such speculative and amateurish research. If this is the type of research you did for your entire book then I would see little value in giving any credence to the information contained in it, but it does show a blatant and intentional disregard for the truth. Since I was Pastor in Lakewood it would be inappropriate for me to release specific information about any individual's employment or service at the parish. (You would most likely point out such an impropriety and ask yourself if you would you expect someone you worked for to release such information about you?) I can say your reporting of the "facts" is inaccurate, incomplete and unsupported. Your email of 2/28/2012 at 9:40 PM, states that I made claims "about Father James Selvaraj which were unsubstantiated and undocumented about his inappropriate behavior while you shared a parish." I can assure you that the claims about inappropriate behavior are substantiated and completely documented. If it is decided that statements in your self published book are slanderous or libelous by my attorney then I would imagine the documentation will in fact come out. While I have no knowledge of what happened to James Selvaraj after leaving Lakewood, I can say with certainty, honestly and sincerity, he did receive warnings about behavior that would eventually cause him trouble. Those warnings are documented as well as the testimony of individuals who made complaints. The fact that he received warnings can also be testified to by others who I am sure will tell the truth should they be forced to do so under oath - these include individuals whom James Selvaraj claims as being those who were his friends – including the person who was the Director of Priest Personnel at that time. As to the accusations about treating Selvaraj "like a slave and denying him food and basic necessities" I have plenty of proof that such was not the case. Documentation that attests to the food that was available to him will certainly reveal the truth. Those who were present in the Rectory during Selvaraj's assignment in Lakewood will paint a completely different picture. I do consider such false accusations to be libelous and slanderous and will seek the advice of professionals to determine if action will be called for.

As an observation, if your chapter 8 is the final version I would recommend different people to proof read your work. It is written very poorly. I am sure the literary critics will have a field day.

And as information, I have sent blind copies of this email to several people in the event you claim that I never responded and take that as some kind of liberty to print your misinformation as "fact." Let's face it, while I have no knowledge of the validity of the rest of your book, or that part of chapter 8 which talks about anything other than that which occurred in Lakewood, there is information in chapter 8 which has to be classified as a work of fiction.

Rev. Michael P. Lang

In April 2006, with charges dismissed by a Grand Jury, Marc Fliedner turned Kamensky & Cohen case number 504022.000 over to canon lawyer Father Michael L. Maginot of Merrillville, Indiana. He summarized the case in two pages and in closing added a telling editorial, stating: "If I can provide further information about my recollection of these events, please do not hesitate to contact me directly. As the events of this two-day period have had such an dramatic impact on Father James' employment and life in general, I can assure you that they are events I will never forget."

Father Maginot is a canon lawyer that works for a not-for-profit organization called "Justice for Priests and Deacons." Justice for Priests and Deacons was founded to create a referral program to offer advice to priests and deacons about their rights under canon law, which many are unaware of. The priest or deacon has nowhere to turn for help, support, or advice when he is accused; Justice for Priests and Deacons strives to fill that void. The organization assists the priest or deacon in the preparation of his case, his defense, and to process his appeal if necessary. Another part of the ministry is to offer assistance to those priests who may find themselves abandoned by their bishops or in prison. In an interview I had with Father Selvaraj for this book, he related that Father Maginot was appalled at the case and went on the immediate offensive on his behalf. Though many encouraged Father Selvaraj to civil action following his acquittal, myself included, Maginot encouraged him to stay the course under the canonical process.

Father Selvaraj and his supporters began writing the Vatican in 2006, asking the Congregation for the Doctrine of the Faith (CDF), a tribunal evolved from the Roman Inquisition, to force Bishop Smith to reinstate the priest's ministry and good name: "I want him to restore my dignity," the priest explained, "so wherever I go this won't haunt me." For nearly three years, Father Selvaraj received no response. Father Maginot believes the CDF decided Selvaraj's case during that time, but only informed Smith of the ruling, which the Bishop buried in a file. "The problem is, they never communicate with us," the attorney said of the Congregation. "If they gave us a copy of what they give the bishop, they could never get away with this."

This is true. The CDF and Rome are under no obligation to share, beyond the bishop of the relevant see, any rulings decided upon. They leave it to the bishop to decide how (and if) information is shared. The faith, integrity and honesty of a direct successor of the Apostles to tell the truth are assumed under canon law, albeit a primitive and naive assumption in reality. The Diocese's withholding of the findings is in direct violation of canon 220 which states: "No one is permitted to damage unlawfully the good reputation of another person enjoys nor to violate the right of another person to protect his or her own privacy."

How does this canon apply to the case of James Selvaraj? The priest's reputation was unlawfully damaged by the actions of a racially motivated individual. She pressed the case into and through the legal system and lost. She left the Saint Raphael/Holy Angels Parish in the immediate aftermath and is the sole cause of the schism that divided the congregation as a result.

If a priest is falsely accused, the bishops' guidelines say that every effort should be made to restore his reputation. According to Teresa Kettelkamp, Executive Director of the Office of Child Protection, the U.S. bishops' abuse prevention office, "it's nearly impossible," she said, "[it's] like pouring out a pillow from the top of a mountain and trying to collect the feathers, but it can be done." For instance, the bishop could say Mass with the priest and use his homily to talk about how the allegation was unfounded, or he could meet with the local media to get the word out, Kettelkamp said. "Anything he can do to show his support for the priest."

According to Father Selvaraj, after the Grand Jury exonerated him, Bishop Smith did none of that. Instead, the Bishop tried to pack the priest off to India. In May 2006, parishioner Janet Zito wrote to the Very Reverend Bishop Yvon Ambroise, now head of the home diocese of Selvaraj in India, expressing support for the unfairly maligned priest:

> [A]fter being cleared by the United States judicial system, Fr. James' treatment in the diocese did not change. In fact, they "disowned" him as quickly as possible. As Catholics, we are taught to act with justice, no matter how much suffering we may endure. The easy thing for Father James to do would be to return to India where he would be able to enjoy his ministry once more. However, there are many of us here who feel that Fr. James is being led by the Holy Spirit for another purpose. Our diocese is in need of someone who is not afraid to stand up and fight for what is right. Although I have great respect for Bishop Smith's office, I am disturbed by what is going on throughout the diocese. I feel that the people of the diocese have lost their voice. We speak, but no one listens....

The final word on Father James Selvaraj comes from his canon attorney, Father Maginot, who wrote to me in November 2011:

> Bruce, I don't know if you heard that we recently received a reply that they (Rome) are backing the bishop and ordering Fr. James to return to India. I think that is your bigger story that would appeal to a world wide audience beyond Trenton. I give you permission to place all the documents of the ecclesiastical case in an appendix to your book which would be most rare since this is usually prevented from being done

by the Pontifical Secret, where I will take the heat in arguing that it doesn't apply in this case. If Fr. James can't have his good name restored, no priest falsely accused will be able to do so, and who is going to want to dedicate their life to such a pathetic example of leadership at all levels just to take a bullet for "the team" and disappear like a clerical "Jimmy Hoffa." Even if it is agreed to include the documents in the appendix, which may be hundred or so pages, it would be a good idea to at least summarize those steps taken these past almost six years.

Beginning with my warning to Bishop Smith that I would report his abuse of power to the Vatican if he didn't allow Father James to return to ministry and at least complete his final two years in Trenton before returning to India as was agreed upon before deciding against his Incardination to the Diocese. Then came Bishop Smith's attempt to contact the Bishop in India to call him home. When we received no word from the CDF, we tried to take the case to the Apostolic Signatura, the Supreme Court of the Church, which told us that they didn't have jurisdiction since it was still in the hands of the CDF. After warning the CDF if they didn't do anything, we would report their inaction to the pope, which we did, where the Secretariat of State got involved eventually forcing the CDF to resolve the situation. The only thing the CDF did was affirm the bishop's right to decide for or against Incardination, and that we had the right to appeal for $1000, which we did. When they didn't cash our check, we reported this to the Apostolic Signatura who reaffirmed their lack of jurisdiction, but did force them to resolve the case and the check was cashed. We warned the CDF if they don't resolve the case in a timely manner, we would report this to the pope, which we did. When the Pope named a coadjutor for Trenton, we *thought the case would be soon resolved, except there was a delay in accepting the resignation betraying the whole concept of naming a coadjutor. When the resignation was finally accepted, we were shocked when the new bishop refused to meet with Fr. James. When he took away his insurances, we could legally act once again and warned Bishop O'Connell that we would report his violations to the pope, which we did.*

Father Maginot has been in contact with Bishop David M. O'Connell and the exchange has not been cordial. It has turned into a battle of who can out "canon" the other. The new Bishop now finds himself on the receiving end of what Maginot believes are canon law violations and Rome needs to decide the severity of the charges.

Bishop O'Connell suspended all the insurance and support lines Father Selvaraj had been receiving from the Diocese of Trenton since his arrival in New Jersey. This was done via email from the Bishop to Father Selvaraj on July 15, 2011. Father Maginot responded to the unlawful act (by canon law standards) three days later in a letter to the Bishop dated July 18, 2011. In the letter, he informed the Bishop that Rome (the Pope) had issued a directive that all of Father Selvaraj's insurances were to remain in place until the issues facing the priest were resolved. The not-so-subtle reminder to the Bishop was punctuated with the end sentence of "what the Holy Father has to say no longer seems to be of a concern [to the Trenton Diocese]." He then cited the canon laws that he intended to report to Rome. In a confidential letter dated August 1, 2011, sent to the Holy Father and His Eminence William Cardinal Levada, Maginot asserted that Bishop O'Connell was in violation of the following canon laws:

- Defamation of character (canon 220)
- Denial of due process (canon 221)
- Denial of living expenses (canon 281)
- Denial of adequate means of livelihood and social welfare (canon 384)
- Abuse of Power (canon 1389)
- False assertion (canon 1391)

Wasting no time in replying, in a letter dated July 25, 2011, the Bishop deferred all issues of the Father Selvaraj matter back to Rome, still refusing to meet with the priest or his attorney and calling Father Selvaraj "disobedient" in his refusal to return to India. He ignored the charges levied against him by Father Maginot, but pointedly remarked that the "Diocese (of Trenton) has no obligations – legal, canonical or otherwise – to provide him with Diocesan insurance…"

What escapes the Bishop is that "otherwise" denies a fellow priest, who was wrongly and criminally accused of a touching a child inappropriately, internal due-process of a fair hearing and the basic necessities to live as a human being. These strong-armed tactics are employed to smoke-out Father Selvaraj, and force him back to India.

And so the battle of an innocent man continues. Falsely accused and abandoned by his Church, a broken man continues his worldly purgatory. Today, Father James lives on the kindness his loyal supporters afford him still, some seven years later. He remains local to the parish that he last served. It's almost a defiant gesture to remain in such close proximity, but he doesn't see it that way. This is just another outward sign of a priest that refuses to run.

The love his supporters have for him is evident and sincere. Fundraisers are frequent and well-attended. I attended one in 2010 because I was more curious at the time than supportive. What struck me at the firehouse in Mercerville was not the quantity of the people so much as the demographic; the vast majority were in an age group and from a generation that revered the Church and its hierarchy. They are now the people that see that it's okay to ask "Why?" and not to conform to the outdated mold of the Church where "pray, pay and obey" was de rigueur.

On the night I first met Father Selvaraj, Janet Zito spoke of the journey they went on with him. All the while the supporter had her hand on the shoulder and back of the priest. When the menu came she reminded him of what he liked, how it was prepared and what he could do without. She also answered the majority of questions posed to him by me. Janet wrote me later:

[I] initially contacted him just to let him know that we supported him. Of course, there was a small seed of doubt in my mind regarding why these accusations were made, but as soon I saw him, I was convinced that he was truly innocent. I tried to visit him at Villa Vianny about once a week for about 30-45 min and our friendship just grew. I still am inspired by the depth of his faith. Unlike me, he does not seem to question Catholicism. The political make-up of the Church, he questions, but not the teachings of the Catholic Church…"

The priest from India says little. A rejoinder to his ordeal, he is still guarded with strangers. Towards the end of the evening I looked at him and pointedly asked, "Father, why not just go back to India?" He said to me with a soft smile and with expressive hand gestures, "Bruce, this is my ministry now. This is God's plan. He has this in mind for me. I have support and love from many and I can't explain it."

With humility at being "chosen" for literally trial on Earth, this was a man that didn't feel abandoned by God, but felt honored by being selected to be part of His higher plan.

9
Father John Bambrick: Advocate or Adversary?

"There's a saying in the law that justice delayed is justice denied, so it's about bringing about justice and healing for people who have been abused and stopping these individuals. The best way to stop them, I think, is putting them in jail. There are no children in jail."

-Father John Bambrick, Abuse Survivor/ Priest

"With every day, and from both sides of my intelligence, the moral and the intellectual, I thus drew steadily nearer to the truth, by whose partial discovery I have been doomed to such a dreadful shipwreck: that man is not truly one, but truly two."

-Robert Louis Stevenson, Dr. Jekyll and Mr. Hyde

I avoided this chapter for as long as I possibly could. In the end I decided that "full disclosure" was the only option that was afforded me.

I first read of John Bambrick in 2005 when I began my research on the Trenton Diocese after exhausting my reading on the Archdiocese of Boston. Father Bambrick's name kept jumping off the screen with every Google search, and I knew that my local research had stumbled upon someone extraordinary. After further reading, I realized I had found the man who wore a red cape and "S" emblazoned on a shirt under his priestly vestments for the victims of priest sex abuse. My respect was solidified; here was a priest who relentlessly hunted down his own priest-abuser. John Bambrick was a rockstar.

As a teen, John Bambrick met the Reverend Anthony Eremito at a wedding ceremony performed by the priest in his home parish in Monmouth County, New Jersey. Eremito was a priest in New York but was performing the wedding of an acquaintance with John serving as the altar boy. The two "clicked," and Eremito began calling the Bambrick home. In the 1970's and 80's, this was perfectly normal behavior for a priest to cultivate a boy's potential vocational calling under his tutelage; today, suspicions would be aroused; back then, it was considered an honor.

According to an interview with Bambrick posted on the "Voice of the Faithful" website, the relationship was strictly mentoring until he and the priest attended a movie together. During the movie, Eremito held Bambrick's hand for two hours. In shame and confusion, John rushed from the theater but was unable to call his parents because he had no money. Eremito told him not to be uncomfortable because everything was fine, and assured him that physical contact was "normal" within the brotherhood of priests; all they had were each other and the bond was special and acceptable. The boy, who had wanted to be a priest since he was 5 years old, closed his eyes as the hand holding progressed to other more intimate physical transgressions, escaping in his mind to other places as he was being abused.

The abuse lasted for six months, with the teen silently objecting. John Bambrick said years later that he vividly remembers the grinding of the priest on his body, the kissing, the rubbing and embracing. At 15, John had enough and rebuffed Eremito's pressuring advances to have sex; the latter grew frustrated and moved on to a "more willing" partner. Bambrick was no longer pursued by Eremito; twenty-two years later the tables would turn.

As he was about to be ordained in 1991, Father Bambrick said he had "a crisis of conscience:" "My whole life is sort of poised for this moment, and all of a sudden, I don't know if I can do this..... All the things the church was supposed to be about -- to speak the truth, to protect the poor -- how can I do that when I know this man is still molesting kids? I felt that I would be a phony." Bambrick found Eremito in New York City and broke his silence to the nation's preeminent cleric of the time, John Cardinal O'Connor of the Catholic Archdiocese of New York. O'Connor promised the young priest that Eremito would be "an unassigned priest, absent on leave," and "not allowed to wear the collar or use the title." Satisfied, Bambrick left the Manhattan Archdiocese's Madison Avenue office.

But Eremito resurfaced, first as a priest in a church in Westchester County, New York, and then Atlantic Highlands, New Jersey, before skipping town, Bambrick hot on his tail. Bambrick was unaware until later that the Cardinal had signed a letter of limited reinstatement allowing Eremito to minister with restrictions as a hospital chaplain in Texas. Loyal to O'Connor and noting that the aging Prince of the Church was dying of cancer at the time, Bambrick trusted, "I really admired Cardinal O'Connor and I really, really hope that it was a diocesan official that wrote that letter, that someone slipped it on his desk and he signed it." It was enough for Bambrick to see, however, that he had to take matters into his own hands. When O'Connor died in 2000, Bambrick doggedly hunted Eremito down from New York to Texas.

At the time Bambrick first approached Cardinal O'Connor, Eremito was serving a ministry in midtown Manhattan at Holy Cross Church on West 42nd Street, located across from the New York City Port Authority bus terminal. Its site made the parish the unofficial welcoming mat for adolescent runaways seeking refuge and a fare home, a circumstance ripe with opportunity for Father Eremito. Indeed, other complaints were made against the priest and it was then that the Cardinal "suspended" Eremito. O'Connor knew, and Bambrick realized, that if the request to defrock or laicize Eremito went to Rome it would take years for the Vatican to act on it. Bambrick left the Archdiocese of New York office satisfied that the Cardinal was acting in the best interest of any future victims and not thinking of Church interests. Anthony Eremito was out of a job and not in a position to harm other children, or so Father John Bambrick thought.

But Anthony Eremito was not going away quietly, and he ran into an adversary of equal drive in Father Bambrick. What came next was a "catch me if you can" game played out from New York to Texas. At the time Father Bambrick began to hear the rumblings that Eremito was in Texas, Bambrick was serving as pastor at Saint Thomas More Church in Manalapan, New Jersey. Bambrick brought his complaint to the New York District Attorney's office hoping that they would lead the charge to find other victims of Eremito. The legal battle commenced, but in an unexpected forum; it was Eremito that filed a "letter of information" against Bambrick for defamation of character; in the church's canon law, a letter of information is similar to filing a complaint or suit in civil court. Bambrick knew if he were found guilty he would lose his parish and quite possibly his priesthood. Bambrick had every reason to be concerned on an additional front because Eremito hired a high profile and respected monsignor and canon lawyer, William Varvaro, pastor of Saint Margaret's Roman Catholic Church, in Middle Village, New York.

Varvaro was seasoned and took full advantage of the situation; he knew that what he was about to embark on was so rare in canon circles that his filing put him squarely in the driver's seat. First, he would not alienate himself within the New York Archdiocese and filed the complaint in the Trenton Diocese. Secondly, and most importantly, by naming Bambrick as the defendant he was taking full advantage of the fact that a priest versus priest proceeding was not familiar territory for even the most battle-tested of canon attorneys. Varvaro was savvy and had the lead-time prior to filing his "letter of information" to prepare his case, however the onus was on Eremito to prove that the molestations did not occur and that his character was thus defamed. The weighing of the respective advantages/disadvantages continued and in its favor the plaintiff had Varvaro, who had at the time held the title Protonotary Apostolic, the highest-ranking level of monsignor. He was much sought after for his advice and counsel on matters of abuse.

Bambrick saw this as a counteroffensive not only on the part of Eremito, but on the hierarchy itself who he was convinced wanted him banished for being so outspoken. What helped and hurt Bambrick at the same time was the fact that Bambrick says his were not the only charges leveled at Eremito. The Archdiocese of New York told him there was close to a dozen more accusations against Eremito, but would never elaborate on them. Bambrick was told that Eremito had professed his innocence, and under canon law, those recorded complaints against Eremito were sealed. But Bambrick made the accusations of others part of his public campaign against Eremito and so they went unfiltered into the public perception. To the further advantage of Bambrick's defense team were the very words of Varvaro himself who downplayed the charges as being uncorroborated, but then proceeded to give them credence as harmful to Eremito: "The church has said Eremito has been severely disciplined at some point in his career and removed from at least two parishes, but it continues to refuse to discuss the case in detail. Whether [Bambrick's claims] are true or false, I don't think he should be repeating them over and over again, as he has been doing since June," Varvaro said. "I think to do that harms Father Eremito's reputation."

    The wildcard in the whole mix was the Bishop in charge of the canonical trial; the Very Reverend John Mortimer Smith. Smith knew that he had time well on his side. His relationship with Bambrick was cordial at best and at times disapproving over Bambrick's public displays of what he saw as unbecoming "cable-TV showmanship." The Bishop knew of the priest's allies within the media and in particular with the local Asbury Park Press, to whom Bambrick was known as "Father Sound-bite." However, he also knew that Bambrick was keen to Smith's past practice of knowingly and willfully transferring abusive priests, as he did with Joseph Keith Symons while Bishop of Pensacola-Tallahassee.

    Bishop Smith also knew that Bambrick would not shy from sharing this information as soon as the first microphone was put within tonsil range of the outspoken priest. Smith knew he could not intimidate Bambrick who publically said that the "(Trenton) Diocese always believed the [abuse] allegations to be true," knowing full well that Diocese officials would never comment to affirm or contradict the statement. This was a constant cause of frustration to the Bishop. Most likely acting out of self-preservation and the desire to remove the Bambrick thorn from his side, and to a lesser extent because he knew the abuse allegations to be true, Smith chose not to provoke the very vocal, very knowledgeable Bambrick, and dismissed Eremito's defamation charges as "without merit." The day after his verdict, the Bishop put a continent between himself and Bambrick and left for Africa.

Father Anthony Joseph Eremito eventually did become Mr. Joseph Eremito, but his arrogance continued as did his pursuit by John Bambrick. In 2006, John Bambrick wrote the following letter to Mr. Robert Lefton, President & CEO of Odyssey HealthCare based in Dallas, Texas:

January 3, 2006
Mr. Robert Lefton, President & CEO
Odyssey HealthCare
717 North Harwood Street, Suite 1500
Dallas, Texas 75201

Dear Mr. Lefton:
I received a call today informing me that your corporation has hired Mr. Anthony Joseph Eremito (aliases; Rev. Anthony Eremito, Fr. Anthony Eremito, Andy Eremito) as a Hospice Chaplain in Philadelphia, Pennsylvania.

The above mentioned is a priest of the Archdiocese of New York currently on Administrative leave without faculties and not permitted to serve in ministry. He has been suspended since the spring of 2002 (his second suspension) due to allegations of sexual abuse of minors. A simple Google search would have revealed this to your corporation. I am one of those who filed a formal complaint.

For confirmation of this information you may contact the Archdiocese of New York's Priest Personnel Office, Rev. Msgr. Desmond O'Connor, Dir. 1011 First Avenue New York, New York 10022. Phone number 1-212-371-1000 or the Office of Victims Assistance at the same address and phone number.

Lynne Abraham, District Attorney for the Philadelphia, has recently concluded a long and thorough Grand Jury Investigation, in part showing the shuffling of predatory priests.

Your corporation must certainly have clients who are children or clients who have children. I am sure your corporation would not want to put vulnerable individuals at risk; certainly that is something contrary to your mission.

Here in New Jersey we have successfully removed a shield that previously protected Non-profits who harbored perpetrators who sexually abuse children. Pennsylvania has no such shield in place either. I pray you will be attentive to this matter and be more vigilant in your hiring practices across the country so that children are not unwittingly placed at risk during a particularly vulnerable time in their families lives.

Rev. John P. Bambrick

Three days later The *Philadelphia Inquirer* ran the following story:

A local hospice provider yesterday dismissed a Catholic priest it had hired as a bereavement counselor, saying it did not know he was an accused sex abuser. Odyssey HealthCare of Philadelphia Inc., based in Blue Bell, said it immediately removed the Rev. Anthony J. Eremito, who is about 63, after learning that he had been suspended from ministry nearly four years ago by the Archdiocese of New York. "He was in our employment for about three months as a bereavement counselor or coordinator," said Brad Bickham, general counsel for Odyssey's parent company, based in Dallas.

Bickham said Odyssey had conducted standard background checks on Eremito before hiring him but found no evidence of wrongdoing "because he was never criminally charged" with sex abuse. "Unfortunately, this kind of conduct is not easily ascertainable," Bickham said.

Eremito could not be reached for comment.

Bickham said Odyssey had "absolutely no" complaints of improper behavior lodged against Eremito during his employment. He said that he did not know whether Eremito's job would have taken him into private homes and that Eremito "probably spent most of his time in an office." He said he did not know whether Eremito had presented himself as a Catholic priest when he applied for work with Odyssey. Joseph Zwilling, a spokesman for the New York archdiocese, said yesterday that Eremito had had no assignment since the early 1990s and that his faculties as a priest were removed in 2002. Priests whose faculties have been removed are not allowed by the Catholic Church to present themselves as priests or wear clerical clothes.

Eremito has denied abusing minors and is legally challenging efforts by the archdiocese to strip him of his status as a priest. His employment at Odyssey was revealed yesterday in a statement released by the Survivors' Network of Those Abused by Priests, the activist group known as SNAP, based in St. Louis.

Among those who have publicly accused Eremito of sex abuse is the Rev. John Bembrick, 22 pastor of St. Thomas More Roman Catholic Church in Manalapan, N.J. Bembrick, [sic] 38, says Eremito abused him for about six months in 1980 when he was a 15-year-old altar boy in Matawan, N.J., and Eremito was assigned to a Bronx parish. "He does move around," Bembrick [sic] said in a phone interview yesterday. Bembrick [sic] also serves as SNAP's legislative director in New Jersey. "Whenever I find him," Bembrick [sic] said, "I notify his employers." He said bereavement counselors and hospice chaplains "have access to children, and they need to be protected."

SNAP said in its release that Eremito had worked as recently as 2002 at Covenant Medical Center, a children's hospital in Lubbock, Texas. Covenant Medical Center did not return a call seeking confirmation of that information.[42]

The ordeal finally ended for Father John Bambrick in 2006 when Eremito was removed from the priesthood under the Vatican's *Charter for the Protection of Children and Young People*. He later stated: "[F]or me at that point, the matter was settled and over."

Father Bambrick was quickly becoming a folk hero to abuse victims, and his fight to bring his own abuser to justice led him to become involved in other cases as well, including, that of a 9 year-old congregant who said he had been molested by a former Saint Thomas More priest, the Reverend Joseph McHugh. With the help of Bambrick, McHugh was convicted in 2006 and sentenced to probation. While it appears to be a slap on the wrist, it could very well have been nothing had it not been for the intervention of John Bambrick.

When I contacted Father Bambrick in 2005 my expectations were way high. A little nervous, a little intimidated by his now caped-crusader-like legendary status, I thought what a better place to start with than him, seeing as I was ready to come out with my story of October 1973. I wanted to tell him how I was saved from Jack Banko, and get the information I needed on Father Jerry Brown to move forward with my own healing. Father was cordial yet abrupt when I reached him by phone. I didn't fault him because he must have been getting dozens of phone calls from victims for advice and counseling and at the time was still in the middle of his own ordeal with Eremito. Yet, admittedly, I felt put off and couldn't put my finger on it. It would be years before my uneasiness was confirmed.

In November of 2009, I attended a meeting of the alumni association at my former high school, Saint Joseph School (Monsignor Donovan High School) in Toms River. Afterwards, I went to a local bar with six fellow alum that were still connected to the school in some capacity, either as teachers, staff, or parents of current students. Naming them here serves no purpose, yet that evening they served a very real purpose, opening my eyes to the Jekyll/Hyde which is John Bambrick.

In June 2008, Father Bambrick came to the parish as pastor and to oversee the schools and cemetery associated with the parish. From the very beginning, it was a stormy relationship that was predicated on hostility. Bambrick was assigned to do a job; clean up the finances of Saint Joseph parish, cemetery and schools. The way he went about doing this job caught many off guard, left many without jobs, and some without a desired Catholic education.

I listened intently that night, and when I left the bar, I stopped in the parking lot of my high school alma mater and prayed for the strength to do what needed to be done. This pastor's firing without cause of the people who built this school and parish would not be swept under the ecclesiastical carpet if I had anything to do with it; at the very least we would expose the reallocation of funds and demand an answer for just where the money was being spent. It was near Thanksgiving, and I vowed to my friends that I would use every means afforded to me to separate the myth from the facts and fight fair with the pastor, yet knowing Father Bambrick's reputation as a demanding bully, I went on the offensive right away and penned the following email on November 21, 2009, to both Bishop John M. Smith and Father John Bambrick:

Most Reverend Bishop Smith,

I heard the homily that Your Excellency gave at my daughter's confirmation this week at Saint Gregory the Great. The overriding theme of which was "do the right thing." I hope his Reverence will do just that and meet with concerned parishioners of Saint Joseph, Toms River and parents of the Monsignor Donovan High School.

Father Bambrick,

I'm always up for a good fight, but I believe in a fair fight. That said, I want you to know my concerns as an alum and a benefactor of the Diocese at both an individual and corporate level prior to my next move. This letter will serve as a cover to all that is described in this email that I have been assured will be hand delivered (as a package) to Bishop John Smith.

I have recently re-engaged myself in the fund raising efforts at Saint Joseph/ Monsignor Donovan High School. On-line social networks have afforded us the opportunity to reconnect with friends and organizations from the past. As such, as a token of remembrance of my sister (Rose/ SJHS '76) who passed last Thanksgiving, I began reaching out to people connected to the school and parish to find where my family and company would be best placed to assist in athletic fund-raising and a scholarship endowment in her memory. Father, to be candid, the feedback I received is disturbing and the 32 pages of letters, emails, inappropriate bulletin rants and belittling of individuals and families that built the foundation of the school and parish under Lawrence Donovan is disgusting and unsettling.

Father, I want to make this abundantly clear: Saint Joseph is not your own personal Idaho. It belongs to the people that have devoted time, energy and capital to its brick and mortar and the traditions and values we carry when we leave. This is what makes a parish a community. This is what makes a community a family. This is indicative by the many people who go to the school as children and return in both service and staff. My research, two meetings and supporting materials have shown you to be divisive and callus. Your dismissive attitude is not reflective of a Parish Priest and is more in step with a schoolyard bully.

I don't think I need to delve into the details but the case of a 37 year employee whose wife suffered from cancer being demoted to the point of leaving his position, a woman being told to discard a food donation to the trash and the refusal of a blessing on a parishioner because of time constraint is really all I needed to hear. Hearsay? Perhaps; but nothing could come close to the "Dear Parishioners" letter that appeared in the August 30 bulletin. Father, this was tantamount to the singling out of an individual for ridicule and embarrassment. Using your words in that letter I have read the Footprints and the bulletins and I'd like you to publish a clear and concise explanation and complete accounting for the approximate $12,000 in alumni association funds (as of 3Q08) raised with the understanding that those funds would be used exclusively for the benefit of the children within and connected to the Saint Joseph/ Monsignor Donovan schools. Using the caveat that the Alumni Association "uses the Parish tax exempt status" does not constitute card-blanch/ zero oversight to the redistribution of those funds by any individual, yourself included. The benefactors were assured that each dollar donated would be directed to a specific cause. By you acting as *judge and jury with that money, with no input from the Alumni Association, has caused irreversible damage to those members reputations and to their efforts to raise funds in the future - and remember Father (as you stated in the "Dear Parishioners" letter), "lies are still a sin."*

As someone who is very active in fund raising for the grade schools Diocese of Trenton, Allentown (NJ) High School and Methodist University (NC) and is personally responsible for cash, goods and services of over $250,000 in the past three years to these institutions, one would think my main course of disillusionment would be over those capital raising efforts, stymied by your disregard for their original intent. You could not be more wrong. My concern is for the people that are dismissed and belittled because you view them as part of the problem. You have a forum of the pulpit (where you give PowerPoint presentations for some unknown reason). You have the bulletin and you have Footprints. You have a closed door when it comes to debate or policy decisions and intimidate via those forums and in person when you are disagreed with. Many affected by your words and deeds will not confront you because of the perceived power over them. The worse you can do to me is to cancel my subscription to my Alumni Newsletter; I'll take that chance. This letter is the shot over the bow. Come December 4, it will be the included in the package that will be hand delivered to Bishop Smith, the Vicar General of the DOT, the Chancellor of the DOT, the Secretariat of the DOT for Catholic Education and the Director of Priest Personnel for the DOT. I will use the local press for any reason deemed necessary to make these points known as well as my website that reaches over 500 daily readers at my website I have a list of over 70% of *living alumni members and I have the on-line social networks that will reach over 2100 "friends of Saint Joseph and Monsignor Donovan" that will be used if we cannot set up a meeting with Bishop Smith and/ or Monsignor Ronald Becovin [sic[the Director of Priest Personnel for the DOT. My intentions are simple. If a meeting cannot be arranged and/ or the approximate $12,000 is not restored to the disposal of the Alumni Association, I will take immediate steps form a 501-C (with gaming license) Friends and Alumni Booster Club and committee. Based on my participation in two previous efforts of not-for-profit organization founding, approval will not be an issue. My fund raising will be aggressive and profitable and it will fit the needs of the children in the schools and parish as seen fit by those who administer and live in the values and traditions of Monsignor Lawrence Donovan. I remain committed to the Catholic Faith and those who serve.*

Bruce Novozinsky
SJHS 1979

For the next 18 months, Father and I would cross swords. In the middle of it all stood Monsignor Ronald Bacovin, Director of Priest Personnel for the Diocese of Trenton, and Monsignor Gregory Vaughn, Vicar General for the Diocese of Trenton, both men of good intention and candidness in their response to issues and both as frustrated as me with the arrogance of John Bambrick. They stood clearly in the corner of the people of the Catholic community of Saint Joseph, but were powerless to take action because Bishop John Smith had gag ordered them with references to "anything Bambrick." Why? John Bambrick had the "goods" on Bishop Smith and Smith feared him going public on the events surrounding his transfer to Trenton from Florida. The *Asbury Park Press* was on Bambrick's speed-dial and he knew that all his calls would be taken and the aging Bishop (who was by this time, ill) did not want the last few months of his tenure sullied by scandal that was about to break wide open in Toms River. It became readily apparent that the "fix was in" and Smith would segway into retirement without addressing this issue; the newly named Coadjutor Bishop David M. O'Connell, would inherit that task.

In January 2010, I met with Monsignor Ronald Bacovin. Accompanying me was Mrs. Peggy McGarry – herself a parishioner of over 40 years, a graduate of the school, and parent of beautiful twin girls that were active altar servers. The meeting, convened to address the "Bambrick situation," was cordial. Monsignor was well aware of all of the calls coming into the Diocese of Trenton Pastoral Center concerning Bambrick. He assured us that the Bishop was "aware and concerned." Among the complaints was the redirection of capital from individual fundraisers (of teams and clubs), inappropriate comments made to staff members about the Blessed Mother "making out" with Saint Peter, the duress resignation of a staff member that he accused of forging another staff members signature ("resign or I will call the police"), and inappropriate homily content wherein he spoke of the breast mutilation of a saint in front of first-graders. Father Bambrick took any and all opportunities to publically embarrass his predecessors on what he perceived as their money mismanagement; he dissolved the Parish Council, which he was entitled to do, but never reinstated it within the one year timeframe as mandated in order to keep control over the accounts payable and accounts receivable. So I asked, "Monsignor, what about the reallocated funds raised by kids for their activities?" Bacovin didn't look up. He was not being dismissive but he wasn't going to overcommit either. "I'll talk to John," he replied, dropping the formal "Father" attached to Bambrick's name.

Mrs. McGarry and I pleaded with Monsignor to come to Toms River and listen to the people that were responsible for the 300+ emails, letters and phone calls that Bishop Smith ignored. Whereas Mrs. McGarry's plea was more emotional based on her family's history at the school, mine was more business-centric. No one around that table was accusing John Bambrick of any criminal activity whatsoever, although that was what he was playing up in and around the community of Saint Joseph.

And he went further. Bambrick accused me of never graduating high school (I did); of being an ex-convict (I'm not); lying about my personal experience with Jerry Brown and Jack Banko (I didn't); and for being an outsider that was poking around where I didn't belong (I wasn't). Contrary to what John Bambrick was trying to portray, I was not on a Bambrick smear-campaign. The facts are what they are. The older community members of the parish by and large supported the pastor. He redecorated the church, upgraded the sound systems and put in the outside landscaping using the school fundraising activities to subsidize the repairs and improvements, while grousing that the church was over $1,000,000 in debt due to his predecessor's lack of money management skills. When made aware of this, I called on the Diocese to audit the parish and Monsignor Bacovin agreed to do just that. Simply stated, we demanded an accounting of what was "coming in" (and from where) and what was "going out" (and to where).

As Mrs. McGarry and I laid out the facts, which included the direct violation of Diocese mandates for fundraising. Monsignor listened, appearing that day well over his 70 years of age. He was athletically built and handsome, but he was worn on the topic of John Bambrick; each story that we voiced corroborated an email or letter that he had seen in his four-inch folder marked "John Bambrick." As any good priest would do, Monsignor counseled and advised us. He sympathized with us and befitting his corporate position, didn't lead us to believe that any decision would be forthcoming; the Monsignor knew his boss. But what came towards the end of our conversation was something I had not at all considered, and which was very telling in regard to how the Reverend John Bambrick was actually perceived by his superiors.

  I looked across the conference room table at Monsignor Bacovin and Mrs. McGarry at my right and said, "no one feels for the 15 year-old kid (Bambrick) more than I because I felt what he went through, but...." It was right then and there that Bacovin cut me off and pointedly said to me with a wave of his hand, *what John allegedly went through.* I sat back, stunned. Mrs. McGarry picked up the conversation from that point, but as she started speaking, the passive Monsignor eye-glanced my way – his message delivered and received. I was dumbfounded that an "executive" of the Diocese of Trenton had so openly and purposefully conveyed doubt that the priest was telling the truth. Bacovin knew full well exactly what he was doing and saying. His knowing look spoke volumes. He was handing me, to insert into my widely read web-blog, the "reasonable doubt" that was the consensus among Bambrick's peers and superiors. As Peggy McGarry and I left the Pastoral Center, Monsignor Bacovin assured us that he would arrange a meeting with concerned parishioners and parents in Toms River in the near future, welcome progress for sure, but at that moment, definitely not my focus;

as we got into the car, all I wanted to know from Peggy was did I hear what I thought I heard? I did.

That meeting never came to fruition. Hundreds of emails and calls and letters and petitions flooded the Pastoral Center, none were answered.

I am a parishioner and the single mother of 3 children who attend or have attended St. Joseph's Grade School and MDHS. Due to the inappropriate actions and spoken words of Father Bambrick I do not attend mass at St. Josephs nor do I have my children attend mass at this church either. They continue to attend MDHS only so as not to disrupt their educational process. However, that too is getting quite difficult.

I am aware of various actions involving Father Bambrick which I find wrong, however my closest concern is the inappropriate misdirection of funds allocated for certain sports programs. My child is on two of the teams in which we were told funds could not be allocated to them even though they were originally directed to them along with specific fund raising. Along with that he is continually selecting which sport teams can move forward...cheerleading which leads me to thoughts and wonders of selecting such a specific team even if they are not of equal caliber as other teams.

His words and actions in connection to Mass and his inappropriate bias is disgusting. I am unable to sit through a mass in which a man speaks to others in the tone and vocabulary in which he does. Although there are other masses at St; Josephs that I am able to attend in which he does not preside over, I do not want to attend a church which honors and maintain such a man. I do not contribute as a parishioner at this time and will not do so until he is not within the walls of St. Joseph's Church. I have begun to find it difficult and am questioning my faith at this time due to his so called Christian behavior.....

I prefer this to be anonymous for the fact of retaliation by Father Bambrick, since I still have children who attend MDHS, for the time being. That concern itself should be a bell for the Diocese. When a parishioner cannot feel safe within the walls of a church then something is wrong with its so called leader....

In and of itself, this email is bad enough, but could it not be attributed to a lone disgruntled parishioner or school parent? The problem with that theory is that it does not stand alone - I received 207 more emails, letters, and phone calls voicing similar complaints against the pastor within two months' time, parents and parishioners lamenting the fate of their beloved community at the helm of Bambrick. Bishop John Smith received over 300 emails, letters and phone calls as well. The difference is that I responded to each and every one of them; Smith chose to ignore each and every one of them. As one parishioner related: "When I called the Diocese to complain about something Father

Bambrick did, I was told, 'He is like the CEO of a company. He can do anything he wants.'"

Bishop Smith also ignored the email I sent him that read in part:

Very Reverend, Bishop John Smith,

You are well aware of the way I approach things, methodically and looking carefully at both sides. You and I have disagreed on events in the Church that led you to Trenton as well the approach taken in the Jack Banko situation and his vile lifestyle while an Associate Pastor at Saint Mary of the Lake and his Pastor assignment when transferred to Metuchen. Our odds are serious but I believe that the respect is mutual and this is why you need to address the very serious issues at Saint Joseph Parish (Toms River) Monsignor Donovan High School before it becomes headlines.

John Bambrick has destroyed the legacy of Monsignor Lawrence Donovan, what he built and what he died for: tradition and faith through service. Today, Fr. Bambrick dismisses our valued traditions at Monsignor Donovan High School as trite "nostalgia." We take our traditions seriously. So much so that we incorporated it in our school motto ("Rich in Tradition").

When I left the Seminary in 1978, (then) Saint Joseph HS welcomed me. The second person to approach me on my awkward first day was (then) Father Donovan. He said to me "it won't be easy, but I live right over there. You are still one of us." I never forgot that. It took me years to come back but when I did one of the teachers there said "you're still one of us." A cord was struck. I was home again. I thought that under

John Bambrick, (a man I admired for his involvement in CNJ-SNAP and bishopAccountability.org) the community was in very, very good hands - I was drastically and resoundingly wrong.

Excellency, you have the letters and emails from frustrated, deflated and defeated parishioners and staff of the schools. What this man has done is to destroy the foundation of that Parish and School community and Trenton sits idly by. The Parish community has been financially rocked and I believe raped of our core values, traditions and Griffin-pride. This is turning into another Saint Raphael (Trenton of the 1990's) and I will not allow it to happen without a fight and I have plenty of that in me. The Parish and school is being ruled by a schoolyard bully that needs to be stood up to.

The children and parents have been classified as a "drain" on the Parish and the fabric of community spirit has been diminished by nothing short of zero-oversight and borderline corruption.

Bishop Smith, is it any wonder that Mass collections are down in a community such as Toms River and its surrounding areas? Why are empty envelopes going into the collection baskets and why are people retreating over the bridge to Mass in Seaside Heights that have been ingrained on Hooper Avenue for generations? Why are children being robbed of fundraising money to pay for statues that never needed replacing? Why are long standing benefactors turning their backs on the school and Parish functions? Toms River is affluent. Every street corner has a shingle of a professional practice hung out. A significant percentage has close ties to Monsignor Donovan the school or

Monsignor Donovan the Man. It's also the people that have been in the schools teaching, cleaning, serving food, administrating, watching kids go from K to 12 that are effected and that watched the flagship school for religious common sense, tradition and faith be destroyed by dictated and forced Doctrine. We have decided that we cannot stand for this anymore.

The time for talk is over. The time for frustration and tears has come to an end...

The Catholic community of Saint Joseph, which dates back to the 1800's, now encompasses a grade school, Monsignor Donovan High School (the only Catholic high school in Ocean County), the two churches (including Saint Gertrude in Island Heights) and a cemetery. One priest in the Diocese of Trenton calls this bustling community a "family business" because of the low turnover for staff and the high percentage of graduates that come back as staff, teachers and parents of a new generation of students within the schools. With so much to manage, it's also a stepping-stone for the purple of a Monsignor, a fact not lost on the many ambitious priests that have passed through these gates.

For this reason, among the inner-circles of the Diocese, the Saint Joseph community is a "choice assignment," yet not without challenges. The ledger book was positively bleeding red when John Bambrick replaced Monsignor Sean P. Flynn in June 2008. Admittedly so, the three prior pastors, starting with Monsignor Lawrence Donovan in the 1960's and passing through the next three decades with Monsignor Casimir H. Ladzinski and Monsignor Flynn, were not "money men."

That was not their calling. They were called to be priests and to offer what they could to whoever was in need. What they lacked in business acumen they made up for on the altar and with their parishioners and students. Rich in tradition and steep in Catholic generosity, the community of surrounding businesses and families answered the call to the good men that were the guardians of their churches and schools and cemetery for over 40 years. The money, like any church, parish or school was used for the purpose it was intended. If cheerleaders sold cupcakes for $1.00, that dollar went to the cheerleaders. If the intent for that money were for new uniforms, new uniforms would be purchased. These were guidelines set forth by the Diocese and regardless of the situation; no funds were diverted from the ledger line that it was intended for. That was pre-Bambrick.

7/15/10 9:06 AM, "<name withheld>:

My name is <withheld> and I am a parishioner at St. Joe's and I feel our parish is being destroyed from within by an outsider no one respects, no one believes and all wish was somewhere else.

I had an interesting "go 'round" with Bambrick one day after mass when he decided that instead of preaching the Word of God, he put Bishop Smith on the Jumbo-Tron to beg for money in his "Annual Appeal". Well, first I walked out in the middle of mass and then after mass, I approached Bambrick over the necessity of this.

I stated to him that I come to mass for enlightenment and to hear the word of God. I told him that it is absolutely hypocritical to have masses where you rail against wealth and privilege while shaking those very people down for donations. He didn't see it that and felt it was a necessary mission to fulfill the financial obligations of the Parish and the Diocese. I (for the sake of furthering the debate) agreed with that but asked why does it need to be in place of why we come to church in the first place? I then asked him how he felt that he was asking for money twice in roughly a 10 minute period. He reiterated his stance about financial obligations...yada yada yada.

Now all of this is happening while he told the band that they could have their "Strike up the Band" yard sale but he got he got a percentage off the top before the band saw a dime. Even worse is what he tried with the Mon Don hockey team. Mon Don hockey is SOLELY parent financed. Not a dime to support the team comes from the school. Parents pay over $500 for their son to play high school hockey. Bambrick tried to come in and raid that money stating because it was Mon Don, it was his money.

Sir, I stand with you and appreciate what you are doing. My son graduated Mon Don this year but for the fall of 2010, my daughter is going to East as Mon Don got too expensive and Bambrick took away ALL of the discounts we used to enjoy which helped make Mon Don borderline affordable. We used to have a Parishioner Discount – Gone; Multi-Child Discount – Gone; The Fund Raising Cards Discount - Gone.

This man is pure evil and needs to be dealt with.

I entered Saint Joseph High School for my 1978-1979 senior year. We had yet to be renamed Monsignor Donovan High School. I had just left Divine Word Seminary and was roaming the halls on my second day when (then) Father Donovan stopped me. "Another Novozinsky?" he inquired, making a reference to my sister Rose who preceded me there. "Yes," I answered, and offered my hand. Father took my hand and pulled me in close and said "you're one of us now, find me if you need anything, now how about a haircut," he chided, laughing. Six weeks later, and hair much shorter, I did need this larger-than-life priest but he didn't wait for me to come to him.

To the shock of many I tried to keep a low profile. I wanted to finish my senior year in high school, make a few friends along the way, date, and if all that came with a "D" average, that was okay; the way I looked at it, "D" equaled diploma. I was keeping it all under the radar so to speak. All of that ended when just before Halloween I looked at the Diocese newspaper, the *Monitor*, and saw my face splashed on the front cover. My photo was displayed in a publicity shot authorized by the Diocese vocation's office with the caption, "a seminarian," an outdated reference to what I once was at Divine Word Seminary. By second period, the barrage of questions started. For a kid trying to fit in and be ordinary, this was unwanted attention. Why did I have to be the poster child for vocations? I made certain that the *Monitor* was taken from the school library and office areas and brought the copies that I grabbed into Sister Kathleen Marie – a wonderful and loving soul that related well to children, knew my sister, and was sympathetic to my plight. She also had some influence with Father Donovan and she approached him on my behalf. When he found out what had happened he called Father James Roach at the Diocese office and from a closed door I heard him on the phone: "Jesus, Jim give the kid a break. You people toss him out because of the shit going on in Lakewood (Saint Mary parish) and then use him for an ad to get kids into Divine Word just because he dresses nice and has long hair? What kind of bullshit is that? He's here now and you're not making it any easier for him."

My faith in Father Larry Donovan was not misplaced. He was a man that knew your name, your siblings' names and your parents' names. When I irreverently called him "Larry" he knew the ribbing was actually a sign of my utmost respect, and he would just smile and pretend to throw a punch to my nose. His handshake was that of an Irishman's bond to his word and you just knew that you could trust him. Larry Donovan was a man that looked out for his own and almost 35 years after I first met him, I adopted this often-repeated tag: "We need to look out for our own," giving silent acknowledgment to my last known true pastor-priest each time I evoke the refrain.

The Diocese of Trenton ordered an audit to look into Bambrick's practice of reallocating fundraising efforts of the school's athletic and social clubs away from those organizations to the parish coffers where it was not intended. Money raised for cheerleading uniforms, ice time for the hockey team and student trips evaporated; worse yet, no explanation was being given by the pastor and the business manager of the parish community, Jacqueline Mack. The arrogance was as galling as the stealth accounting. Satisfied that there was absolutely no criminal intent or activity involved, my team (now called the "Committee of Ten," despite twelve members) continued pressing the issue for financial transparency and requested an accounting of what money was being used from what account and for what. The accounts receivable were logged by the administrators and passed to Mack who alone would enter it into the ledger system. No one else had this access. When calls came to the parish for funds to be released to a club, organization or athletic team, it was left up to Mack or Bambrick to answer and allocate. The audit was completed and the results while seemingly in his favor, ultimately proved disastrous for the priest and his puppet public relations team. This is how it played out.

Like a straight-A student boasting of his report card, the pastor posted an 18x24 laminated poster board at the entrances and exits of the churches in Toms River and Island Beach featuring the blown up letter from the auditor that the requested audit from "a person outside of [the] parish" (me) has been conducted - and passed. I attended the Mass that Saturday night celebrated by John Bambrick and the entire sermon was devoted to the audit and the high praise he received from the independent auditor. Upon leaving Mass that evening, the pastor, full of braggadocio, passed by me, looked at me, and gave me a Cheshire cat smile. I was sitting with my attorney at the time, Dawn Ritter, herself a member of the parish.

There was only one problem for Father Bambrick. I did not request the audit that he spoke of at the Mass or represented on the poster boards; the audit that he was speaking of was conducted 14 months prior. He still had a lot of explaining to do to the community and we expected him to do so through Monsignor Bacovin because Bishop Smith was not responding to the calls and letters coming into the Lawrenceville Pastoral Center. However, in a phone call I had that week with the Monsignor, he advised me, "John has stopped taking my calls." A slight-of-hand combined with smoke and mirrors on the behalf of Bambrick, but he fooled no one, least of all the Committee of Ten.

Immediately following the Mass, this email was sent to the Diocese's Pastoral Center by a parishioner and school parent (who happens to be a CPA):

Subject: Monsignor Donovan High School is OUR SCHOOL!

Good morning, as a parent paying over $10,000 a year to send my Daughter to Monsignor Donovan, you have a fiduciary duty to at address our concerns. You can no longer bury your (collective) heads in the sand.

Saint Joseph parish, school and cemetery and Monsignor Donovan High School is in a complete state of ruin and the conditions deteriorate with each passing day. This is a direct, complete and pointed result of the culture of hostility brought about by Father John Bambrick. Under this pastor the following has transpired:

1) The teachers have been forced to unionize as a last resort to answering the whims of a pastor out of control in his inappropriate words and deeds;

2) Enrollment is down by 30% in a school that used to have lines outside the door when it came to registering;

3) Over 300 mails and emails have come into the Diocese directed to Bishop John Smith and he has not uttered one word or addressed the crisis with the parishioners and parents;

4) Father Bambrick continues to use inappropriate pulpit bullying (and racial epitaphs) to describe Filipino parishioners that left the parish out of embarrassment;

5) Father Bambrick continues to use inappropriate pulpit lecturing to grade school children on the ripping of saints breasts;

6) Father Bambrick, in a public setting, made a "joke" about Saint Peter and the Virgin Mary "making out in the corner;"

7) Funds raised by school clubs, teams and organizations are being reallocated to the pastor's projects with no oversight by those organizations or explanation in direct violation of Diocese policy.

I personally would like to know how you plan to address these issues. I grew up with a Pastor like this and this was not acceptable 30 years ago. How is it acceptable now?

The courtesy of a reply would be greatly appreciated.

No response ever came. Throughout the ensuing months, more and more emails came into the Pastoral Center and each and every one remained in the folder, unanswered. The meeting promised by

Monsignor Bacovin with the parishioners and parents of the Saint Joseph Community was never held because Father Bambrick went directly to Bishop Smith who berated Bacovin for "over-committing to a small group of disgruntled people, one of whom is not even a parishioner." Bambrick was told, however, that he was not to respond or speak publically about this matter (at that point viral on the internet when I released 90 of the over 200 emails in my possession) and he was to report all expenditures over a specified amount to the Diocese office. He was not at all happy with this, but he complied.

Dear Mr. Novozinsky, Your blog and letter regarding Fr. Bambrick has come to me through my connections to the school. Since I am a former staff member of over 20 years and they knew I would be interested in reading it. I left the school recently after teaching there for many years, hoping to achieve a better salary and retirement, but also due to the dictatorial leadership in the parish and schools. My children graduated both and the grade school and high school. I totally agree with you. St. Joseph School and parish was a happy, nurturing and caring place. My children still recall the great education and values instilled that they received there. It is no longer that happy place and I believe Father Bambrick is progressively destroying the schools and parish. You need to know that he also has since his arrival been disrespectful, threatening and demeaning towards the grade school staff. His homilies for the children's masses have often been inappropriate. The enrollment is way down, which is not totally attributable to the economy. I know firsthand, that the moral of the faculty at the school and parish offices are very low due to his bullying. A few years ago they too tried to form a union, but were intimidated into dropping it. They still remain prohibited from speaking up because they are literally afraid for their jobs. I am alerting you to this so that you may seek out some people who know the grade school stories and may help the cause. I wish to remain anonymous due to my connection with the staff, knowing that swift repercussion will befall them.

On June 4, 2010, David Michael O'Connell was appointed Coadjutor Bishop of the Diocese of Trenton and officially succeeded Bishop Smith in December 2010, the latter having reached the mandatory retirement age of 75 and in failing health. Smith's transition from Bishop to Bishop Emeritus was swift. O'Connell chose as his episcopal motto: *Ministrare non ministrari*, meaning, "To serve and not to be served." The sign to the Saint Joseph's community was positive and hopeful. The new Bishop welcomed representatives to his office from the parish and school as well as the Mayor of Toms River at the time, Thomas Kelaher, in March 2011, to personally hear the mounting complaints against the pastor. The Bishop was candid, though the pastor's immediate removal was not on his to-do list. It would be foolish to think that a Bishop, new to the position, would make a decision of this magnitude in a short period of time. It would be bad precedent, triggering every parish that had a gripe with any pastor to launch a similar campaign and expect a similar result. I was not at this meeting (by choice) but in a personal meeting I had with O'Connell, it was clear to me that in his short time as Bishop, he had already mastered the fine nuances of his own his episcopal motto: "Bruce, there are times that 'to serve' means saying 'no.'"

As an almost afterthought of the efforts of the parish and school members fighting for the perseverance of the same two entities were those of Saint Joseph Cemetery. To this day, the stories that flooded my inbox from those who created the community on Hooper Avenue and those fighting for its survival are almost upstaged by those whose families were now interred at the resting place Saint Joseph managed.

I was asked to meet "Mary" at the cemetery in March 2010. It was a raw, wet Saturday afternoon. Mary was in her seventies yet still worked. Her husband and only child had passed and as part of her holiday ritual, she visited them at the mausoleum of Saint Joseph cemetery.

Mary contacted me via postal service mail. She didn't have email and at the doctor's office where she worked, she was kept apprised of the events of the efforts to rid Saint Joseph of Father Bambrick by co-workers. Her request for us to meet was attached to a letter and a petition. The letter described the closing of cemetery after certain hours and holidays. The petition had over 300 signatures obtained over three weeks in protest of the abbreviated hours all under the order of Father Bambrick. The petition went to Father Bambrick and Bishop John Smith, and neither of the two responded to the petitioners. After walking for a few minutes, Mary took my hand and laid it on the engraved lettering of her son and husband. The softness and sincerity in her eyes were reflected in the touch of her hand: "This is all I have left and the priest took it from me and won't even tell me why. It's all I have left." I embraced a woman like a son to a mother and I had only met her 40 minutes prior.

Many thought that the Committee of Ten formed to "oust" Father John Bambrick from Toms River abandoned the efforts after the March 2011 meeting with Bishop O'Connell. Nothing is further from the truth. I wanted to end this chapter with a final email exchange I received after the meeting was over with the Bishop in March – it comes from "Chelsea."

[I] am new to Toms River. Having recently moved here from Bergen County, and I was "Church shopping." My neighbor, who is also Catholic, suggested St. Joseph's or St. Justin's, but that she goes to St. Joseph's and likes it there better. Anyway, in checking online for things about the parish, I came across your website. It has been fascinating as well as disturbing reading (the clergy sex abuse), but I was also troubled by some of the things that were said about the Parish financial situation. Having already been through something similar in the Newark Archdiocese I am not looking to go through that again.

You stated: "From our first meeting in July 2010 to our publishing of "The Package" in November we have pressured the Pastoral Center to take action. Those who wanted to see it, saw it and those who want a copy in the future, can email me." Anyway, I would like to know what is or has been going on before I decide on this parish and before I decide how I want to participate in parish stewardship with my contributions.

As an aside, I had heard some good things about Fr. Bambrick, a former abuse victim, who was standing up for other victims of clergy abuse. The tenor of your article seems to indicate that this abuse-survivor is repeating those patterns of abusive behavior (not uncommon) in how he relates to his staff. It's all about power and control, really. He should seek counseling if that is the case. So, may I have a link to that parish information so I can make an informed decision as to how I want to support the church locally? Thanks...

At this point the "package" of emails was removed from my website (by that point renamed www.novozinsky.com) so I emailed the file to the letter writer stating: "St Joseph, is an amazing place. Don't discount it. Here is the package; judge for yourself. I wish you and your husband the very best of luck."

Chelsea replied:

Thank you very much for the attachments. I must say I am not so sure that St. Joseph Parish is the place for us (at least while Fr. Bambrick is there) given the emails you shared. One email in particular, I think, says it all: I am a parishioner at St. Joe's and I feel our parish is being destroyed from within by an outsider no one respects, no one believes and all wish was somewhere else.

I don't know that I have the energy necessary to endure what appears to be a very unhealthy parish situation. And I mean no disrespect to the parishioners when I say that. I just don't think I want to subject myself and my husband to an environment where such hostility exists - especially when the source of the problem appears to be the very person who should be the peacemaker and embodiment of the Lord in our midst.

I wish you all well. But I think at least for now, we will attend Mass either at St. Justin's or somewhere else until this is resolved. You are all in my prayers. I hope the new Bishop is a better Shepherd than Bishop Smith (who we knew from our former Archdiocese in Newark.) I would have expected better from Bishop Smith....

10
The Curious Cases of Patrick Newcombe

"... Laws govern us I grant you that. Give me an hour with him and a baseball bat in a room...."

-Bishop David M. O'Connell on Terence McAlinden

----- *Forwarded email Message* -----
From: J P <j.krams@yahoo.com>
To: [Patrick Newcombe]
Sent: Friday, September 9, 2011 11:02 AM
Subject: Bruno
Don't take this as a threat. take this as advice leave this Bruno situation alone, NOW. tell this novzinsky to back off. J

Six days later, on September 15, 2011, taped to the plastic wrap on my Trenton Times that gets delivered to my driveway each morning, was a picture of my oldest son and me at a golf outing. It was taken off my Facebook page and photo copied. In green Sharpie, my eyes were "X'ed" out.

I live in the Soprano State. I have heard the name Bruno before. Two days later I applied for a handgun license.

Seven months prior to my receiving these warnings, on a Monday afternoon in February of 2011, Patrick Newcombe, Robert Markulic and Chris Naples stood in front of Saint Theresa Roman

Catholic Church in Little Egg Harbor Township, New Jersey, a trio united by the sins of one man, Father Terence McAlinden. Patrick Newcombe's intent was to remain in the background and absorb information, and clad in a mundane tweed jacket, head lowered, hands clasped in front of him, his inconspicuous attire and demeanor allowed for this. He was mostly there for support. The day belonged to Chris Naples who, standing two people down from the staid sports jacket clad Newcombe, appeared out of sorts, unkempt and nervous.

"Father Mac" had abused Naples, Markulic and Newcombe as boys. It was difficult to place young, almost angelic faces of innocents on the withdrawn and bitter scowls that now stared into the cameras this day in southern Ocean County, New Jersey. All three stood in support and solidarity of the other two victims that were coming forward, demanding that McAlinden be defrocked immediately and that the church be held responsible. One of the victims, Bob Markulic, 56, of White Township in Warren County, claimed that he was sexually assaulted by McAlinden in the late 1960s at age 14 at the rectory at Our Lady of Victory Church in Sayreville, New Jersey, where he was an altar server. Markulic continued: "The next morning after the abuse, I was given absolution by my abuser and told to keep it between ourselves. Others would not understand. What I couldn't understand was why I was being given absolution — and what about the priest who had committed the abuse on me."

Patrick Newcombe found out about Naples after reading about Naples' sexual abuse claims against McAlinden on the Internet. The Diocese of Trenton repeatedly insisted that they were made aware of the accusations first in 2007 and then only from one victim, in an obvious reference to Chris Naples; yet, Newcombe repeatedly insisted that a decade earlier, in 1989, he reported to the Diocese that McAlinden had sexually abused him. Newcombe said he was sexually abused by McAlinden for five years, from 1980 to 1985, and he told his parents in 1989: "The abuse had catastrophic consequences in my life. I didn't go to police because the church pleaded with me not to. Then when Chris came forward with his allegations, the Diocese said that was the first report they had gotten about McAlinden and that there was only one victim. That's not true. Participating in the cover-up is one of the biggest mistakes of my lifetime."

The Trenton Diocese kept up the defense that implied Newcombe was lying, without coming right out and saying he was lying; Rayanne Bennett, spokesperson for the Diocese dismissed, "on the question regarding past allegations, there is nothing in any of the records, including correspondence from Mr. Newcombe and his representatives that makes any reference to Father McAlinden."

Newcombe maintained, however, that he had filed a notice of claim of intent to file a lawsuit with the Diocese, which forced a resolution: "A month later the church settled, but the settlement we signed doesn't mention any names." He said the settlement included the Diocese paying him, but would not say how much. The week prior to the news conference at Saint Theresa, Newcombe claimed to have met with numerous Diocesan officials, including Monsignor Walter Nolan, who according to Newcombe, recalled his 1989 accusations: "Monsignor Walter Nolan told me on Thursday that he remembers me talking to him in 1989 about McAlinden abusing me."

That night in his hotel room and admittedly under the numbing influence of alcohol, Newcombe took to his laptop and started posting unfiltered posts, at first as "Oh No" and then as the night wore on, under his full name, his final rant of the night, the most disturbing read:

I will stay silent no longer... My name is Patrick Newcombe. McAlinden abused me as a child, I was 13, he is a pig. I used to be 'OH NO!' Now I'm Patrick. Fuck him. I hope you rott in hell Mac..HA HA HA HA he who has the last laugh laughs best....HA HA hAFuck you scumbag

    I had seen this pattern of behavior before in my research; a victim at a press conference, in the spotlight with the most intimate, personal and embarrassing events in their lives being played out in the press. They feel shame, albeit unwarranted, and are almost contrite. When the cameras leave, they feel abandoned and the need for attention once again. They need to be reassured that they are not at fault. This can go one of two ways; first in organized advocacy and crusade or, second, down a self-destructive path of substance abuse and withdrawal. As it played out in the case of Patrick Newcomb, neither path was mutually exclusive of the other.

    Patrick Newcombe was on the brink of both and had no clear path to turn. You see, Newcombe's encounter with "Father Mac" was not his only encounter with an abusive priest; years prior to McAlinden, Patrick Newcombe met Father Frank Bruno.

    Father Francis "Frank" Bruno came to the home parish of the Newcombe family, Saint Martha's in Point Pleasant Boro Beach, New Jersey, in the early 1980's. Bruno saw a vulnerable, shy and awkward boy in Patrick and struck up a mentorship-like relationship with him because of Patrick's obvious devotion to the church and the nuns associated with his school. Patrick and his best friend Walter Weidmont spent many hours at church events. Setting up for bingo, Patrick and Walter would be there. CCD classes, Patrick and Walter would be there. Patrick thought of the priesthood as an obvious extension of this devotion to the church and looked to the young priest as a role model for his vocation.

In a secretly taped conversation with Diocese of Trenton deacon representatives in 2011, Deacon Charlie Moore told Newcombe that he had warned Newcombe's mother about Bruno when he saw how friendly the new priest was becoming with her son. Moore related that he told her to be aware because Bruno "had been transferred from a church in Matawan because of a problem with young boys" and it wasn't the only time that he was moved for this reason. "Unfortunately," Newcombe said in retrospect, "we choose not to believe this."

Prior to his coming to Newcombe's parish, Frank Bruno was assigned to Saint James Roman Catholic Church in Woodbridge, New Jersey. It was during this assignment that a young man by the name of John Crowe claimed to have been sexually assaulted by Bruno both at the rectory and at the Stella Maris Retreat in Long Beach Island, a seaside resort of the Diocese of Trenton at the Jersey shore.

Crowe alleged that during the period of 1978-1981, Bruno routinely invited him and other boys to play poker and offered them beer and cigarettes, which ultimately led to sexual assaults in the priest's bedroom and rectory sitting room. He also alleged that other priests and bishops at the time were well aware of Bruno's habit of keeping teenage boys for sexual purposes and had given him the nickname "Chicken Hawk." Crowe filed a suit against Bruno, which also named Trenton Bishop John C. Reiss, Monsignor Joseph LaForge, the Reverend Harry Flynn, the Reverend Thomas Rittenhouse, the Reverend John J. Scully, the Reverend Vincent Treglio, the Reverend William McKeon, Bishop Edward Kmiec, Monsignor Francis Krine, and the Rev. Richard Lyons.

And under a "known or should have known" theory of liability, the suit went on to name Bruno's seminary school and the churches he was affiliated with. According to bishopaccountability.org, Bruno was moved from one major seminary to another when his sexual behavior was discovered. This called into question the recruiting and retention policies at major (college) seminaries. This disputed the claim made by many dioceses in the same legal predicaments, that it is only after ordinations that many of these tendencies began to resonate with newly ordained priests. In the case of Frank Bruno, his reputation was common knowledge at his churches, too; he was transferred from the Trenton Diocese to the Metuchen Diocese and under the care of Bishop Theodore McCarrick. [43]

In October 2011, I received this email. It read:

I am not sure how to begin this except to simply begin. This past weekend, while doing a Google search on another subject, I came upon your website. I was intrigued by tab entitled "Purple Reign-The Book," so I had to click on it. I could only imagine what my eyes and facial expressions were when I got to reading the parts about that monster who tortured many--including myself--Frank Bruno and his associate John Scully. Every word I read made me sick, horrified, and angry, but I realized that this beast was real and got away with so much. I thank you for taking up this cause so that the truth be told.

There...I've said it. There is only one other person besides you that I have ever told about this evil man--that's my wife. But after reading that section, I knew in my heart that I had to confirm this with you. I, too, was abused by Bruno when I was an altar server. I suppose, like most, I simply put it out of my memory to the point where I believed and convinced myself that nothing ever happened. I have suffered privately, but I always wondered about what happened to Bruno, and I found out a few years ago that he was indeed working in the state corrections system. How ironic! I knew in my heart that he was not defrocked and simply left the priesthood on his own accord and with the full knowledge of this horrible diocese.

I hope this helps you to further realize that you are correct in your assertions of this beast. If there is anything else you may want to know, I would be happy to correspond with you further. Be well.

Bruno left the priesthood but not before he was investigated internally by the Diocese of Trenton after Patrick Newcombe's mother contacted them via Father Walter Nolan in 1989. In a February 2011 conversation, secretly taped by Newcombe and released to me by his attorney, Newcombe discusses his earlier allegations with Monsignor Nolan, Diocese Victims Assistance Coordinator Maureen Fitzsimmons and his boyhood friend, Walter Weidmont, there for moral support; Monsignor Joseph Rosie and Bishop O'Connell joined the group later. Below are the transcripts of the meetings that took place that day. They are unedited except for the parts where the tapes were inaudible or unrelated conversation took place.

Why make these public? Why now? The conversation will not declare a "winner." It will not bring you to the conclusion that good conquers evil. It does offer insight to several areas covered in this research. It introduces the reader to contradictions on the sides of all parties. In the case of the Diocese, it shows an apparently concerned (and newly installed) Bishop that is either woefully ill-informed or had been lied to; a Monsignor that willfully covered up the past transgressions of abusive priests and feigned ignorance as "just following orders," and a process so laden with flaws that at several meetings on abuse claims, no notes were ever scribed. Like it never happened - the abuse *or* the meeting. The victim is flawed as well. His memory faded by time and nightmares that carried over to his waking hours and dulled by years of substance abuse.

What is transcribed below represents no less than four rewrites. Editors fought with the author over the content and the author fought with his conscience over validity of the entire chapter.

Is the entire meeting transcript necessary? Yes. So often a word left out or put in based on assumption will corrupt the entire content of the conversation; in the end, completeness trumps all, and whereas it may be mundane in portions, the entire recording, from the point it starts to the point it finishes, is necessary to ensure that the integrity of all parties remains intact and that the conversation is relayed verbatim.

The meeting took place in the Pastoral Center of the Diocese of Trenton in early winter 2011. In the room for the first part of the meeting are Newcombe and Weidmont, Monsignor Nolan, and Fitzsimmons.

NEWCOMBE (to Monsignor Nolan): I happened to Google McAlinden's name on the internet about six weeks ago. When I first made contact and saw that this other man made accusations against him, and I saw where this Ms. Bennett (Rayanne Bennett, Director of Communications for the Diocese of Trenton) made the statement in an article for the Star Ledger I think it was - that no other victims have ever come forward and that the Diocese has hired a private investigator to investigate this and that's simply not true – its simply not true that no other victims came forward – because I came forward to you back in 1990 I told you about these things I have recordings of those telephone calls that were made from my mother's living room and I, um, -this especially with – Bruno apparently I was told by Monsignor Rosie that he was removed from the priesthood which I found out to not be true he left the priesthood

FITZSIMMONS: Bruno was sent right after your accusation - at that point he was sent to a residential place where they do a battery of tests and make recommendations, and in June of 1989 he was removed from active ministry after a six-week stay at that facility

NEWCOMBE: Okay. So, he had been removed from active ministry prior to me even contacting you

FITZSIMMONS: Uh, yes

NEWCOMBE: Because I didn't contact you until 1990

MONSIGNOR NOLAN: Probably so, but I don't know to be honest with you but, yes, Bruno was removed from ministry

NEWCOMBE: So, a year prior to him…

FITZSIMMONS: It was your mom's letter that prompted that and when this was received it was actually received up north (to the Paterson Diocese) they sent Bruno away to the residential place where he was tested and when he came back he was removed from active ministry in June

NEWCOMBE: Um, that was done prior to me coming forward, prior to this letter for sure, but also prior to me coming forward to you, Monsignor Nolan. I remember the phone call like it was yesterday that we had when I was sitting in my mother's living room and me telling you about Bruno and about all his friends, John Scully, Richard Lyons and all the people that knew that he was abusing me because it was public knowledge in their circles of people or friends and at that time you had already apparently dealt with Bruno – it was kind of interesting that no one had reached out to me, I guess, because you hadn't at that point. I contacted you after a suicide attempt from remembering all this stuff from all the…

FITZSIMMONS: So, that was after your mom wrote the letter…

FITZSIMMONS: Is that when - I know we made an arrangement for you to go into…

NEWCOMBE: That was on April 1, 1990

FITZSIMMONS: 1990

NEWCOMBE: Which in this letter it was dated April 26, 1989, so it was a year later that I had come forward and then when I did, like I said, come forward it wasn't just Bruno that I came forward about. I came forward about these other men that abused me and also gave you a lot of information about other priests that knew. Then, I see then in 1994 its also on the Internet that someone sued the church a guy named John Crowe about being abused by Bruno and mentioned some of the very same names that I mentioned as far as knowing about the abuse, not necessarily being abused by them, and even some that I didn't mention, Patrick McGee, he walked in on us one time so I know he knew. [NOTE: Father Patrick McGee has not been named as an abuse suspect]. *He never touched me, but I know somebody that he did, Tommy [name withheld by author] if you're familiar with him at all because he came and told me as kids and I didn't say anything back. I guess I've done a lot of talking I'll be quiet now. I feel that participating in this cover-up has been the worse thing that I've ever done by signing this confidential settlement agreement was the single worse mistake I ever made in my life and not for financial reasons. I'm saying that in 1990, the criminal Statute of Limitations was not up and Bruno could have been charged with rape, McAlinden could have been charged with rape, James Scott could have been charged with rape and by my failure to proceed any further, at your recommendations that you would take care of it internally, I feel somewhat responsible for these other kids that were abused and I don't know how you could...*

MONSIGNOR NOLAN: Didn't I and again please I'm going back in my back of mind I don't have anything verbatim in my mind...

NEWCOMBE: I understand

MONSIGNOR NOLAN: I certainly do remember that period of time the whole Bruno thing and I thought that we looked into that pretty quickly and took care of Bruno. Do I know that some names were mentioned that knew about some of that were some of those priests talked to, yes, were some not from the Diocese if I recall correctly and I do remember that somewhat vaguely I just remember that somewhere along the line we had a conversation, in fact, we had a few conversations on the telephone or in writing and I remember even asking could we meet or to get together and exactly where you were at the time I don't know and I do remember your mom asking for some help for you, I think we kind of quickly, I think, took care of that. Correspondence back from us about that saying thank you or whatever the words actually were - I do have a recollection I'm not going to say it was you, but I'm going to say so but probably so I don't ever remember that McAlinden's name being mentioned with the Bruno thing meaning with the other names you or someone else mentioned about Bruno that knew or hung with Bruno that kind of thing. I do remember something about saying and almost and its just my recollection I don't even know when this was, but I do remember saying and I don't know when this was after the settlement, when you were in treatment or after treatment and I do remember by the way make that seemed to me anyway where's McAlinden to me anyway coming from in this particular scenario. I do recall talking to McAlinden about that accusation or whatever, of course he denied it completely and I kind of think if I recall that there was some correspondence back saying could we get together some more, I didn't have enough to go on or there's not *enough there and I heard nothing about McAlinden up until his name was thrown out and I do kind of remember that's what I remember, gee, where'd that come from in a sense like it was almost like by the way*

[NOTE: It's at this point that Monsignor Nolan admits that the press reports were false that no claim against Terence McAlinden came in prior to 2007. He did in fact remember that Newcombe came forward in a letter from his mother prior in the late 1980's]

MONSIGNOR NOLAN: And then I'm going to say that after that I don't remember conversations you and I had about McAlinden I remember a conversation where McAlinden's name was brought up. It was after that I looked into it at least we addressed it a little bit, maybe not enough, but I do remember

NEWCOMBE (interrupting): Do you know how many victims that I have found of McAlinden's?

MONSIGNOR NOLAN: No, I don't...

NEWCOMBE: Its going to sicken you when you find out I think your getting ready to– again, my lack of action by not going to the prosecutor is something that I'm having a hard time personally dealing with because if I had he would have been properly investigated and at that time this guy that I read about on the Internet his abuse was taking place at that point in time in 1990 when I reported that to you and if something was really done his abuse would have stopped and possibly other people's abuse that took place after that wouldn't have taken place at all. I'm pretty angry about that –I know what I said it's almost verbatim what you just said. It was after we talked about Bruno and my words were I'm not done –not by the way I'm not done, I have more to tell you and that's when I told you about James Scott who was the Paterson Diocese and McAlinden, I haven't been able to find anything on James Scott what happened to him or if there was any other victims that have come forward, um, but, uh, I guess that would be just standard operating procedure that you would contact the accused priest and if he denied it you would let it go

MONSIGNOR NOLAN: Well, you know Pat at the time a lot of this was new to us and even myself I don't you know - I fully understand your anger. I hope you have at least a little faith - this stuff kills us to and kills me to a little bit and I'm not trying to make your feelings mine or mine yours – because they're totally different and if you ever want to know just ask Bruno, they hated me because of me going (asking) ' how do you prove this.' you know it wasn't easy for any of us and certainly not for yourself, okay. I feel also that to very, very much so I've had many conversations about how we either helped each other, ourselves probably a part of me that was very, very pleased this is not an area where anybody can be pleased, but when I thought that you were helped, and your parents seemed okay, I felt very good about that – so don't think I don't get concerned or didn't get concerned about anybody who was certainly involved with something

NEWCOMBE: Excuse me, I'm going to say how I feel because I haven't for twenty years so I'm going to – I don't think the church's concern for me was in the forefront when they put him in treatment without even contacting me. It was a year later that my mother instigated a phone call between you and I and that's when I got help. It wasn't from the church reaching out and saying that we sent Bruno to treatment and we realize he's a child rapist and now we're going to see if we can do something to help the kids that he raped, uh, that didn't take place. It was my mother reaching back out because I had attempted to commit suicide and that's when they did make the offer to send me to alcohol and drug treatment, which I went to and I succeeded at. This has been a lifelong problem for me. This has caused chaos in my life in my relationships with people in general, and especially with my relationships with men, with God, my faith got blown out of the water still is. I'm 44 years old I can't believe because of the things that happened to me as a child. I can't believe in the God that you believe in I can't and I don't blame anything I've done in my adult life, but I never raped any kids and you know I think that my anger especially after seeing the date on this letter and my mother's letter and the series of events which took place after that with Bruno. Yeah, my anger is directed towards you a little bit, the church in general. After I went to treatment it was two years later that I wrote the next letter almost to the day kind of strange, and, um, during that two years there was no contact. I completed the treatment center and that was it. I was left to fend for myself, which I did. I went through the struggles of - Walter knew me all through this, he knows McAlinden, he knows Bruno, he knows Scott. He knew all these people so there's not a need for me to explain any of this to Walter any further. He didn't know the abuse was going on – but we've been friends for 35 years. I didn't even tell him (Walter) about this until three weeks ago because I told him I was coming up here and that I was going to need some support because this is something that is really dangerous ground for me to tread on emotionally, mentally and spiritually, but I felt that I needed to - these guys were monsters and I'm going to include the guys who knew about it that you mentioned before, John Scully, Rich Lyons, Vincent Treglio, these guys all knew there was no —when we were down at the Stella Maris Treatment Center at Long Beach Island there was no hiding some of them had their own boys. I didn't see them abusing any of them, but they knew I was being abused because it was talked about it, was joked about and these guys are still priests today, but McAlinden is still a priest today as we speak. That is not acceptable that man raped me and you guys protect them and that's not acceptable to me. You know I've been watching the news especially recently across the river here in Philadelphia with the huge cover-up and the bishop is on TV talking - I can't understand how you guys live with yourselves knowing that you protect child rapists because by not doing anything further especially with the people that knew Lyons, Treglio and all these other guys, McGee, um, that knowing about a crime that's taking place in the position that they were in, knowing that a child is being abused, and not doing anything about is just as bad as abusing a child. If I visited a friend's house and saw that he was abusing their child and I did nothing about it, I would be guilty of a crime. Um, I spoke with the Ocean County Prosecutor's Office and she said it was a crime that I reported this to the church in 1990, and that the church did not turn around and report it to law enforcement that was a crime because the criminal statutes were still in place then. They could have been prosecuted. Um, your explanation that the church was just learning how to deal with these things I guess I could buy that to a certain extent, but to protect the church and the priests seemed like to me was a taller order

MONSIGNOR NOLAN: *You know that I can tell you look at you I never, never, never did something just to protect the church – I would take care of it - if it wasn't done right or something I can tell you that I never do that*

WALTER: *My burning question really is if after his mom wrote you the letter he spoke with you - you said you made a phone call to Mac he denied it and forgot about it. If the church did not know how to deal with this, why didn't you deal with it the way the rest of the world would and turn him over to the authorities? What's the explanation I mean these guys are monsters and you're just protecting them and moving them somewhere else or say no you can't be a priest anymore but that's all we're going to do. Why wouldn't you turn them over to the authorities? Why don't you call the police and say we have a complaint about this individual and let them investigate it because you guys aren't investigators your priests - cops do what they do because they don't believe anybody you have to prove to them*

MONSIGNOR NOLAN: *And I think what you are saying Walter is wrong we do talk to the prosecutors, we do right away if some complaint comes in...*

NEWCOMBE: *Now*

MONSIGNOR NOLAN: *Yes now – yeah, and actually going back then I don't know the dates of all of this I don't keep that in my mind or haven't really done that we have also started in our Diocese weren't the first to even start this put a group together to understand all of this, but not to understand it in a way – but to talk about it all of this let somebody come in and talk to us, other minds involved in this you know so it did evolve to this point and now I think we do have a pretty good system and I think we do make sure that all the dots are covered, etc., etc., were they all covered then I'm not going to sit here and look at you and say yes they were...*

NEWCOMBE: Well, this man that came forward in 2008 against McAlinden you guys removed McAlinden immediately from his position, because you said this other guy had credible evidence, but he's still a priest

FITZSIMMONS: Can I just explain and I do I totally understand where your coming from with that question

NEWCOMBE: He's still on your payroll

FITZSIMMONS: This has to do with canon law

WALTER: It doesn't apply to law – that's church law correct so what about legal?

FITZSIMMONS: We're looking at McAlinden is still a pastor and McAlinden is still the pastor because he has refused to resign and he is covered by Canon Law so that's not something that you should pick and choose who can stay – we've had

WALTER: You know what I don't mean to interrupt you but - I live in Manahawkin – I grew up in Point Pleasant with Bruno and when I went to Manahawkin my whole half of my family lives in Tuckerton so St. Theresa's was our parish so I half grew up going to that church on the weekends. You have people that live there still have faith in that man because no charges were ever filed against him and he's still the pastor even though he doesn't actively in the church preach there anymore. They still believe him - I talked to my relatives about this

NEWCOMBE: He's still holding mass on Sunday mornings at his house I know this to be a fact

MONSIGNOR NOLAN: Well, maybe you do, but I don't know if we can stop that - I don't know that I know if a guy does stuff in his house we're not authorizing any of that stuff. And he's told not to because I'm going to guess at this - I don't do this stuff now, but I'm sure there's a letter saying you can't do this and you can't do that and what he does or what anybody does...

NEWCOMBE: And then the spokesperson for the church, Ms. Bennett, responded to the reporter that no other people have ever accused McAlinden of anything and we've hired an investigator to figure this whole thing out...that's a bold face lie. If you go to bishopsaccountability.com [NOTE: "org"] and pull up abuse tracker and pull up McAlinden and read the articles that are next to his name about this other guy that came forward, its in those articles that Ms. Bennett says that no other victims have come forward -that we have hired an investigator to see if there's been any other victims. No investigator has contacted me that was two years ago. If this was handled properly, and I'm sure that notes would have been made in McAlinden's holy file, that someone has accused him of abusing them so that if it happened again that you would maybe have some credible evidence and say wait a minute maybe there's a pattern we see here and this guy is the Director of the CYO. This might be an issue that we have there now. I would think that accusation would have been taken extremely seriously. He was the worst of them all as far as being a monster. He and Bruno were in cahoots and he knew that Bruno was abusing me and he knew I was an easy target. When it happened it was like a foregone thing, that it was going to happen – and when I told Bruno about it he laughed and said "oh, Mac"

[NOTE: At this point, Patrick Newcombe begins to tell of the priests he alleges to have witnessed the abuse he endured and did nothing about it]

NEWCOMBE: Vincent Treglio, I know he's in Florida now. I believe he was in the Diocese of Metuchen when this happened. John Scully is a pastor in your Diocese. He knew very well what was happening to me – no ifs ands or buts about it - that Johnny, as they called him knew about – and Treglio's nickname was grandma, I remember telling you that to, James Scott was Scotty. They all had these nicknames, granted these guys like I said didn't physically do anything to me but they knew this was happening to me – Bruno sleeping in the same bed with me at the retreat center down at the nun's place down in Long Beach Island and them being there – they were there - I was 14 years old that's atrocious that they would allow that –even if they weren't guilty themselves – John Scully is not one I ever saw a boy with him, the other *ones were all of the other ones - I never saw John Scully bring a boy with him down there – but he knew that not only from there he knew it from coming from Point Pleasant and us going to Our Lady of Lords where John was pastor at for a while back in the 80's or 90's*

NEWCOMBE (visibly upset, speaking to no one in particular): James Scott, he abused me. He was a teacher in Wayne. He was a high school teacher. I thought he was from Metuchen, but I've come to find out since that where he was located was in the Diocese of Paterson, but yes I was told that. I don't remember exactly when I was told that, but this settlement agreement here has nothing to do with any other diocese. And you know reading some of this stuff here even that my mother wrote what Charlie Moore, who was a deacon at our church, told us when Frank (Bruno) first arrived he saw him becoming friendly Patrick and was told to be aware because Frank had been transferred from a church in Matawan because of a problem with young boys. That wasn't the only time that Bruno was transferred because of a problem with young boys, unfortunately, we choose not to believe this. I know about Steven, I know about Matthew, I know about Jimmy, I know about all these kids because Bruno told me about them. I don't know their last names, but I know these kids. John Crowe I know about the seminary that he was in and he was removed from for having a sexual relationship and placed in another seminary. The church had plenty of warning that this guy was a sexual predator and kept moving him around without warning anybody, and even here what would happen was he was transferred from St. Martha's to St. Joachim's? And he was a priest there before he went to treatment or whatever the case may be – so even right after this he was still in a position where he had contact with children...

Patrick's day was far from over. Fitzsimmons and Monsignor Nolan brought them in to meet the newly installed Bishop of Trenton, David M. O'Connell, and Monsignor Joseph Rosie. Upon entering the room and prior to the Bishop joining the group, Newcombe advised Monsignor Rosie that Monsignor Nolan questioned Father McAlinden about the letter Newcombe's mother sent and the allegations of sexual assault against him.

NEWCOMBE: I just learned from Monsignor Nolan that he remembers me telling him that McAlinden abused me and yes they did talk to him about it and he denied it and they let it go at that. I come to find out that while that was happening he was abusing someone else. This other man that was on the Internet that I saw, and I participated in the cover-up of it by agreeing to this confidential settlement, which is something that I regret more than anything else in my life was agreeing to that and I can't sleep at night - knowing that by participating in this cover up other kids were abused nothing was done. And I read a letter today that my mother had written back in 1989 regarding Frank Bruno I was given a timeline today where he had been immediately taken out of service, and put in a treatment center and that's how you guys dealt with him, and when we got the results from testing that he was put on administrative leave

[Enter Bishop O'Connell]

MONSIGNOR JOE ROSIE: How old were you Patrick when the...

NEWCOMBE: When this all started around 13 I believe or 12 if I'm not mistaken - I have to look at the dates

BISHOP O'CONNELL: You were eighth grade or seventh grade

NEWCOMBE: Right or even younger then that. When I met McAlinden, I was going out and doing the sacrifice to the suffering and doing different service weeks here and service weeks there and that's when that abuse started - McAlinden and Bruno were friends and Bruno told McAlinden that he was abusing me and, um, I learned this later because Bruno told me that he told him and he laughed when I told him that McAlinden had

BISHOP O'CONNELL: Did he say why he told McAlinden this?

NEWCOMBE: He was giving him a heads up because he knew I was going to Trenton on this weekend to the sacrifice of the suffering and that's when McAlinden abused me for the first time and that was on Lawrenceville Road somewhere at a conference center, and then McAlinden took me to Keyport to the Jeremiah House and I was abused there, and then at a home that he owned that was nearby the Jeremiah house and then at his parent's house in Tom's River and on his boat in Tom's River. I called McAlinden in 1985 for the last time, and told him I was in trouble with alcohol and drugs. I was doing Heroin that Bruno was supplying for me and I asked him for help and he came and picked me up and took me to Tom's River to his boat, and took me out on the boat and abused me for the weekend and gave me alcohol That was the last time I saw him. Shortly after that I joined the Navy to escape all this and it worked, fortunately, for that part. You know I know that you probably have an idea of what - maybe you have an idea of what survivors go through, but quadruple it the idea that you think you have – and these people to still be in place in your employ is horrific - that McAlinden is still collecting a pay check from you guys is disgusting– he raped me – he physically held me and raped me – um, the priest that knew that I was being abused and did nothing about it, John Scully, is a priest here today in your diocese – he's a pastor - knew that I was being abused by Bruno saw it happening and nothing was done. I reported these names to Monsignor Nolan back in 1990 and he just told me that he talked with these people and they just denied it – and it was left at that. I can't remember why we didn't do anything else about is what he said – I know why nothing more was done about it was they certainly didn't want anybody to know. That was the standard operating procedure in 1990 with the church, unfortunately, was don't tell anybody. Let's not have anybody find this out - you know. If Monsignor Nolan had reported these crimes to the District Attorney's Office in 1990 when I reported them, people would have been arrested because the Statute of Limitations was not even up yet it was still within that period even. I've been in contact with the Ocean County Prosecutor's Office now and with Colleen Lynch she's a sergeant/detective and she told me that by the church not reporting these crimes in 1990 it was a crime - in itself. I'm not going away until these people that are on your payroll are no longer on your payroll. If I have to go to the top of the tallest building and tell them what happened to me, I'm going to do that. Um, I can understand at some point when a young man like I was in 1990 *comes forward of maybe you guys not being sure whether or not you can believe everything that's being said, but then when other victims come forward and tell you the same story – when I read this stuff on the Internet I had to literally go vomit because it was the same story this other kid had gone through that I did and your spokesperson, Rayanne Bennett, said no other victims have come forward. So now the people in that church, which Walter happens to be a parishioner of, still believe that McAlinden is innocent because your representative said that no other victims have come forward. He's still listed as the pastor. I called and asked who the pastor was?*

MONSIGNOR JOE ROSIE: Patrick, I mean he is the officially the pastor because he has not resigned the parish. I will - I can only say that the process that has come out following the Charter in 2002 and the subsequent rules that the Vatican asked us to do we are following here – as a matter of fact that process on our side absolutely continues as you probably might know there was an issue with McAlinden and the Diocese in Delaware, there is a civil procedure still continuing against him in Delaware because of the Statute of Limitations changes that took place in Delaware. The Diocese is cooperating in that investigation down there. He does continue to receive some support from us

NEWCOMBE: Why, he's a rapist...

MONSIGNOR JOE ROSIE: He will lose his pension, as this process is still ongoing from here because we will continue to pursue the canonical procedures that we need to do here - because Bishop Smith did write and request of Rome that a canonical process take place here in the Diocese of Trenton believing that the allegations made against him are true and that he should be – that part of that punishment should be and including dismissal from the clerical state – you cannot collect a pension - a priest does not collect a pension from the Diocese of Trenton unless they are in good standing because that's part of our process....

NEWCOMBE: But that process that you're talking about was done in 2008 it's 2011 now

MONSIGNOR JOE ROSIE: Well, and part of the very difficulty is that at the time the other victim was the only victim that we were in communication with

WALTER: Isn't that enough...

MONSIGNOR JOE ROSIE: What I'm trying to say – but there was also a difficulty in his coming forward. He was talking to us for a little while, he would step back because he much as I certainly respect and have heard and truly believe what you say the pain and the difficulty this was making him <inaudible> think process not just being determined by expediency in terms of coming to some canonical process but also the recognition that we don't want to – pardon the phrase because I don't' know what better phrase to use -to re-victimize –he said I need a little bit of time. We felt we needed to respect that. What was happening was from the very first moment when that first allegation came forward, within the week Bishop Smith was at the parish, there was a parish meeting and at that time he told them that soon as read those allegations – he effectively said you cannot function as a priest. So he held the title *of pastor, okay, because he has a canonical right a right within the ecclesiastical <inaudible> – he was not allowed to do anything that a pastor could do*

NEWCOMBE: *Do you know that he still does that at his home on Sunday's...*

MONSIGNOR JOE ROSIE: *My understanding is and we have written to him numerous times and told him to stop and every time we are made aware of that we tell him to stop – I cannot – I mean the difficulty that we run into, frankly, is that he says to us that he's not advertising this and people come to his house and he does this. We tell him you can't, but we do not have any police force or anything that is going to go in there and say because Bishop says that you can't say mass with people – don't say mass with people – we have - the only way we can continue to do that is to keep writing to him as we do and telling him to cease...*

NEWCOMBE: *There is only one victim that Rayanne Bennett said that has come forward - that's a lie...*

MONSIGNOR JOE ROSIE: *All I can say is that I do know – and I mean I can't answer for what was going on in 1990. I do know that I was involved in 2002, 2003 when we were going through our files and because I can tell you about various things there was a group of us and literally there was not a note of some kind – because we did flag many obscure notes or something if there was a obscure reference in a file or something and we did look through all the files and I don't know in all* honesty what happened back specifically with what Monsignor Nolan was telling you and stuff today because I just was not here. I don't know what was going on. I can say with certitude that as I was responsible to look at files here I did not recall a note or a reference in any of that file that took place in 1990. I'm not saying that doesn't mean that it didn't take place in 1990, but I did not see something because I wrote to let you know that files were fine and things were looked into because of what might have been and I mean that I regret that situation

NEWCOMBE: I don't know what Monsignor Nolan wrote down when I reported it to him, what took place back in 1990

WALTER: He didn't write anything

NEWCOMBE: Right. I can't control what he wrote down, but I can control the conversation that took place because I have tapes of the conversation that took place in 1990, and so I know that I reported McAlinden then, and Bruno and James Scott, who was a priest in a different Diocese and I reported the other priests that knew I was being abused to Father Nolan then and he just confirmed that to me in there that I do remember calling these other people and asking them about it and then I don't remember what happened - why it didn't go anywhere else and that was Vincent Treglio and John Scully, who's a priest here now, James Scott who was a priest in Paterson and Vincent Treglio who was a priest in Metuchen I believe and now he's in Florida. These men knew that I was being abused. Patrick McGee, who was the pastor at St. Martha's walked in on us. McGee never touched me and I never claimed that he did, but he knew that I was being abused. He saw it with his own *eyes, as did John Scully, and nothing was done and so even when you did have or even when your office did have someone report things it wasn't handled properly. It wasn't flagged properly that's for sure. If you look at Bruno's case, it's disgusting. It goes all the way back to the seminary, the first seminary that he was in and was removed from for sexual misconduct, with a minor, and then moved around throughout several different parishes. I know the kids' names that he abused. I've met them when I was a kid and the church moved him from place to place. Alright, he's in trouble here we'll put him over on the other side of the state, put him over here in Point Pleasant and then we'll bring him back to Trenton where we can keep a close eye on him here at St. Joachim's and then they sent him to treatment and still didn't contact the person that he was abusing, but we took care of the priest – let's get him in treatment, let's get him help, let's get him counseling, the victim, we're not going to contact him victim. We're not going to contact him, but we'll get a hold of the priest and help him – to me that's deplorable behavior and sadly it has colored not only my faith in the church in general because my faith in the church in general, my faith in anything that's coming out of this conversation is zero. That this will influence your decision-making process or whatever I believe that this conversation is nil. It's only making me feel better and that's just from my past experience is why I feel that way. I believe that if Bishop Smith or Bishop O'Connell now got on the telephone to the Vatican or to the Canon people and explained that we have a child molester, a rapist on our payroll; this has been confirmed. We have credible evidence – they were your words from the other person. I would like to think that my evidence is pretty credible to [inaudible]. I can tell you how many ceiling tiles were on the bedroom - I can tell you that right now – in the Lawrenceville Conference Center –*

I can give you details about this man's life that I would not know about. I would think that a telephone call from someone in a position of authority saying we have got to do something - this man has to be defrocked or whatever the other word is laicized...

MONSIGNOR JOE ROSIE: Laicized...

NEWCOMBE: I would think that if your office made enough noise about this that would happen and I don't think your office has done that. I have no interest at this point and I understand that from a financial point of view. I settled with the church and that's done and over with, but I'm a loose canon you don't want me on the other side of this where I'm telling everybody what I know because I'll mail copies of my confidential settlement agreement to the press if you want me to - I'm not intimidated anymore...

MONSIGNOR JOE ROSIE: Well Patrick, I would ask you to you consider today and recognize in actual sincerity that in order to laicize defrocked McAlinden, we need the help of people like you willing to tell that story to the tribunal, that would be part of here that it would not be priests of the Diocese of Trenton, but it would be priests. We certainly would need witnesses that would come forward and share their story in order for there to be a final resolution to a situation like that. Much as - it's not the same procedure wise, but I don't want to lead you down a line – but I mean in the same way that civil courts need witnesses and stories and collaboration of stories; church tribunals require the same assistance of people to come forward and I think certainly as tomorrow with the Review Board and stuff part of the reason we invite you to do that is so that we can have your story that you can tell us

NEWCOMBE: *Again*

[NOTE: According to Newcombe, up to this point, Bishop O'Connell remained silent. He was taking it all in. He sat in a straight back chair, hands clasped with pointer fingers pressed to his lips - the church and the steeple. This is typical O'Connell contemplative fashion. He lets others speak before interjecting his observations or his opinions]

BISHOP O'CONNELL: *As you said, you know that I'm new here. So I don't have the benefit of – I mean these people - I'm just hearing their names for the first time so I don't know Bruno, I don't know Mac, I don't know these people I've never laid eyes on them. I'm just learning this for the first time. It's not an excuse I'm just telling...what I understood*

[NOTE: This is absolutely not true. One month prior to this meeting, I sat in the same room on the same couch that Patrick Newcombe and Walter sat in as this meeting was taking place. What remained on my lap during the hour and 10 minutes that I met with the Bishop was a folder with a single sheet of paper inside; this was the list of names that I knew of, of credibly accused clergy members. I said to the Bishop, "These are the names you need to know. Do you want the list? We need to work together. I have the nine names that your predecessor – or predecessors – knew of and sealed with the Mercer County Prosecutor's Office. Additionally, I have three other names. We need to share lists,

Excellency. One name that is going to come back again and again as a result of my book is Francis Bruno." At this point, the Bishop said to me, "I think you've given me enough information for one meeting"]

[The Bishop continued]

BISHOP O'CONNELL: *He's suspended which is the first step that the church takes...that is the Canon Law, the church law, that's the process that you follow, you suspend them, but I will say you know I don't know in terms of controlling what he does other than just telling him your not allowed to do this that you'd have a whole lot of legal – because its not like a civil society where you can send someone in and lock him up*

NEWCOMBE: *No, but you could have him defrocked. It's been going on for three years*

BISHOP O'CONNELL: *Well that's the process. Father Charlie Cavanaugh in the Archdiocese of New York had a case and he was a big fundraiser for the archdiocese – it took six years...*

WALTER: *Why?*

BISHOP O'CONNELL: *From the beginning to the end*

WALTER: *Why?*

[NOTE: The Bishop offered no concrete reply to the "Why?" being posed by Walter. The conversation went back to the process of defrocking McAlinden and the perception people have of the priest while the process dragged on in Rome. The subject of Chris Naples came up regarding his suit against McAlinden that was going to trial in Delaware]

BISHOP O'CONNELL: I understand the process (trial) is moving toward it a trial in Delaware. A church trial, hopefully with the evidence all presented so there'd be judges that would be assigned and can make a decision and once that decision is made the outcome would be the man would be defrocked. But you have to - I mean its like even civil law you can't just go in and say okay this guy's a rapist/killer this guy's a rapist you put him in jail, he can make bail and he can be out on the street the next day and there's a trial that takes place that trial is going to take a while. Our system is parallel to that....

NEWCOMBE: If you were any other business and you had an employee that was accused of the crimes that he's been accused of and you received credible evidence that these crimes were true and you heard repeated allegations over the years he would be fired

BISHOP O'CONNELL: Maybe so....It would not be with this business with these processes - laws govern us I grant you that. Give me an hour with him and a baseball bat in a room... I mean that's what an emotional level and I have to tell you how I feel. I mean I'm sitting here calmly because I want to make sure I hear what you say. There's a lot of stuff that makes me want to throw up about this you know. Just the fact that I'm wearing this, I'm wearing it today, I'll wear it tomorrow the guy wears the same uniform and I have to look at him and say he's the same as me, absolutely not - he's a monster. You used the word monster that's what he is and you indicated you're not the only person that has been subject to this. I can honestly say as I sit here listening to you and it's the first day I've met you first thing I mentioned and the first that I've had a conversation with you - we've had - there's absolutely nothing I can do about the past, nothing its happened its historical. The thing that I have to do is say is from this point forward how do we deal with this how do we handle this

NEWCOMBE: And that's why I agreed or asked to speak with you because I knew that you were new here and you as well had nothing to do with anything that happened when I reported this stuff in 1990 or who had the settlement in 1992, and then when I called again. I know that you weren't here, but I want you to know that it all took place. It seemed that the more I reminded Monsignor Nolan of the more he remembered as well taking place - me asking or saying about the different priests that knew that Bruno was abusing me - no one else knew that McAlinden was abusing me so tomorrow that won't come out in the Review Board. But the priests that knew that Bruno was molesting me are still active priests in your diocese...

BISHOP O'CONNELL: Do we have some record of that these priests knew about it or...

NEWCOMBE: Yes

MONSIGNOR JOE ROSIE: Yes, yes

BISHOP O'CONNELL: And they're still on the job?

MONGSIGNOR JOE ROSIE: Mm mmm

NEWCOMBE: John Scully is a pastor in your diocese, Vincent Treglio was not in your diocese, but he was transferred to Florida. James Scott was a high school teacher with the Paterson Diocese. He also molested me down at the Stella Maris Retreat Center. Patrick McGee is still a priest in your diocese

MONSIGNOR JOE ROSIE: No, Patrick is not

NEWCOMBE: He's been defrocked?

MONSIGNOR JOE ROSIE: Uh, he's suspended

NEWCOMBE: I know a boy that he abused when I was a boy because at the time when we were kids he came and told me. Again, he's suspended, but he's still a priest. I understand with him that there was a big deal over in Ireland that his abuse path went way back

BISHOP O'CONNELL: Is he Irish?

MONSIGNOR JOE ROSIE: [inaudible] Yeah

NEWCOMBE: He never touched me, but he walked in on Bruno and I in bed, naked, in the rectory so he knew it was happening. He was the pastor of that church and nothing was done. That was early on to that could have stopped this track of abuse that went on in my life for the next four or five years...

BISHOP O'CONNELL: How old were you when the abuse stopped?

NEWCOMBE: 17

BISHOP O'CONNELL: 17 and how did it stop?

NEWCOMBE: I joined the Navy...

BISHOP O'CONNELL: So you took yourself out of the situation...did you ever hear from these guys after that...

NEWCOMBE: Yes, yes

BISHOP O'CONNELL: What did they say?

NEWCOMBE: I got a phone call from Mac when I got out of the Navy. I was living in Summerville at the time and wanted to know if I'd come see him and you don't want to know what I said to him and I hung up and that was in 1987 or 1988 and that was the last I heard from either one of them – I've never heard from any of them. So, I don't even know how he got a hold of me there to be honest with you

BISHOP O'CONNELL: How did he found out where you were

NEWCOMBE: Nope, I have no idea. I had just gotten out of the Navy. But, uh, like I said I don't know how he did that, but I didn't go see him I know that...

BISHOP O'CONNELL: And the priests who abused you were this Father Bruno and this Father Mac?

NEWCOMBE: And Father (James) Scott.

BISHOP O'CONNELL: Father Scott is with...

NEWCOMBE: Paterson Diocese

BISHOP O'CONNELL: Is he still around, did he die?

NEWCOMBE: I believe he's still a priest in the Paterson Diocese

BISHOP O'CONNELL: I do not know

NEWCOMBE: He was a high school teacher then I don't know what he does now

MONSIGNOR JOE ROSIE: I'm aware that you came forward you know after the Bruno situation and mentioned (James) Scott from what I understand

NEWCOMBE: Right

BISHOP O'CONNELL: And that I would assume, Monsignor Nolan, at the time since he was still working with - referred you to the Diocese of Paterson

NEWCOMBE: I actually called the Diocese of Metuchen because that's where I thought he was and I received a call back from Michael Herbert, your attorney [NOTE: Michael Herbert was the long standing Diocese of Trenton attorney who died in 2011] saying that I had a confidential settlement agreement and I need not to be talking about this – that's what happened – that was after my settlement. When I called to find out because I was tracking what was done and when I called to find out what was done with Scott, I wanted to know why I didn't see his name anywhere on any of this stuff that I had and that was – that was the answer that I got from Michael Herbert, your attorney, was that I better keep my mouth shut. I better let sleeping dogs lie or we're going to sue you is what he told me for the balance of the annuity that was paid to me. When I contacted my attorney about it, he said if I were you I would let it lie…I'm not letting it lie

MONSIGNOR JOE ROSIE: May I ask so you don't think anything has happened to Father Scott up in Paterson I mean

NEWCOMBE: I know nothing's happened – nobody has ever contacted me. I reported him in 1990 the day that I reported Bruno and the day that I reported Mac I reported him as well and then I called back again I think it was 1994 I don't' have the date on that conversation, and that's when I received a call back from your attorney saying that I better let this lie…that I had already settled and that was part of the settlement

– its actually not if you read the settlement agreement. I've settled with the Diocese of Trenton, but I didn't settle with the Catholic Church and he wouldn't be included in any confidentiality part of the agreement that I had

BISHOP O'CONNELL: Who's this (James) Scott?

NEWCOMBE: Right. So me asking questions about what was done about that doesn't break that agreement that I have with the church in that the confidential part of the agreement that I have with the church doesn't concern me anymore

BISHOP O'CONNELL: [inaudible] you don't' have to get it for me...

NEWCOMBE: I have it - no, its saying that I can't talk about this – admitting that the church is admitting to nothing wrong, but they are going to (give) me x amount of dollars and pay my attorney x amount of dollars and that I release the church – the Diocese from all wrong doing and from any future, present or former employees and it just goes on and on and on – and that I can't talk about this to anybody I man anybody. I can't mention it...

BISHOP O'CONNELL: When was that?

NEWCOMBE: In 1992. I reported this stuff in 1990 and was sent to alcohol and drug treatment in 1990... I was sent – Monsignor Nolan - Father Nolan at the time offered this alcohol and drug treatment center which I did attend I did go to and which I was successful then I heard nothing from the church for two years and then I wrote a letter...

BISHOP O'CONNELL: To?

NEWCOMBE: Letter to the Diocese – to Walter Nolan basically saying that my life at an early age was interrupted and I believe that I should be compensated and he wrote me a letter back saying I need to get an attorney, which I did within a matter of weeks I had a check with a confidentiality agreement that I can't talk about this. I'm just trying to bring you up to pace because I know that you don't know of any of this. So that's what taking place with that

BISHOP O'CONNELL: And since then what's (been done) and again I'm just asking this just to try understand what precipitated now coming forward

NEWCOMBE: Okay, about six weeks ago I googled McAlinden's name on the Internet -still on my mind I'm 44 years old and I just happen to google his name and was horrified by what I saw. That you know that this man had come forward and that the Church was denying that anyone else has ever come forward and I'm sitting there saying - I'm thinking to myself, I'm sure you heard it in my e-mails that I sent you initially that first day. I was flabbergasted. I just could not understand how the church could stand there and say that no one has come forward. When I came forward and I came forward 20 years ago or at the time would have 18 years ago, but Raeann [sic] Bennett saying that no other victims have come forward and we're even going to hire an investigator to see if there are any other victims. Come on - no investigator of yours contacted me that was three years ago that this man came forward and that Ms. Bennett said that an investigator was going to be hired...

BISHOP O'CONNELL: Was one hired?

MONSIGNOR JOE ROSIE: Yes

BISHOP O'CONNELL: And what was the outcome of the investigation?

MONSIGNOR JOE ROSIE: Going off the top of my head that I know from his word that there were no other names that came forward

BISHOP O'CONNELL: This is what the investigator said to you other than

MONSIGNOR JOE ROSIE: Other than mister...

NEWCOMBE: No, other than the man that came forward in 2008 – Naples

MONSIGNOR JOE ROSIE: 2008 - Naples

BISHOP O'CONNELL: Was he, do you know, pursued?

MONSIGNOR JOE ROSIE: He has, and that's the case that's the case is currently given...

BISHOP O'CONNELL: So that's the one that's pushed this to the...

MONSIGNOR JOE ROSS: Pushed this to the forefront...

BISHOP O'CONNELL: I see

NEWCOMBE: And there's other victims as well and I'll just give you a heads up on that...

BISHOP O'CONNELL: Of Father ...

NEWCOMBE: Of McAlinden....

BISHOP O'CONNELL: Will they be coming forward?

NEWCOMBE: Yes, but they're not coming to you they're going to the Prosecutor's Office, um, and, uh...

BISHOP O'CONNELL: And today they have that right and we encourage them even if they come to us to go to the prosecutor's

MONSIGNOR JOE ROSIE: Absolutely, and even if they came to us we would send them there also

NEWCOMBE: Yeah, it's a shame that wasn't done in 1990 because these men would be in jail right now...McAlinden after every episode made sure to grant me absolution and forgive me for what I have done –

this was as a kid, um, I forgive you my son. God forgives you. God wants you to please father. Yeah, this is what I was told and you listen to that crap long enough you believe it....

BISHOP O'CONNELL: *You were a kid*

NEWCOMBE: *Yeah, I was you know and then as an adult in 1990 even when I reported this stuff the level of embarrassment, shame and guilt was still there you know you guys didn't get all the dirty details. You only got part of them and that did the trick for Bruno to get him out of there. He was stealing from the church I can tell you things that he did that probably would have gotten him laicized sooner than sexual abuse would have and that was his crimes against the church...*

BISHOP O'CONNELL: *Is he dead, Bruno?*

NEWCOMBE: *I hope so. No, he's not dead he works for the Department of Corrections in Youth Control because nothing was done - he's a youth counselor for the Department of Corrections. Um, and you know - and he's somebody that it wasn't just me. It was me and John Crowe, the kids Steven, Michael, Jimmy and Matt and the seminary and there was a long, long, history that the church had with Bruno, but being that nothing was done...*

BISHOP O'CONNELL: *Well, he was just defrocked wasn't he?*

NEWCOMBE: *No, he was not*

MONSIGONOR JOE ROSIE: *No, Bruno was defrocked.*

NEWCOMBE: *No, Bruno left the priesthood and got married.*

MONSIGNOR JOE ROSIE: *No, no, no, he's officially (defrocked) – he is married I do know he is married, but he is at the same time defrocked – he's laicized...*

NEWCOMBE: *When did that happen?*

MONSIGNOR JOE ROSIE: *I will tell you that it happened after the year 2000, but I don't know off the top of my head, but I do know that he is defrocked he is more than [inaudible]...*

BISHOP O'CONNELL: *I wonder why - why would the state hire somebody who was on the record as being a child molester?*

NEWCOMBE: *He's not on the record you guys didn't report him to anybody. That's my whole point*

BISHOP O'CONNELL: *You know all day long I've had my stomach in knots to meet you. I have nothing to say to you in the sense that could even begin to lift the burden of how you feel nor do I expect you to believe anything that I say just because of your experience and how terrible it's been. I must say to you that I find this whole chapter in the whole history of the church is one of the most sickening, disgusting, horrific things that I could imagine, but even saying that I couldn't even begin to know what you've been through and what you've felt - and as you say think of the worse case and multiply it by four and maybe get some sense of it. All I can say is thank you for telling me. You have helped me to understand this much more clearly from a personal point of view as opposed to reading about it in the paper or whatever so I appreciate the fact that you had the courage to come forward. As the bishop, I had nothing to do with any of this stuff. You know… I'm just so sorry that your life went this direction at the hands of one of our own guys – one of our own priests…*

NEWCOMBE: *Three of them*

BISHOP O'CONNELL: *Three of our own – three of our priests – destroyed - stole really stole that part of your life. I apologize for what they did not just for what you feel, but for what they did. I can't even ask your forgiveness. I'm just sorry - sick to know that your conversation if nothing else you've made it clearer to me. I can't possibly look at this the same way as I did before you walked in the door*

[End Tape].

Frank Bruno was never prosecuted for the allegations against him. He left the priesthood, got married and was never held accountable for the crimes of sexual assault against minors. As irony would have it, Bruno was appointed the Director of Youth Counseling for the Department of Corrections for the State of New Jersey. Bruno skulked away to assume the life of a married civil servant and he wanted it to stay that way.

In February 2011, Patrick and his loyal friend Walter may have actually believed that a sense of vindication was achieved. But very little has actually happened since that day and today Patrick Newcombe remains a bitter man; his health continuing to deteriorate and his nightmares refusing to subside.

In the time between the Bishop's meeting with Newcombe and what I considered "the end" of this chapter in early 2012, many more questions than answers came to mind with respect to the curious cases of Patrick Newcombe. In March 2012 when I submitted this chapter for review and critique to my proof-reader, she came back and said (without coming out and saying it) "this (chapter) is shit. I didn't come all this way with you to put in this lazy effort." The truth is that I was beginning to doubt if the Newcombe file was all about justice and regret for "settling" his cases with the Diocese or more about "the money has run out, I need more." Why?

Patrick Newcombe settled his case with the Diocese of Trenton. He received over $50,000. He says he regretted it. He claims that by taking this money, he himself contributed to the cover-up. I asked Newcombe who signed the check? Certainly Bishop John Reiss didn't cut a personal check to the victim. This is the smoking gun that is missing. The Diocese of Trenton refused comment when the same question was posed to them. Patrick Newcombe can validate his credibility by contacting the bank where the check was cashed to support his timeline of events and the Diocese could support any counterclaim by issuing the same evidence. Why this is not happening is beyond me and after asking each party twice, it is a moot point to press the issue further.

In 2011, Patrick settled once again and that was with the Diocese of Paterson. He asked that the conditions of the settlement be sealed because he was going through a divorce at the time. I agreed. What gnawed at me was the fact that Newcombe repeated the same "greatest mistake" of his life by settling once again with a diocese.

I never harbored an iota of doubt that Patrick Newcombe was sexually abused, tortured, raped and pimped-out by two priests, Francis "Frank" Bruno and Terence McAlinden. Both have, so far, escaped justice in a civil court of law. Neither shows remorse. McAlinden continued to live on the property line of his former parish after being removed and placed on administrative leave. Bruno has been sighted on the grounds of Saint Gregory the Great Parish and School as recently as March 2012, knowing full well that this is my parish. The Bishop and Catholic Church hierarchy are satisfied Bruno is married and thus, no longer a "church issue," and that McAlinden remains insulated within the canon law process in Rome.

How is it fathomable that canon process remains a shield for Terence McAlinden and those like him? The canon law of the Catholic Church is a fully developed legal system, with all necessary elements: courts, lawyers, judges, a fully articulated legal code and principles of legal interpretation. It lacks two fundamental and critical elements of justice however - the right to a speedy trial and the necessary binding force present in most modern day legal systems. Imposing canon law in the court system would carry as much merit (and outrage) as implementing sharia law. Canon law is a tribunal process that was devised by bishops to protect bishops. It is nothing short of a non-binding set of rules that are enforced by the hierarchy to ensure that their rules are obeyed. Each priest takes a vow to obey his bishop and when the bishop instructs his underlings to obstruct justice, justice is obstructed. The faithful are assured by "the Church" (in most cases by the diocese officials) that the process to remove a priest from active ministry is underway; that justice will be realized. The canon process, as it drags through the local diocese to Washington, D.C. to Rome, back to Washington, D.C. and then relayed to the local diocese, all but ensure that the applicable statute of limitation for any civil case is exhausted.

Why is this happening when we, the Diocese of Trenton, have a canon officer at the helm? Bishop O'Connell is a problem solver and a delegator of issues to his vicars, or various department heads. And his track record bears this out. While President of Catholic University, he stared down the powerful American Association of University Professors (AAUP) who placed the university under censorship for academic freedom violations and to this day, the censorship remains in place. He banned anti-Catholic speakers from campus while making a general policy statement that the academic freedom of faculty and students will be respected. He denied political candidates with pro-choice platforms on campus and would not let the student production of *The Vagina Monologues* be performed. More recently it was rumored that the Bishop naively banned the production of *The Laramie Project* within his Diocese because of his belief that it promoted a homosexual agenda.

David M. O'Connell geographically connects the Archdiocese of Philadelphia to the Archdiocese of New York, a triangle of ecclesiastic command. Philadelphia is engaged in the largest sexual abuse cover-up in the United States since Boston and second only to Ireland, worldwide. New York is governed by Timothy Cardinal Dolan, currently the

President of the United States Congregation of Catholic Bishops. "Powerful" would be downplaying Dolan's role in the Catholic Church in America and "influential" demeans his place in the professional and private life of the current Pope, Benedict XVI. But if Dolan is the favorite son to the successor of Peter, O'Connell, being strategically placed over the 800,000 souls of Trenton, certainly places him as Dolan's little brother. David M. O'Connell will not disappoint his older brother or father over the Patrick Newcombe's of the world, that is a given.

Patrick Newcombe suffered most horrific abuse. His is a story that as I look at, read my notes and emails about and reflect on, I'm sure will end sooner than it should, with his legacy being reduced to a file in three of the five dioceses in New Jersey. This makes me sad.

In January 2012, I closed this book. Ten was the final chapter to be put on paper and I was looking forward to its publishing date scheduled for May 2012. Then a casual acquaintance made over the Internet defied the odds of each and every sad story of 14,000 pages of research, and hope jumped off the paper:

Open> WORD
Save As> Jenni DRAFT_1
Resolve.

11

"Uncle Ronnie"

"Be a good priest, I'll be praying for you in heaven."

-Father Ronald Becker's aunt, as she lay dying

When two year-old Ronald Becker's sister Dianne was born in 1947, a rivalry began which lasted until his death, ultimately claiming Dianne's only child in its insidious reach through the generations. One of Ronald Becker's first memories of his baby sister was when he almost cut off her finger at the sewing machine while their mother was changing the bobbin. A few years later Dianne threatened to ruin Becker's First Holy Communion by forcibly stuffing his mouth with puffed wheat on the morning of, sending Becker into a panic that he had transgressed the "no food after midnight" rule of fasting Sister Julia Agnes had drilled into them in preparation for the sacrament. Sibling shenanigans make for the stuff of memories, but in the case of the Becker kids, not everyone's memories were free of resentment. Becker, overweight and awkward, begrudged the ease with which the "pampered princess" moved through life and how she escaped the wrath of their father, who alternated between being distant and detached and berating his son's with taunts of "fat slob" and "fucking pig," always criticizing that his best "wasn't good enough." While his mother was generally supportive and loving, the Becker house was for the most part governed by the state of his father's temper.

This dysfunction stood in stark contrast to the warmth and affection that was "Bobshie," his mother's aunt, who he and Dianne considered their grandmother. Becker and his sister, who grew up in Jamesburg, New Jersey, were left with Bobshie in neighboring Helmetta when their mother accompanied their father on trucking hops. Becker enjoyed being there because of the big yard, the woods, the two dogs, the good Polish food and the extra attention from Bobshie. It was the attention of her two twisted daughters that he could have done without.

In an undated "journal" written in his own hand entitled *The Secret's Out,* Becker alleged that his two female cousins started sexually tantalizing him while they were of school age, playing a game called "*Little Baby,*" which involved pulling his pants down to masturbate him several times a week. Though he claims he hated the experience each and every time, he felt that he no recourse but to submit because his cousins were eight to 10 years older than him and his protests and tears only brought on threats and more physical abuse. Becker alleged that he was undressed and talcum powder was rubbed on his genitals and buttocks, and that one of his cousins took out her breast and put it in his mouth chiding, "If you're going to act like a baby, I'll treat you like one." The cousins would also hold his penis while he urinated and inspect him after defecation. Becker claimed that this went on until the summer of 1950. While the 5-year-old Becker was attempting to escape from his then 13 and 15 year-old cousins who were trying to take his clothes during "play," he fell and broke his arm. The girls heard the snap of the bone and ran for help. Something must have snapped in their warped conscious as well, because inexplicably, the abuse stopped right then and there. School started in September that year, and the cousins moved on, but not before irreparably damaging Ronald Becker, and in the process dooming his great niece who had yet to be born.

The cousin's abuse rendered the socially impaired and prematurely sexually stimulated child yearning for another playmate. Enter "Butchie." In a neighborhood of girls, the only two boys formed an inseparable bond that lasted through high school. Butchie was a year younger than Becker, and what started with more "games," including the little boys comparing "Junebugs" (penises) in the sandbox, flourished years later for the libidinous youths into a routine of mutual masturbation sessions; in his journal Becker mused, "we shared more than just a friendship." Butchie became Ronald Becker's first homosexual partner. When a third boy, "Vern," moved into the neighborhood, he brought with him the knowledge of his older brother David, the "walking encyclopedia of sex." Taking the "curious" to a new level, Vern introduced Becker to oral and anal sex. What Becker learned, he passed on to Butchie. Vern eventually phases out in the Becker journal, but Butchie endured. Theirs was a homosexual relationship that lasted through 1963, the year Ronald Becker entered the seminary.

Becker asserted that he remained celibate through his seminary years. He acknowledged that he was attracted to other seminarians, but maintained that he never acted on the sexual impulses. At both Christ the King and Saint Bonaventure's, Becker stated that oral sex was commonplace, but maintained that he refrained from participating when invited. His outlet became chronic masturbation, engaging in the act sometimes up to five times a day. He would fantasize mainly about those men he was in close contact with; these fantasies included being masturbated by an acquaintance or performing oral sex on that person. He felt an overwhelming physical and emotional love for a classmate, Jerry (last name withheld), and even slept in the same bed with him on an overnight trip to Jerry's parents, but nothing ever happened between them and Becker never admitted his love or his fantasy to him. Jerry went on to become a priest, too, slightly ahead of Becker, and it was at this time that Becker says that the interest of being with teenage boys began to intrigue him.

In May of 1973, Father Ronald Becker was ordained and assigned to the Church of the Incarnation in Ewing Township, New Jersey. Father Becker's assignment at Incarnation was frustrating for him. He was under the guidance of Monsignor John DeCoste, who Becker described as "a vicious drunk," and a "Father Liam," who would drink with the Monsignor. Becker stated that he complained to the Trenton Diocese about his long work hours covering for the two priests, but even feeding off the affection of his parishioners, he felt tired and anguished. Still, he continued his ministry enthusiastically. He did so for two years, when, in his hand he wrote, "and then it happened."

"It" happened in June 1975. Father Becker claimed that he only went to Jimmy's house to visit him because he had heard he was ill. Jimmy was 13 and his home was a sanctuary of sorts to Becker. No yelling or fighting – it was a refuge from the boozy rectory life he had tolerated for these past two years. The priest says that leading up to this June night, Jimmy always made a point of sitting close to him, of parading in front of the priest in "just his Jockey's," and cuddling with him at times while watching TV at his home and in full view of his parents. With this as context, Becker entering the sick boy's bedroom and closing the door raised no suspicion. What took place next was passed off by Father Becker as "building" sexual tension. According to Becker's journal, he reached under the boy's pajamas, took out his penis and masturbated the 13 year-old. All Jimmy did was smile and swore to never tell anyone. Later that summer, Father Becker and Jimmy's family went on a two-week vacation driving through Canada, Becker's fantasies of former schoolmates at the seminary taking a backseat to the adolescent boy. In fact, Becker's predilection for sex with youths was well-solidified at that point, and he was willing to risk anything to fulfill that desire.

Jimmy and Becker maintained what Becker insisted was a "relationship" for over two years. True to his word, the boy didn't tell anyone. The two remained in close contact through the years, and Jimmy even visited Becker in 1998 when he came home to Trenton with his new wife. Jimmy was the priest's first adolescent victim and may (or may not have) been involved in the settlement of $1,000,000 the Diocese of Trenton paid to five now-grown men in 2011, only the first names of which were made public. All were 13 years old and all were at Incarnation; one victim stated that he was abused by Becker over 150 times. But these were not the only victims. Becker wrote in his journal that there were "too many to keep track of."

Proximity provided opportunity and so in 1977, Becker volunteered with the Boy Scouts and took up giving "wedgies" to the Scouts that, by his own admission, aroused him and offered him a new set of fantasies. In the mid-1980's, still involved with the Scouts, Father Becker was assigned to Precious Blood in Monmouth Beach, New Jersey, as Pastor. He admitted that the pressure of ministering to a bourgeois congregation, intransigent in their ways of worship, and an "over-zealous, pro-life obsessive" associate unnerved him – he looked for relief and turned to the voyeurism that roughhousing with the Scouts offered. This time, however, parishioners and Scouting parents started to call the Diocese offices about the priest. Those calls were ignored at first by the eighth Bishop of Trenton, the Very Reverend, John Reiss, and turned over to his Human Resources director, Father Walter Nolan.

According to Becker's journal, Father Nolan called him about the complaints in June of 1987 and told to him "clean up his act." This stands in direct contradiction to the statement released by the Diocese of Trenton in 2011 when the Incarnation settlements were announced. At the time, spokesperson Rayanne Bennett maintained in several interviews: "The first complaint against Becker emerged in 1989, and that while he was not charged with a crime, the church removed him from the ministry and sent him for medical treatment. When he was released, he was given a desk job with no interaction with children."

The Diocese received complaints about Becker at least two years earlier than the press statement acknowledged. But in 1987, Bishop Reiss saw his job as to protect the Church from scandal and Monsignor Nolan saw his job as to protect Bishop Reiss. Sadly, no one saw their job as to protect the children.

On one afternoon in January 2012, I opened a large sealed manila envelope in my dining room containing family photos that were sent to me by a woman in Florida. There were 11 pictures that told a story on the back of each, such as "Jennifer Beth with Uncle Ronnie dressed as Santa," "Jennifer Beth on Uncle Ronnie's shoulders," and "Jennifer Beth with Uncle Ronnie at Jennifer's baptism." Under the latter picture, this personal note was inscribed to me by the "Jennifer Beth" in the picture: "Bruce, My Baptism (abuse started at this point according to Becker in police tapes)."

I first learned of Jennifer "Jenni" Beth Hermanski Franz in 2009 through the local newspapers, as did thousands of others in New Jersey, when she exposed the sexual abuse she endured at the hands of Father Ronald Becker. In Jenni's case, the "uncle" referenced on the reverse of the pictures was not simply a respectful designation sometimes bestowed upon a close family acquaintance; it denoted an actual blood relationship. Jenni Franz is the daughter of the former Dianne Becker, sister of Ronald Becker.

I looked up Jenni via the normal avenues these days, Facebook and Google, and we exchanged emails. I had already built a teflon wall around me after speaking to dozens of victims over the years; therapists call it "compassion fatigue," a common coping mechanism among mental health providers, social workers, law enforcement, even journalists and authors. It's basically a numbing response. I felt that I had heard it all and was immune to the next story or the next victim's tears' effect on me. By and large, when I spoke with victims, their eyes were downcast, their voices in a whisper. Anger would flash on occasion, but pain always won out. Not long into the process of writing this book I realized that scars fade but nightmares are forever. There were no "happily-ever-afters" in the over 14,000 pages of notes taken, books and articles read, emails received and letters written. Until Jenni.

When I phoned Jenni Franz in November 2011, I was immediately caught off guard by her vivacious greeting: "Hi Bruce, its so nice to finally speak with you!" This wasn't simply about the pleasantries of a first introduction. Jenni's vibrancy remained constant throughout this and subsequent conversations, as if we were discussing a spring picnic or the milestone of a child, rather than the most God-awful experience of her life. Her pictures convey a similar radiance, and her smile is what one is drawn to; even in a large group photograph, she stands out. Jenni and I spoke a few times over the next few months, her positivity never ceasing to amaze me.

But here is where I stood on January 9, 2012. I was done with this book. Eight years in, ten chapters, an Introduction, Prologue, Epilogue and Afterthought all ready for attorney review, yet at 6:20 p.m. I kept staring at the pictures again and again. Earlier, I had showed them to my wife and daughter who remained stunned in silence. Really, what can you say? Then my editor, Linda Alexander, came over to pick up a draft of Chapters 1 through 10 for review. She looked at the pictures, looked and me, and said laconically: "Eleven."

I had known in my heart once I received the pictures that clearly this book was not done. I spoke to Jenni that very night, and to her attorney, with whom I had exchanged emails. Twenty minutes later, I opened up a WORD document and with that, "11" was underway.

And that was where I froze for three weeks straight.

A blank screen.

Texts to Linda Alexander, all caps: "BLOCKED."

A condition born out of not only thinking I had crossed the writing finish line a few days earlier, but this nagging internal fear: "Could I do this amazing person justice? What about her husband? Will one day her children read this? I was unnerved.

A much needed break.

Then the purpose became clear. Jenni was sexually abused by her uncle, Father Ronald Becker, in her bassinet, at her baptism that he presided over, when *she was a mere three months old.* She had not merely survived unthinkable abuse, but had thrived in spite of it. Nothing about this Chapter 11 was "bankrupt" of hope.

Victims needed to know that there could be "happily ever afters." Jenni had entrusted me to tell you about hers.

And so it begins.

The Irish belief that if one gives birth to a priest one secures a place in Heaven is proudly shared among every culture, with slight variation, upon the ordination of a favorite son. It was no different in the Polish Becker family. In the pecking order of family pride, members serving nobly as teachers and police officers, such as Jenni's parents, while well regarded, couldn't hold the proverbial candle to a priest in the family. Father Ronald Becker was the one-way express to the pearly gates for the Becker family, carrying their sanctification and salvation faithfully on his shoulders. As if they could make up for the void of being graced with his physical presence, the displays of Uncle Ronnie photographs in their home, by sheer number alone, spoke volumes about the esteem in which he was held, only to be outdone in impact by one single oil painting of the priest, hanging prominently, almost beatific, in his mother's home. Becker's ordination even transformed his rocky relationship with his father, who was now "in his glory" that his son was a priest.

Jenni was born in Princeton, New Jersey, on September 10, 1977, the only child of Dianne Becker and Ronald Hermanski. At age five, the Hermanski's moved from New Jersey to Florida and as Jenni remarked always seemed to be the case with her family, there are two versions as to why the family left town. According to Jenni's mother, Dianne, they moved because her fiancé before her dad was murdered by his brother and was then diagnosed with schizophrenia and was driving school buses in their town of Princeton. Fearing for their lives, the Hermanski's moved to a secluded property in Jupiter, Florida, and remained unlisted. Story two, courtesy of Jenni's dad, was that they moved because he loved Florida and his brother Stan lived there. Most of Jenni's younger years in Florida were spent with her maternal grandmother because of the busy work schedule of Ron and Dianne.

In any event, the Hermanski household was not a happy one. Jenni describes her mother as "manic," prone to shopping sprees and hills and valleys of mood swings. Her father was removed and reserved, and her parents made no overtures to make friends. Dianne's rants were hurtful to her daughter, who she constantly referred to as a "slut" and "bitch." According to Jenni, her mother lived in a paranoid world where all women were out to get her; Dianne's seclusion was her selfish refuge from the outside world, but little did she know that it was an insider she had to worry most about.

Jenni was in graduate school and working as a Speech & Language school-based therapist when she met SeaWorld employee Jon Franz. Embracing their cliché courtship, Jenni called it "love at first sight:" "We almost eloped after dating a month, [we] moved in together by May, [we were] engaged by November." The couple married in 2003, two years after they met, with Jenni's mom commandeering the entire wedding planning process, from the choice of bridal gown to officiate; Uncle Ronnie would be celebrating the wedding Mass. It was Dianne that pressed her brother into service to marry the couple and it was Dianne that had to tell Jenni and Jon that that at the last moment, Uncle

Ronnie could not marry his only niece because of "health reasons." Jon recalled: "Something never added up. I thought it was very strange; I had never met him but always heard about him. I heard he was a highly respected priest in New Jersey – nothing more. At the time of our wedding planning, we were both Catholic and I remembered thinking that it was neat that we would be married by her Catholic uncle. I remember it was really odd that all of a sudden he was not able to even come to the wedding. Now I understand the reason."

Ronald Becker had been defrocked. Trenton Bishop John Smith had barred Becker from ministry a year earlier. Not the first correction for the priest, but still a long time overdue. Over a decade earlier, in 1989 - two years after Monsignor Nolan told Becker to get his act together - Bishop John Reiss removed Becker from parish assignments, posting him in the Diocese headquarters, away from minors, evaluating requests for annulments. Jenni's mother and father knew this, and did not share it with anyone else in the family.

Whether her uncle's absence at her nuptials was disappointing to her or alternatively relieving to her was not ripe for the asking on that day. The 26 year-old bride had yet to even recall let alone begin to process the damage her Uncle Ronnie had inflicted on her as a child.

Memory repression is a strong and validated medical infliction. Dr. Elizabeth F. Loftus of the University of Washington – Seattle, is a foremost authority on repressed memory and its impact on the legal system today. In her abstract on repressed memory, Loftus explains: [44]

Repression is one of the most haunting concepts in psychology. Something shocking happens, and the mind pushes it into some inaccessible corner of the unconscious. Later, the memory may emerge into consciousness. Repression is one of the foundation stones on which the structure of psychoanalysis rests. Recently there has been a rise in reported memories of childhood sexual abuse that were allegedly repressed for many years. With recent changes in legislation, people with recently unearthed memories are suing alleged perpetrators for events that happened 20, 30, even 40 or more years earlier....

To support her abstract, Loftus cites a 1990 landmark murder trial in Redwood City, California. The defendant, George Franklin Sr., 51 years old, stood trial for the murder of an 8 year-old, Susan Kay Nelson, which had occurred more than 20 years earlier. Franklin's daughter, Eileen, only eight years old herself at the time of the murder, provided the condemning evidence against her father in the form of a repressed memory.

Eileen's memory did not come back all at once. She claimed that her first flashback came one afternoon in January 1989 when she was playing with her 2 year-old son Aaron, and her 5 year-old daughter, Jessica. At one point, when Jessica looked up and asked her mother a question like, "Isn't that right, Mommy?" a memory of Susan Nelson suddenly came back; Eileen recalled the look of betrayal in Susie's eyes just before the murder. Later, more fragments returned, supplying Eileen with a rich and detailed memory. She remembered her father sexually assaulting Susie in the back of a van. She remembered that Susie was struggling, and plead, "No, don't" and "Stop." She remembered her father saying "Now Susie," and she even mimicked his precise intonation. Next, her memory placed the three of them outside the van, where she saw her father with his hands raised above his head with a rock in them. She remembered screaming and walking back to where

Susie lay, covered with blood, the silver ring on her finger smashed. Eileen's memory report was deemed credible by her therapist, several members of her family, and by the San Mateo County District Attorney's Office, which chose to prosecute her father. It was also believed by the jury, which convicted George Franklin Sr. of murder in the first degree.

Long-repressed memories that return after decades, often while a person is in therapy, have become highly publicized through popular articles. A year after the Franklin trial, *People* magazine reported a story about former Miss America Marilyn Van Derbur, who had repressed all knowledge of sexual violation by her father until she was 24 years old, telling the world about it only after his death. Similarly, Jenni's memory began to take shape. Recall was slow and at first uncertain because "Uncle Ronnie" stopped molesting her when she was about eight. But her recall of the events of her early childhood years was accurate, and what she lacked in actual memory - for how can one remember what happened when they were three months old at their baptism - she relied on "cellular memory" for - instinctively "just knowing." Along with the memories came the realization that her parents did little to shield her from Becker, her colloquial reference to "Dianne" and "Ron" indicative of her deteriorating relationship with them:

I always felt strongly uncomfortable around Becker. I had all sorts of pelvic issues that Dianne would take me to the doctor for. I would beg, even as a 29-year-old I would plead not to have to talk to [Becker] on the phone. Dianne would force the issue and I would cave, as I hate conflict.

That was my first minor clue. The second was the panic attack I had at the age of 26 after driving in from the city to see Dianne. She was at his Becker's condo tried to leave me alone with him and I completely fell apart crying and begging her to not leave me there while she shopped. I was an adult and very calm typically so this was a Red flag. Dianne's response: "Push him off your a big girl," which looking back, WOW!

That stayed in the back of my mind. I feel like with cellular memory the body always knows.

I always had horrible nightmares and they were horrible if we [Jon and Jenni] ever stayed with Dianne and Ron in that horrible childhood bed! The next red flag was visiting with Dianne and Ron in 2007. Ron and I were extremely close after I went to college. We were talking about how much I hated talking to Becker. Dianne walked and started screaming, "what did you tell her" at my dad. She then broke down and confessed that Becker had "credible allegations against him" she then turned on Jon and I, said we ruined her birthday and after a full day of her being horrible, I left to go home. She did not speak to Jon and I from July until almost Thanksgiving, which became her typical pattern. At this time I deep depression set in. Nothing gave me joy which for me anyone who knows me I get overjoyed over the smallest things. I started therapy with Barbara Coffee. She was the one who first said, "you were abused."

Jenni continued:

Professionally, I had a case of a (six year old girl with limited language and a feeding tube) who was being molested by her stepfather. I worked closely getting the language out of her. The same day Becker sent me an email. It was a 'forward' [email from someone else] but still enough so I responded with "I know you are a pedophile so never contact myself or my family again." To me that was a God-thing! The timing was crazy! It was November and Becker sent Christmas presents and asked Dianne if she could get us in touch because he and "Monsignor John" were going to be on a Disney cruise."

Jenni and Jon Franz had enough of living in a depression-infused nightmare induced by the onset of her memories. Jenni had committed her life to helping other children but could not heal the child within. Now Jenni was 30 years old and had insight into her past propelling her to pursue this pedophile and to make sure that he never hurt another child again. With the assistance of the Winter Park Police Department and the support of her husband, Jenni set about confronting Ronald Becker. As difficult as it would no doubt be, it was the only way the Franz's saw that could set the wheels of healing in forward motion.

In March 2007, Jon called the Diocese of Trenton. After being put off for several weeks by Diocese officials including the Victim Assistance Coordinator Monsignor Walter Nolan, who fielded the concerned phone calls from Scouting parents and parishioners about Becker in the 1980's, Jon received a return call. Monsignor Nolan, now aware of the vile and reprehensible acts of incestuous pedophilia against Jenni Franz, nevertheless tautly told Jon that it was "a family matter." He then hung up the phone.

What the Monsignor didn't know was that 1100 miles south of Trenton, more phone calls were being placed. In March 2007, the final conversations between niece and uncle were taking place and the police were listening in.

[NOTE: The unedited transcript below is day two of the conversations between niece and nephew with uncle. The previous night, Ronald Becker confessed to his abusive sexual assault towards his niece. Largely, those tapes are inaudible.]

ANSWERING MACHINE: *Hi, this is Ron. I'm not here right now, but if you leave your name, telephone number and a short message, I'll get back to you as soon as I get back.*
Thanks. Have a great day.

MS. FRANZ: *Hi Uncle Ronnie It's me again. I'm calling to check on you. I want to make sure that you're okay, when I talked to you earlier and at this point I'm going to give you two choices. The first choice is you can apologize for hurting my feelings today and not telling the truth or I will be calling the police and asking that they give you a lie detector test, which you will promptly fail, so these are your choices because you really hurt me when you lied. I've been in therapy to get help for what you did and I have some closure and you did not have the right to take it away from me. All I wanted was some more information, which I deserved, so this is your choice. If you can text me and apologize for the way you behaved today and for what you did or I will be calling the police and you'll be taking a lie detector test, so it's your choice. My phone number is --. I will be here all night. Jon will be home in a few* hours. *I suggest you call me before he gets home because I'd rather he not get wind of this. Thanks. Bye.*

PHONE CALL CONNECTED

MS. FRANZ: Hello?

MR. BECKER: Hello, Mrs. Franz?

MS. FRANZ: Hey, how are you?

MR. BECKER: Hello.

MS. FRANZ: I want an apology. Why are you lying to me? Choice one that's that. Choice two I call the police. And you know what? That affects me, too. It's just as unfair for me because then family gets involved and it gets ugly.

MR. BECKER: I'm sorry. I just walked in the door.

MS. FRANZ: Why are you lying to me today? Yesterday you gave me closure. You gave me what I needed.

MR. BECKER: Jennifer, I told you I cannot talk to you.

MS. FRANZ: Here is your choice. You talk to me or you go in and take a lie detector test and guess what? I'm pretty legal savvy and I have a pretty good background, so don't fuck with me.

MR. BECKER: Jennifer, could you do me a favor, please? Would you call your mother and ask her to call me?

MS. FRANZ: You want to talk to mom?

MR. BECKER: Yes.

MS. FRANZ: Okay. Take a lie detector test and talk to mom.

MR. BECKER: She's not answering the phone for me.

MS. FRANZ: Why do you think that is?

MR. BECKER: I don't know.

MS. FRANZ: Why are you even calling her? Are you going to confess to her or going to try to lie and bullshit to her, too?

MR. BECKER: I need to talk to my sister.

MS. FRANZ: Okay. You can talk to your sister, but you're going to talk to me first. Why did you lie to me today? Why would you do that to me?

MR. BECKER: Jennifer, I told you my psychiatrist does not want me

MS. FRANZ: I don't give a flying fuck about your psychiatrist. Look, I'm a pretty strong girl. Lie detector test and police involvement or you fucking tell me the truth. You choose.

MR. BECKER: Jennifer, please let me talk to your mother.

MS. FRANZ: You are not fucking talking to my mom until you talk to me.

MR. BECKER: Jennifer, I tried to do what my psychiatrist told me.

MS. FRANZ: Okay. Let me go look up the number for New Jersey police. You live in Helmetta. You can have it your way or we can have it my way. What would you like to do? All I'm asking -- you know I just called you today to thank you. I really did and I was generally concerned about you. That's all and then you had to lie to me. You had to lie to your niece who loved you. Who trusted you. Who you actually helped and made a difference in her life. You are breaking my heart.

MR. BECKER: I don't know what's going on.

MS. FRANZ: You --

MR. BECKER: Today you are accusing me of having sexual relations with you.

MS. FRANZ: That's the same conversation we had yesterday. I am not playing games. I don't get why you are playing games. You should *know from yesterday, you can make it easy or you can make it hard, but I'm a fighter and I'm going to get what I need. I'm begging you to be honest like you were yesterday. You helped me. You saved me from hurting myself and that seemed like a good idea because now you're lying to me. In the note I can include what you did to me unless you want to apologize for lying to me today when all I did was to call to check on you.*

MR. BECKER: *I apologize.*

MS. FRANZ: *Why are you apologizing?*

MR. BECKER: *Because you asked me to.*

MS. FRANZ: *No, that's not good enough. You know what? We have a whole kitchen full of knives. I'll be sure to leave a note.*

MR. BECKER: *All right.*

MS. FRANZ: *That's fine.*

MR. BECKER: *Good night, Jennifer.*

MS. FRANZ: *If you hang up on me I will never forgive you.*

MR. BECKER: *Jennifer --*

MS. FRANZ: Why did you lie to me today? You know you already apologized.

MR. BECKER: Jennifer --

MS. FRANZ: You already apologized. I will be calling the police if you hang up on me. Do you understand that? Do you know how embarrassing it would be for my poor mother to have (my) poor uncle or her brother in jail? Do you know what that would do to your mother? I know the laws in New Jersey and the only reason I wouldn't do that to you is because of your mother and your sister and the embarrassment it would put them in. It would be horrible for them. It would be horrible for you. You have health problems and you would die in prison and I don't want that to happen to you. All I asked was for an apology. That's all I wanted and you are pushing me further than you should be. It's a simple request.

MR. BECKER: Jennifer, if I hurt you today, I'm very sorry.

MS. FRANZ: You hurt me when I was a child and today you just really destroyed me. (Inaudible)

MR. BECKER: I can do no more for you than I've already done for you.

MS. FRANZ: No, you can do more. When I called you today to talk to you further you could have said, yes, Jennifer, I don't want to talk or something, but don't lie to me on top of it. It makes me feel like I'm going crazy. I know what I heard and you're not going to convince me otherwise.

MR. BECKER: I'm afraid you're going to have to call the police, Jennifer. I'm sorry.

Becker hangs up.

PHONE CALL CONNECTED

MR. BECKER: Hello?

MS. FRANZ: Why are you doing this?

MR. BECKER: I asked you to call the police since --

MS. FRANZ: I will call the police, but you know how embarrassing that is going to be for my mother?

MR. BECKER: Jennifer --

MS. FRANZ: Do you know what that's going to be like? You are in a position of power. People respect you. People know you in that town. Did you really want this?

MR. BECKER: Yes.

MS. FRANZ: You really want this?

MR. BECKER: Jennifer, you are giving me no choice.

MS. FRANZ: No, I am giving you a choice. It's very clear. Just apologize for lying to me today. That's all I want.

MR. BECKER: I apologize.

MS. FRANZ: For what?

MR. BECKER: For upsetting you.

MS. FRANZ: That's not good enough.

MR. BECKER: Good night, Jennifer.

MS. FRANZ: I do not want to do this to your mother.

Becker hangs up.

PHONE CALL CONNECTED

MR. BECKER: Hello?

MS. FRANZ: I am begging you to not do this to your mother.

MR. BECKER: Pardon?

MS. FRANZ: I am begging you do not do this to your mother, please.

MR. BECKER: Jennifer --

MS. FRANZ: I idolized her. Please don't do this to her.

MR. BECKER: Jennifer, if you want to call the police --

MS. FRANZ: It is a small town. I have the number. I really don't want to play this game. I didn't want to go there because mom really is looking forward to seeing you and going to her reunion.

MR. BECKER: Jennifer, if you need to call the police, please do so.

MS. FRANZ: So you'd rather have --

Becker hangs up.

PHONE CALL CONNECTED

MR. BECKER: Hello?

MS. FRANZ: Please do not do this to your sister.

MR. BECKER: Call the police.

Becker hangs up.

PHONE CALL CONNECTED

MR. BECKER: Hello?

MS. FRANZ: Why do you think mom is not talking to you or Aunt Bernadine?

MR. BECKER: Jennifer, please speak up. I can't hear you.

MS. FRANZ: Why are you doing this?

MR. BECKER: Jennifer, if you need to call the police --

MS. FRANZ: I don't want to do that. I really don't.

MR. BECKER: Well, then --

MS. FRANZ: This is my uncle. I want a God damn apology.

MR. BECKER: Call your mother and have her call me.

MS. FRANZ: Why? What is that going to prove? Are you going to apologize to her?

MR. BECKER: Good night, Jennifer.

MS. FRANZ: You know what you're going to do to her? You're going to destroy that woman and it's not going to happen.

MR. BECKER: Please call the police. Good night.

MS. FRANZ: Are you going to take care of yourself?

Becker hangs up.

PHONE CALL CONNECTED

MS. FRANZ: You are a lying sack of fucking shit.

MR. BECKER: Okay. Yes, I am if that is what you think I am, yes, I am.

MS. FRANZ: Why the fuck would you do this?

MR. BECKER: Are you going to call the police for me?

MS. FRANZ: Am I going to call the police for you? Why are you offering to do it for your fucking self to embarrass your family?

MR. BECKER: Jennifer, is Jon around?

MS. FRANZ: Is Jon around? No, he's not home from work yet, but God help him I am not very calm.

MR. BECKER: When he gets home, have him call me, please.

MS. FRANZ: When he gets home, have him call you?

MR. BECKER: Yes.

MS. FRANZ: Okay. That sounds like a blast. Do you want him to call from his cell phone?

MR. BECKER: Yes.

MS. FRANZ: Do you? Are you going to tell him the truth? Are you going to lie through your fucking rat teeth?

MR. BECKER: I'd like to talk to Jon.

MS. FRANZ: Why the fuck are you lying to me?

MR. BECKER: Excuse me a minute.

MS. FRANZ: No. No. Excuse me a minute?

(Becker answers another call)

MR. BECKER: Okay. Sorry about that.

MS. FRANZ: You need to be honest with me. I don't know why you are doing this, but I'm pissed.

MR. BECKER: Could you ask Jon to call me, please?

MS. FRANZ: I will have Jon call you after you fucking apologize to me. You rather have your whole God damn family embarrassed than you fucking apologize? Why is that? Hello?

Becker hangs up.

PHONE CALL CONNECTED

MR. BECKER: Hello?

MS. FRANZ: Are you ready to apologize to me?

MR. BECKER: Good night, Jennifer.

MS. FRANZ: Don't you dare.

Becker hangs up.

PHONE CALL CONNECTED

MR. BECKER: Hello?

MS. FRANZ: I want an apology and I want it now.

MR. BECKER: Good night, Jennifer.

Becker hangs up.

PHONE CALL CONNECTED

MR. BECKER: Yes, Jennifer.

MR. FRANZ: Hi, Uncle Ronnie.

MR. BECKER: Yes.

MR. FRANZ: This is Jon Franz.

MR. BECKER: Hi Jon.

MR. FRANZ: I was wondering if you could help me out.

MR. BECKER: Can you speak up, please?

MR. FRANZ: Yes. I was wondering if you could help me out. I know I haven't met you in person and all. I've heard good things from your niece.
MR. BECKER: Jon --

MR. FRANZ: And your sister.

MR. BECKER: Yesterday your wife called me and accused me of molesting her. I never did anything to her. Today she called and is *accusing me of having sexual intercourse with her between the ages of three and eight.*

    MR. FRANZ: Now you've got to help me, sir.

    MR. BECKER: I have difficulty hearing, Jon. Could you speak up?

    MR. FRANZ: Yes. Uncle Ronnie, I heard you confess.

    MR. BECKER: I did not.

    MR. FRANZ: I heard you confess. You are a priest. I'm Catholic.

    MR. BECKER: Jon, I told her that --

    MR. FRANZ: No. You cannot -- you can't do this to her. You are killing your niece. You are killing your niece. All she wants -- give her one minute. Just one minute. Get the lie off your back. Confess like you did last night. Just help her out.

    MR. BECKER: I did not confess to anything last night.

    MR. FRANZ: I heard you. You are a Catholic priest. My whole family is Catholic.

    MR. BECKER: Jon --

    MR. FRANZ: That is not how -- that is not how you act.

MR. BECKER: *I told Jennifer that she said that I hurt her.*

MR. FRANZ: *I was there the whole conversation. I was there. I was sitting right there holding her hand. Don't -- you are a Catholic priest. You can't lie. All I'm asking is do this for your niece. Do me a favor. Do her a favor. Talk to her for one minute. Explain to her that it's not her. Okay? Explain to her for one minute. Take one minute out of your life and help her out. Help her out. I pray to God. Please help her out for one minute and then I will -- we won't deal with it ever again. We won't call you. Just help her out and I will help her understand. She only called you today to check on you because I heard you. I heard exactly what you said last night. You screamed it over the phone. You said, Jennifer, I'm going to stab myself. You can't do this to this girl. I love her and you've got to help her out.*

MR. BECKER: *I will talk to her.*

MR. FRANZ: *Please, please just seconds. Just explain yourself. Explain to her how you did last night and we will be done. We'll leave you alone. I pray to God, please help me. Will you please -- will you please talk to her?*

MR. BECKER: *Have her call me.*

MR. FRANZ: *Okay. She's right here.*

MR. BECKER: *I'm not making any promises.*

MR. FRANZ: She is right here. She is right here. I'm with her, please. She is right here and you've got -- this is your niece. Please, I pray to God. Just give her seconds. Explain to her that it's not her.

MR. BECKER: Okay.

MR. FRANZ: Please, here she is.

MS. FRANZ: Hello?

MR. BECKER: Jennifer, you're a good person.

MS. FRANZ: Then why did you do this?

MR. BECKER: You have no guilt.

MS. FRANZ: Why did you do this to me?

MR. BECKER: Jennifer, you are a good person. You have no guilt.

MS. FRANZ: My husband heard you. We couldn't do more than this, but I just want an apology. When I called you today I was just checking on you because I was scared that you hurt yourself.

MR. BECKER: Jennifer, if I hurt you tonight, I apologize.

MS. FRANZ: Tonight is not what we're talking about. Do not lie. I have a witness. Don't fuck with me. You had a choice. He asked you to apologize. Apologize for tonight.

MR. BECKER: I apologize. If you want an apology, I give you an apology.

MS. FRANZ: I do want an apology.
MR. BECKER: I do apologize.

MS. FRANZ: For what?

MR. BECKER: For making your life difficult.

MS. FRANZ: Why? Why is it difficult? Why did you have to hide it for so many years?

MR. BECKER: Jennifer, I'm sorry for anything I may have done.

MS. FRANZ: You are saying "may." Don't be vague with me.

MR. BECKER: Jennifer --

MS. FRANZ: I called to check on you and then you lied to me. Jon told me don't check on him, but I checked on you and then you lied.

MR. BECKER: Jennifer, I'm sorry for hurting you. You are a good person.

MS. FRANZ: Why did it go on for so many years? Did I not stop you? Did I not say enough to stop you? Did I never say that to myself?

MR. BECKER: The question --

MS. FRANZ: You need to answer that question. Do you understand me?

MR. BECKER: I cannot answer that question.

MS. FRANZ: You are the reason I'm crying tonight. You are the reason why I cried for years.

MR. BECKER: Jennifer --

MS. FRANZ: Honey, he won't apologize.

Jon Franz returns to the phone

MR. FRANZ: Sir, you don't understand. You don't understand. You are a priest of all people to lie.

MR. BECKER: I am not lying.

MR. FRANZ: Sir, I was right there.

MR. BECKER: I know --

MR. FRANZ: I was right there. I heard the conversation.

MR. BECKER: I did not admit to any molestation last night. I deny it today.

MR. FRANZ: Sir, you are killing your niece.

MR. BECKER: If Jennifer needs to call the police, let her do so.

MR. FRANZ: This is between you and I and Jennifer.

MR. BECKER: Jon --

MR. FRANZ: Keep my wife alive. You don't understand. You don't understand the years --

MR. BECKER: If I hurt Jennifer in any way, I apologize.

MR. FRANZ: No. No. You don't understand, sir.

Becker hangs up.

PHONE CALL CONNECTED

MR. BECKER: (call) Helmetta police.

MR. FRANZ: Please, Uncle Ronnie, tell her it's not her fault.

MR. BECKER: (call) Helmetta police.

MR. FRANZ: You don't understand. Please, she thinks it's her fault. She doesn't understand. You confused her tonight. Please.

MR. BECKER: I have said all I'm going to say, Jon. Let me talk to my sister. I want to talk to my sister. The line is busy there. I have been trying to talk to her.

MR. FRANZ: You don't understand what you're putting Jennifer through. This is your niece. This is my wife. She doesn't understand. That's all she needs is seconds of your time just to help her understand. Please, I beg you. I pray to God that you'll help her. Just take seconds. Will you do that for me, please? Uncle Ronnie?

MR. BECKER: Thirty seconds.

MR. FRANZ: That's all you have to do. Just help her understand it's not her. She didn't do it. She's going to be a great mom. She's going -- please.

MR. BECKER: Put her on, please.

MR. FRANZ: Okay.

Jenni Franz returns to the phone

MS. FRANZ: Hello?

MR. BECKER: Jennifer, I told you last night you are a good person. You had good upbringing. You will be a good mother. I'm sorry that I cannot be a part of your life any longer, but know that I love you and I love Jon.

MS. FRANZ: But I really need you to tell me that it wasn't my fault and you will never hear from the Franz family again.

MR. BECKER: Nothing – whatever happened, you were not at fault.

MS. FRANZ: Did I try to stop you? Did I stand up for myself?

MR. BECKER: I can't answer that, Jennifer.

MS. FRANZ: Please don't do this to me. Seriously, if you don't want to be a part of my life, this is your ticket out, but if you don't do this, I'm going to be confused about why you told me the truth. You made me heal. You made me happy and you made me whole and hours later you made me feel like I was crazy.

MR. BECKER: Jennifer, you are an innocent person.

MS. FRANZ: I just feel like you're being vague and I --

MR. BECKER: Jennifer, you are an innocent person. You are a good person. No child is responsible for anything that happened -- at *that age responsible for anything that happens. A relationship is based on trust.*

MS. FRANZ: Does it bother you that I trusted you wholeheartedly?

MR. BECKER: Anything that happened for a person to break that trust, it's that person's fault. Not the child's fault.

MS. FRANZ: Does it hurt your heart that I trusted you and you violated my trust after so many years?

MR. BECKER: I am very sad right now.

MS. FRANZ: But why did you --

MR. BECKER: Jennifer, please don't prolong this. It's difficult for both of us.

MS. FRANZ: Why did you lie to me today? That is what I want to know. I called to check on you and you lied to me.

MR. BECKER: Jennifer, I'm trying to do what my psychiatrist told me to do.

MS. FRANZ: And he told you to lie to me?

MR. BECKER: I am trying to deal with this issue.

MS. FRANZ: I want you to deal with it, but don't lie to me and make me feel like I lost it when our conversation --

MR. BECKER: I'm sorry that I hurt you tonight.

MS. FRANZ: You killed me tonight. You have to understand that. I thought I was losing it hours ago.

MR. BECKER: Jennifer --

MS. FRANZ: If my husband had not heard you confess to molesting me I would have thought I was losing it.

MR. BECKER: Good night, Jennifer.

MS. FRANZ: Not good night, Jennifer.

MR. BECKER: Good night.

Jon Franz returns to the phone

MR. FRANZ: Give her seconds. You are not -- help her understand. Help her understand you molested her and it's not her. Just tell her that. It will take you two seconds.

Becker hangs up.

PHONE CALL CONNECTED

MS. FRANZ: Okay. This sounds funny, but I teach special ed kindergarten, okay? This sounds really funny, but humor me. When the kids do something that makes everyone upset, they say I'm sorry. I did whatever. It made me feel whatever and they then shake hands and move on and that's what I need and it's silly, but trust me, it works for my kids. It will make me feel human again. I know you don't want to talk to me anymore and I know you want to move on, so humor your niece here.

MR. BECKER: Jennifer, I'm sorry that I did something that you believe hurt you.

MS. FRANZ: See, now you're lying. That's vague.

MR. BECKER: I'm sorry.

MS. FRANZ: When my kids do it, they're honest.

MR. BECKER: I'm sorry that I hurt you.

MS. FRANZ: When you --

MR. BECKER: I'm sorry that I hurt you.

MS. FRANZ: When you molested me.

MR. BECKER: I'm sorry that I hurt you.

MS. FRANZ: That's not good enough. You are going to keep hearing from us.

MR. BECKER: Jennifer, please call Helmetta police then.

MS. FRANZ: I don't want to call Helmetta police.

MR. BECKER: Then call your mother.

MS. FRANZ: I have a great grandmother and family and it's a small town.

MR. BECKER: Jennifer, I did nothing to you.

MS. FRANZ: Okay. Now you're lying again and here we go again.

Becker hangs up.

PHONE CALL CONNECTED

MR. BECKER: Yes.

MR. FRANZ: Uncle Ronnie.

MR. BECKER: Jon, please do not call me tonight.

MR. FRANZ: No, you are being a coward. Two seconds. Stop being a coward.

MR. BECKER: Don't call me again.

MR. FRANZ: Sir --

Becker hangs up.

PHONE CALL CONNECTED

MR. BECKER: This is the last time I'm answering the call -- the phone.

MS. FRANZ: I think you need to pray with me.

MR. BECKER: If you want to begin legal action, please do so.

MS. FRANZ: You would rather that than just apologize?

MR. BECKER: I'm sorry, Jennifer. I can't hear you.

MS. FRANZ: You would rather legal action than just say I'm sorry I lied to you today. I don't get it. I just don't get it.

MR. BECKER: Jennifer, I wish you well in life.

MS. FRANZ: I wish you well in life and now let's say a prayer together.

MR. BECKER: *I wish you well. I prefer no more contact with you.*

MS. FRANZ: *You're going to keep hearing from me. I will take a flight. I will do what I need to do, but I want my apology. You lied to me when I called and checked on you.*

MR. BECKER: *Jennifer --*

MS. FRANZ: *That's pretty nervy.*

MR. BECKER: *Jennifer, in life*

MS. FRANZ: *Just say I'm sorry. I'm a big fat liar. I'm sorry I lied to you. I'm sorry I made you so crazy that hours ago I made everything better and today I took everything back.*

MR. BECKER: *Jennifer, if I hurt you in any way, I'm very sorry for that.*

MS. FRANZ: *It is not good enough at that point. We are past that.*

MR. BECKER: *That is the best you are going to get from me.*

MS. FRANZ: *What do you have to lose here? I don't get this.*

MR. BECKER: *At this point I want no more contact with you. Your mother wants no contact with me. I regret that. I love you both and good-bye.*

MS. FRANZ: Are you planning on apologizing to her?

Becker hangs up.

PHONE CALL CONNECTED

MR. BECKER: Hello?

MS. FRANZ: What are you doing to my mother?

MR. BECKER: What do you mean?

MS. FRANZ: What are you doing to her?

MR. BECKER: I love your mother.

MS. FRANZ: You are being a coward.

MR. BECKER: Good night.

Becker hangs up.

ANSWERING MACHINE: Hi, this is Ron. I'm not here right now, but if you leave your name and telephone number and a short message, I'll get back to you as soon as I get back. Thanks and have a great day.

MR. FRANZ: Reverend Ron, please stop treating my mother-in-law like this. Stop treating my wife like this. Please stop being a coward.

Hangs up.

MR. FRANZ: This is (inaudible). Pick up the phone, please. Ron, pick up the phone, please.

Hangs up.

PHONE CALL CONNECTED

MS. FRANZ: Hello? Yes.

MR. BECKER: I am very sorry for any improprieties that I gave to you. I regret it very much. You were a good young lady. You will make a fine mother. I love you very much. I wish you and Jon all the (inaudible) that you have and more in the future.

MS. FRANZ: I think for lying to me today I need more than that. You had no right to lie to me today and make me feel like I'm going crazy when I knew what you did.

MR. BECKER: I'm sorry for lying to you.

MS. FRANZ: Wasn't it just easier to admit and apologize than do this? I don't get it. Now you made the entire family upset. I don't understand. Do you know what you put my mother through?

MR. BECKER: *I just talked to your mother.*

MS. FRANZ: *Do you know what she's going through?*

MR. BECKER: *Yes, I know.*

MS. FRANZ: *Did you say I'm sorry that I started molesting your little girl when she was an infant and continued to do it until she was about seven?*

MR. BECKER: *Your mother hung up on me.*

MS. FRANZ: *Can you blame her?*

MR. BECKER: *No.*

MS. FRANZ: *You fucking lied to me all night.*

MR. BECKER: *I apologize.*

MS. FRANZ: *Do you know how ill I feel after doing this all night? You lied to my husband.*

MR. BECKER: *You have every right to be angry.*

MS. FRANZ: Well, here is what we are going to do to make this right. I am going to ask you questions and you are not going to lie to me. That's what we're going to do and then we're done. Okay?

MR. BECKER: Okay.

MS. FRANZ: And the ugliness goes away. How old was I when it started?

MR. BECKER: What was the last phrase?

MS. FRANZ: How old was I when

MR. BECKER: No. No. What was - - I didn't hear what you said.

MS. FRANZ: I said, this is what you're going to tell me. You are going to tell me the truth and then our issue goes away and we all move on and I go to work tomorrow and you go to work and mom goes to work and dad goes to work and it's a new day and my husband and we don't live with this anymore because I can't tell you how big this burden is on my shoulders, so...

MR. BECKER: I want to relieve the burden from your shoulders.

MS. FRANZ: Okay. Let's be honest with each other.

MR. BECKER: Okay.

MS. FRANZ: I remember stuff clearly. I'm not stupid. Don't snow me. How old was I when you started molesting me?

MR. BECKER: I'm not sure. I know that it was -- you were young.

MS. FRANZ: How young?

MR. BECKER: An infant.

MS. FRANZ: An infant. Okay. I remember you putting your finger inside of my vagina. Do you remember that?

MR. BECKER: No.

MS. FRANZ: Are we going to lie here?

MR. BECKER: I'm not lying, Jennifer.

MS. FRANZ: Okay. Then what did you do to me?

MR. BECKER: I'm having a hard time recalling all this.

MS. FRANZ: I've done a lot of research on the subject for many, many years and I never heard of the perpetrator not recalling the molestation. It's usually the victim, but unfortunately for you, I have a pretty good memory for things.

MR. BECKER: Okay.

MS. FRANZ: So don't bullshit me. Okay?

MR. BECKER: I'm not bullshitting you.

MS. FRANZ: Okay. Was I three months?

MR. BECKER: Perhaps.

MS. FRANZ: "Perhaps?" That's a bullshit answer. Was I one month old?

MR. BECKER: You were at mommy's house. At my mother's house.

MS. FRANZ: And --

MR. BECKER: You were in a crib.

MS. FRANZ: Go on.

MR. BECKER: I don't know your exact age.

MS. FRANZ: I'm sure.

MR. BECKER: You were in a crib.

MS. FRANZ: I was in a crib still?

MR. BECKER: Yes.

MS. FRANZ: Did the molestation get worse as I got older?

MR. BECKER: No.

MS. FRANZ: So you always had the same routine?

MR. BECKER: Yes.

MS. FRANZ: Does my routine what I remember differ from what you actually did?

MR. BECKER: No.

MS. FRANZ: Are you more innocent than I thought?

MR. BECKER: Pardon?

MS. FRANZ: I almost remember a break in what actually happened.

MR. BECKER: That never happened.

MS. FRANZ: Okay. Help me understand what did.

MR. BECKER: Help you understand what? I'm sorry.

MS. FRANZ: Help me understand what did.

MR. BECKER: Touching.

MS. FRANZ: Where?

MR. BECKER: In your privates.

MS. FRANZ: Did you ever put your finger inside me?

MR. BECKER: No.

MS. FRANZ: I'm remembering that. Why do I remember that then?

MR. BECKER: To do that would have caused damage and hurt you and I wouldn't do that.

MS. FRANZ: You are being honest here. This is our healing time together. I know what I remember. Okay? Did you stick your finger inside my vagina?

MR. BECKER: I would never do something like that.

MS. FRANZ: Did you stick your finger in my anus?

MR. BECKER: No, for the same purpose.

MS. FRANZ: Did you touch my breast area?

MR. BECKER: Probably.

MS. FRANZ: "Probably" is not going to fly with me right now.

MR. BECKER: Yes.

MS. FRANZ: Okay. Was I one month old? Was I a newborn?

MR. BECKER: You were still in a crib.

MS. FRANZ: Still in a crib means to me under one. What does "still in a crib" mean to you?

MR. BECKER: I don't know how long you were in a crib, but it occurred when you were in a crib.

MS. FRANZ: And I remember it stopping when you came to visit mom and dad's house. I think I was seven or I was eight. Do you remember?

MR. BECKER: I don't remember how old you were.

MS. FRANZ: Okay. What do you remember about it?

MR. BECKER: I know you were a young lady.

MS. FRANZ: What does a young lady mean? Thirteen? Fourteen?

MR. BECKER: No. No. You were a girl. I'm sorry. A girl. Jennifer, I told you this. I'm not good with age. I thought you were actually older than you actually are.

MS. FRANZ: That's fair. We won't get into ages.

MR. BECKER: Thank you.

MS. FRANZ: You never inserted your finger in my vagina? Because I really do remember that.

MR. BECKER: No, I did not. I would not have hurt you. That would have hurt you.

MS. FRANZ: So you just rubbed on the outside area?

MR. BECKER: Any contact was external.

MS. FRANZ: Did you masturbate while you were doing that to me?

MR. BECKER: No.

MS. FRANZ: What did you do while you were touching my genitalia?

MR. BECKER: Nothing to myself then.

MS. FRANZ: Was that later on?

MR. BECKER: Yes.

MS. FRANZ: And you are telling me the truth about everything?

MR. BECKER: Yes.

MS. FRANZ: Because as you can tell, I'm tough. I'm calm. I can handle it. This is what I need to hear to heal. This is why I'm afraid to be around babies. I get it now.

MR. BECKER: I hope that you heal after this.

MS. FRANZ: I hope I do, too, and I hope you do, too.

MR. BECKER: I love you very much.

MS. FRANZ: We're not done with the conversation. Don't try to get rid of me.

MR. BECKER: I'm not.

MS. FRANZ: Did you ever touch my bottom area?

MR. BECKER: Yes.

MS. FRANZ: But you never inserted fingers?

MR. BECKER: No.

MS. FRANZ: Did I cry when I was an infant and you were doing this?

MR. BECKER: No.

MS. FRANZ: When did I finally stand up to you? What did I say? Did I even have the balls to stand up to you?

MR. BECKER: You didn't have the balls to say anything.

MS. FRANZ: Okay. I remember just kind of laying still and zoning out. Is that the way you remember things?

MR. BECKER: Yes.

MS. FRANZ: Just kind of mentally checking out. Did I ever cry?

MR. BECKER: No.

MS. FRANZ: I remember this happening all the time.

MR. BECKER: Pardon?

MS. FRANZ: I remember this happening a lot and I just -- it just feels like it happened on a daily basis and it just -- how often did this really happen?

MR. BECKER: Jennifer, I didn't see you that much.

MS. FRANZ: Okay, but how much did this happen?

MR. BECKER: I can't give you a number.

MS. FRANZ: Where was mom? Where was Grammy? Please tell me that neither one had a clue. They didn't or did they?

MR. BECKER: They did not.

MS. FRANZ: Did Pop-Pop have any idea?

MR. BECKER: No.

MS. FRANZ: Did I ever try and tell them that you can remember because I remember trying in my own way. I remember having nightmares and trying.

MR. BECKER: I have no idea. If you did, I would not have been around.

PHONE CALL DISCONNECTED

One Day Later

PHONE CALL CONNECTED

MS. FRANZ: Uncle Ronnie?

MR. BECKER: Hi.

MS. FRANZ: I'm just calling to check on you to make sure you're okay.

MR. BECKER: I'm doing better.

MS. FRANZ: You're better?

MR. BECKER: Yes.

MS. FRANZ: You really helped me yesterday.

MR. BECKER: Thank you. I --

MS. FRANZ: (Inaudible) the sexual abuse.

MR. BECKER: I had problems after you called. I had not eaten since breakfast.

MS. FRANZ: Uh-huh.

MR. BECKER: And my blood sugar gets dangerously low. I got very sick, but I'm okay today.

MS. FRANZ: Good. I'm glad you're feeling better.

MR. BECKER: I hope you are, too.

MS. FRANZ: I am feeling better. You helped me a lot.

MR. BECKER: Good.

MS. FRANZ: Made me feel a lot better by admitting everything and apologizing for the sexual abuse. I just want to know why you would start when I was an infant and --

MR. BECKER: Jennifer, can we -- we had enough talk yesterday.

MS. FRANZ: No, we didn't have enough talk. That's not to my satisfaction.

MR. BECKER: Jennifer, I can't talk to you today.

MS. FRANZ: I think after you sexually abused me from let's say an infant to eight, I think you owe me this conversation.

MR. BECKER: Jennifer --

MS. FRANZ: Would you like me to get on a plane and fly there?

MR. BECKER: I can't talk right now. I'm involved in a project right now.

MS. FRANZ: I think that apologizing further for molesting your niece is more important than any project you might be involved in at the time. I want you to answer a couple questions for me and then I will not call you again and I will forgive you and we will move on.

MR. BECKER: Okay.

MS. FRANZ: I want to know --

MR. BECKER: I cannot answer that question.

MS. FRANZ: You didn't even hear what I asked you. Don't tell me you can't answer the question.

MR. BECKER: You had asked me a question.

MS. FRANZ: I didn't ask you a question.

MR. BECKER: You did a few moments ago. Okay.

MS. FRANZ: I want to know, it makes me feel horrible that I would be the only victim and I would feel so much better if you would tell me that I was not the only victim that you did this to because I feel very isolated that I could be the only one

MR. BECKER: You are it.

MS. FRANZ: So this was an isolated thing. You molested one child and that's it?

MR. BECKER: Jennifer, no one else is involved.

MS. FRANZ: I was also really upset because you had told me about the other priests at church who were also doing this. How many of them are there?

MR. BECKER: I can't give you a number across the country.

MS. FRANZ: I want to know your specific church, your experience and where you worked. I don't care about the rest of the country.

MR. BECKER: In the Trenton diocese?

MS. FRANZ: Uh-huh.

MR. BECKER: Four.

MS. FRANZ: And where are those four now?

MR. BECKER: Some are in ministry. I don't know where they are at. That information was not available to me.

MS. FRANZ: Last night you told me that you had put your hands in my underwear when I was two. Maybe when I was an infant. I just want to know why you would do that.

MR. BECKER: I can't answer that.

MS. FRANZ: Why can't you answer that?

MR. BECKER: Because I don't have an answer. I can't give you an answer.

MS. FRANZ: I think you have an answer. You were there. You were the molester. Clearly you must have an answer.

MR. BECKER: I do not have an answer.

MS. FRANZ: You know, you saying I was ill. I had a preference for infants. (inaudible) something. It would give me some sort of closure.

MR. BECKER: I can't give you an answer. I'm sorry.

MS. FRANZ: You really hurt me. I was just a small little girl when you performed these sexual acts on me and you acted inappropriately and you were in a position of power that you abused and I just want to know why.

MR. BECKER: I can't answer that

MS. FRANZ: I want to know why you can't answer that.

MR. BECKER: Because I don't have an answer.

MS. FRANZ: I want to know if I ever bled when you did that.

MR. BECKER: I cannot answer that.

MS. FRANZ: I think you can answer that and I think you will. Was I bruised?

MR. BECKER: I cannot answer that.

MS. FRANZ: Why can't you answer that?

MR. BECKER: I can't answer it. Give you an answer to something I don't know.

MS. FRANZ: You don't know? That's pretty insensitive. I think I would notice if one of my students had cut their hand and they were bleeding. I certainly would know if the child I was rapping was bleeding.

MR. BECKER: Jennifer, I cannot answer your questions.

MS. FRANZ: Would you not check on me when you raped me?

MR. BECKER: You're saying I raped you now?

MS. FRANZ: You want to clarify what you did?

MR. BECKER: I did not rape you.

MS. FRANZ: Okay, then what did you do?

MR. BECKER: I don't know what I did.

MS. FRANZ: So you don't remember. (Inaudible) dealing with your life. I want to know did you check on me? Was I bleeding?

MR. BECKER: Jennifer, I spoke to my therapist this morning.

MS. FRANZ: And?

MR. BECKER: He advised me not to speak with you any longer.

MS. FRANZ: So your therapist knows that you molested a very young infant all the way until what, seven, eight and they advised you to not speak to me?

MR. BECKER: That was his advice this morning.

MS. FRANZ: I would seriously question the therapist. I don't think that is appropriate advice.

MR. BECKER: Well, until I go in and see him and talk to him.

MS. FRANZ: You really helped me last night and I want some closure. I want to finish the conversation that we had last night and I was genuinely concerned that you were no longer on this earth.

MR. BECKER: Jennifer, again, I am not in a position to speak to you today.

MS. FRANZ: I don't think that is acceptable. You made me feel so much better when you apologized to me and told me that you were sorry for molesting me and that you hurt me. I need more of that.

MR. BECKER: Jennifer --

MS. FRANZ: You know as a priest you help families and you can help put closure to this.

MR. BECKER: I am not in a position to speak with you.

MS. FRANZ: I highly doubt that any licensed health professional would advise you to not speak to a victim that you molested. Highly doubt that. I would actually think that they would tell you to apologize because it would be therapeutic for you.

MR. BECKER: I told you what my therapist said this morning.

MS. FRANZ: Well, your therapist didn't molest me and you did and so I don't really care to talk to your therapist or hear what your therapist has to say.

MR. BECKER: Jennifer, I cannot discuss this with you any longer.

MS. FRANZ: Did the therapist tell you this today?

MR. BECKER: Yes.

MS. FRANZ: When?

MR. BECKER: This morning.

MS. FRANZ: Which therapist are you going to that they are telling you this? Is it a therapist through the church?

MR. BECKER: Yes.

MS. FRANZ: Is it another priest that you're going to?

MR. BECKER: No.

MS. FRANZ: Who are you going to?

MR. BECKER: His name is Dr. Fitzgibbons.

MS. FRANZ: And Dr. Fitzgibbons is recommending that you not apologize to your victim any longer?

MR. BECKER: That's correct.

MS. FRANZ: Okay. What did they say about you telling me the truth last night and apologizing and making me feel better?

MR. BECKER: I am not to discuss this with you any longer.

MS. FRANZ: That's your response? I felt that --

MR. BECKER: That is my response.

MS. FRANZ: I felt that you were a better person than that after last night you were being honest with me. I need closure on this so I can start a family. I don't need your actions to affect my marriage.

MR. BECKER: Jennifer, I can no longer discuss this issue with you.

MS. FRANZ: I'm disappointed because I really -- when you apologized and you told me that you were sorry for hurting me and that you were sorry it happened and that Grammy and Pop-Pop didn't know you were abusing me, it really gave me closure and I didn't feel depressed today.

MR. BECKER: I admitted nothing last night.

MS. FRANZ: Admitted nothing last night?

MR. BECKER: I said that you said that I disappointed you. I apologize for disappointing you.

MS. FRANZ: You said more than you disappointed me. Remember we talked about how you molested me starting when I was an infant all the way to seven or eight?

MR. BECKER: I at no time admitted to molesting you.

MS. FRANZ: You know, I have a direct quote from my little brain of things that you said. You said that you were sorry that you hurt me. You said that you were sorry you molested me.

MR. BECKER: No, I did not use the word "molest." I said -- you said that I --

MS. FRANZ: Are we going to go back to this lying?

MR. BECKER: Yes, we are.

MS. FRANZ: We are going back to the lying? How fun for us.

MR. BECKER: Jennifer, good night.

MS. FRANZ: I will fly there.

Becker hangs up.

PHONE CALL CONNECTED

MR. BECKER: Hello?

MS. FRANZ: I'm calling to apologize. I'm sorry that I got upset with you. I was just upset and hurt.

MR. BECKER: I can't speak to you.

MS. FRANZ: Why can't you speak to me? We had such a good conversation last night and you were the only one that could help me and you really have and I just want, you know --

MR. BECKER: I --

MS. FRANZ: -- to finish our conversation.

MR. BECKER: On the advice of my psychiatrist, I cannot speak to you today.

MS. FRANZ: I'm your niece. I'm your family.

MR. BECKER: On the advice of my psychiatrist, I cannot speak to you today.

MS. FRANZ: Your psychiatrist is not related to you. The psychiatrist is not in our family.

MR. BECKER: On the advice of my psychiatrist, I cannot speak to you today.

MS. FRANZ: I don't think the psychologist would say that and I really wish you would treat your niece better.

MR. BECKER: On the advice of my psychiatrist, I cannot speak to you today

MS. FRANZ: I loved you and I trusted you and last night you made me feel all better. What has changed from now until last night?

MR. BECKER: On the advice of my psychiatrist, I cannot speak to you today.

MS. FRANZ: What has changed from now to last night? From last night to now?

MR. BECKER: On the advice of my psychiatrist, I cannot speak to you today.

MS. FRANZ: Are you just going to keep chanting on the advice of your psychologist, you can't speak to me?

MR. BECKER: Pardon?

MS. FRANZ: Are you just going to keep saying that to me over and over because you are really hurting me.

MR. BECKER: I'm sorry if that is all I can say to you.

MS. FRANZ: But you're hurting me.

MR. BECKER: I'm sorry that I'm hurting you. I am not intentionally hurting you.

MS. FRANZ: Why can't we just finish our conversation and then we're done.

MR. BECKER: We finished it last night.

MS. FRANZ: But I still had questions about why and did I put myself in that situation to molest me?

MR. BECKER: Jennifer, I did nothing to you.

MS. FRANZ: You're lying. You and I both know that. What do you have to lose? I don't understand.

MR. BECKER: Jennifer, I did nothing to you.

MS. FRANZ: You're lying again. You apologized. You made me feel all better. What is your fear? Are you afraid I'm going to tell mom?

MR. BECKER: I'm waiting for your mother to call me.

MS. FRANZ: What are you going to tell mom? I mean, you told me everything last night.

MR. BECKER: *I told you nothing last night.*

MS. FRANZ: *Okay. Have I fallen and hit my head because I clearly remember everything you said last night. You apologized. You made me feel better.*

MR. BECKER: *I did not admit to molesting you in any way.*

MS. FRANZ: *Why do I feel like you have a lawyer present or this is getting ridiculous. You told me last night.*

MR. BECKER: *No, I did not tell you last night. All I said last night was that you said that I had hurt you and I apologized for hurting you. Those were my exact words.*

MS. FRANZ: *You really think I'm going to believe that? Do you think that I have forgotten everything you said less than 24hours ago?*

MR. BECKER: *Again, I --*

MS. FRANZ: *Remember when I told you how when I received a gift from you this Christmas my husband had to hold my hands in the car because I wanted to jump out of the car?*

MR. BECKER: *Yes.*

MS. FRANZ: And you remember apologizing to me and comforting me last night or did that not happen either?

MR. BECKER: I told you that you had a fear that you were going to -- you could not be a good mother. I assured you that you could be. You will be.

MS. FRANZ: I'm still feeling like this might be my fault. Is this my fault?

MR. BECKER: Is what your fault?

MS. FRANZ: Is what happened between us my fault?

MR. BECKER: Jennifer, nothing happened between us other than last night's discussion.

MS. FRANZ: Other than last night's discussion, so why are you completely contradicting everything you said to me last night? What changed in 24 hours?

MR. BECKER: At no time last night did I admit to doing anything to you.

MS. FRANZ: Why are you lying again? Where is this going to get us? This took hours last night.

MR. BECKER: Good night, Jennifer.

MS. FRANZ: Do not hang up.

Becker hangs up.

PHONE CALL CONNECTED

ANSWERING MACHINE: Hi, this is Ron. I'm not here right now, but if you leave your name, telephone number and a short message, I'll get back to you as soon as I get back. Thanks. Have a great day.

MS. FRANZ: Hi, Uncle Ronnie. I was checking on you. I wanted to make sure you said you were going to kill yourself last night and, you know, being your niece I was concerned about you. Our conversation really upset you and just calling to make sure you're okay. I hope that you decide to talk to me further and I hope you're feeling better. Thanks. Bye.

ANSWERING MACHINE: Hi, this is Ron. I'm not here right now, but if you leave your name, telephone number and a short message, I'll get back to you as soon as I get back. Thanks. Have a great day.

MS. FRANZ: Hi, Uncle Ronnie. This is Jenni again. I'm just calling to check on you. I'm sorry that I was so upset. Really I just lost my temper. I had a long day at work. If you could pick up, I really would appreciate it. I just want to talk to you one minute. You can time me. I just want to finish our conversation and be able to move on and I really appreciate all of your honesty last night. It really helped me feel better *and I'm sure it will help me be a good mother and help my marriage and I just really appreciate your strength. I know it took a lot of guts to be honest with me and I'm sure it was very painful for you to go through that. If you can I guess give me a call. I just want to talk to you for exactly a minute. All right. Take care. Bye.*

ANSWERING MACHINE: Hi, this is Ron. I'm not here right now, but if you leave your name, telephone number and a short message, I'll get back to you as soon as I get back. Thanks. Have a great day.

MS. FRANZ: Hey, Uncle Ronnie. This is your niece. I was just calling to check on you again. You know, I was really worried about you. You said a couple times you were going to commit suicide, but I will call you later and check on you. Thanks. Bye.

Uncle and niece never spoke again; twenty-four hours, Ronald Becker was placed in custody.

The healing process for Jennifer Beth had finally begun.

Epilogue
June 2012

Father Ronald Becker never saw trial for his offenses against Jenni Franz. He died in January 2009. The Diocese of Trenton spent nearly $1.4 million to settle the claims against him involving not only Jenni, but five altar boys at Incarnation. Jenni Franz was awarded $325,000.

***

Jenni Franz is a licensed Pediatric Speech & Language Pathologist whose primary focus is working with children diagnosed with Autism Spectrum Disorder, Dyslexia, and other developmental and learning disabilities. She lives in Winter Park, Florida, with her husband, Jon and their two sons.

Jenni may have settled with the Diocese of Trenton in 2009 but the issues with the Diocese did not end at that time. In a post-settlement press release, the Diocese went on the attack against the Franz's, confirming the settlement but contesting Franz's version of events. Diocese spokesperson Rayanne Bennett said the Diocese learned of Franz's allegations only in 2007, shortly before Becker was charged. Bennett said the Diocese viewed the allegations as a family problem unrelated to Becker's "priestly ministry or responsibilities."

Rayanne Bennett admitted that prior to 1989 the Diocese had received other, separate "credible accusations of misconduct" against Father Becker and had "resolved" them through cash settlements. Therefore, by the Diocese's own admission, they were handing out money to settle Becker's sexual abuse cases and allowing him to continue to function as a parish priest in good standing during the precise period that Jenni was being abused by him. That they only learned about her in

2007 is a specious argument when you consider that they could have prevented her abuse altogether. Franz and her husband contend in an Op-Ed piece from January 2009 that during the process of mediation with the Diocese, case files regarding Becker were incomplete, pages torn out and other pages "missing."

Dianne and Ron Hermanski are no longer in contact with their daughter Jenni and her growing family. They have never met their youngest grandson even though they live within 40 minutes of the Franz's. They have also cut off contact with any family members that supported Jenni. Jenni's mother called the entire nightmare her daughter endured, "an embarrassment to the family." To this day however, in a bizarre ritual, Dianne and Ron continue to shower gifts and written words of "love" on the grandsons they hardly know. Jon's father has been tremendously supportive of Jenni, but his mother, not so much. A nurse by profession, Jon's mother says this could not have happened because she has never seen it happen and accuses Jenni of ruining her son's life.

Jenni thrives on the love and support of her relatives, friends, husband and children. Many of Ronald Becker victims (all men so far) have reached out to Jenni, mostly via Facebook, and she speaks to all of them; they have formed a close bond that she continues to cherish. Though she was the only female to come forward with accusations against Becker, she remains certain that Becker's other victims were not all male.

In a March 2011 email Jenni wrote:

What I was limited in the way of supportive parents I have been blessed beyond words to have found in my Uncle Stan, Aunt, Cousin,

Grandmother (my aunt's mom), father in Law, best friend whose like a sister, huge group of great friends, and my sweet hubby and babies. Counseling oh my yes! I did it for years and years and loved going because it allowed me to be the person God intended me. Removing toxic people: okay so this was the hardest.

Like most victims I avoid conflict like an art form. I have a really hard horrible nightmare of a time if someone ever is upset with me. I will bend over backwards to not have conflict. For years I put up with a schizophrenic relationship with my father. When I was young he put on a good front around others but although he was physically present he could not have been more emotionally distant. Once I went to college we became extremely close BUT only when Dianne allowed it. She would decide Jon and I were not in her good graces which happened many times a year over much to do about nothing and then " Dad" and I am being generous calling him that would completely freeze Jon and I out for months and months at a time with NO contact with us and would not even return calls.

Dianne would also get very mean about other family members and would say things like "the worst day of my life was when your Aunt became godmother to Thomas" (Jenni and Jon's son) then proceeded to pick apart every since family member despite Jon and I's protests. The final straw came when she slammed the door in my face while I was holding my infant son screaming that " Jon and I are sellouts" because we invited my Aunt and Grandmother to lunch that day. She called us every name in the book in front of the baby and threw one of her many *temper tantrums. I stood there with and had that moment where I woke and said this pattern of dysfunction ends with my generation.*

To this day, the settlement money from the Diocese of Trenton remains in an account, untouched except for investments made for the security of the children of Jon and Jenni; a security that she never had as a child.

Jenni has told me that she will not read Chapter 11. The ghosts continue to haunt.

***

On March 6, 2011, representatives of SNAP came to the Diocese of Trenton and asked the tenth Bishop of Trenton, David M. O'Connell, to release the names of all priests and religious within the Diocese who have been credibly accused of sexual misconduct against minors. On that day, His Excellency committed to "considering the request."

Over a year later, he refuses to release the names or speak publically about it.

The Bishop has listed a toll free number and email address in the Trenton Diocese newspaper for those that feel they have been abused.

***

Sister Harold Phelan is retired, suffers from dementia and lives on the campus of Mount Saint Mary College in Watchung, New Jersey. I visited her in November 2010 just to let her know that she saved so many others with her bravery. To dedicate this book to her would be appropriate but not sufficient. My respect for her is boundless. Sister stood up to the hierarchy when most would have kowtowed, kissed rings and bowed heads as they backed towards the door; she is what myths and martyrs are made of.

***

Doris Kessler, who stared down Father John "Jack" Banko, went on to work at Georgian Court University in Lakewood, New Jersey. Tragically, she died in May 2002 as a result of a single-vehicle car accident. When she left Saint Mary Academy, she converted from Judaism to Catholicism.

***

Tony Conte sat across from me on New Years Eve in 2011, at a restaurant in Lawrence, New Jersey, watching his hamburger get cold. As we spoke for an hour, I tried to reassure him that he was not alone, by steering the conversation back towards the people that supported him after hearing his story. Sadly, today, solitude remains his condition, by choice or by circumstance, who can say.

Tony seeks compensation, not vindication; vindication passed long ago with the death of Brother Deo Gratias. No longer able to work, Tony looks to the legal system to force compensation from the Society of the Divine Word Missionaries and the Diocese of Trenton. His is an uphill and insurmountable climb.

In June 2012, Tony emailed me to let me know he was doing just fine. He moved away from the city streets of Trenton, NJ to a place that gives him peace; Tony writes, *"I am 10 miles south of Interstate 80, at Rt. 80 Chicago is 112 miles east. Again from Rt. 80 the Mississippi River at Iowa is 56 miles to the west. I absolutely love it out here, I am finally living for a change rather than exist. The town is crime free, everyone leaves their house doors unlocked even when they go out!*

It is rather scenic; the area where I live is farmland in the bottom of a valley with lots of trees, meadows, stream, canal. This move has done wonders for my mental well being, just wish I did this sooner."

Anthony found refuge as a boy in the outdoors, I'm happy he's found it again.

***

(Brother) Gary Craanen was confronted with the allegations contained in this book by Saint Catherine's school board president Christopher Olley. Olley issued this letter to the community of Saint Catherine's in January 2012:

An open letter to the SCHS community from President Christopher Olley:

Over the recent holiday break; the Archdiocese of Milwaukee was contacted by Bruce Novozinsky, a New Jersey-based author writing a book entitled Purple Reign about sexual abuse and the abuse of power in the Diocese of Trenton, New Jersey. Novozinsky informed the Archdiocese of serious allegations regarding SCHS teacher Gary Craanen, who was once employed at Divine Word Seminary in New

Jersey in the late 1970s. St. Catherine's immediately addressed the situation with Gary Craanen and began an internal investigation to research how the matter would impact the SCHS community. On Monday, Jan. 2, Mr. Craanen announced his desire to retire immediately. Mr. Novozinsky has recently published allegations on his blog about Gary Craanen's time at Divine Word. The allegations are both serious and explicit. While we are limited in sharing more about this ongoing personnel matter, please know that after being contacted by the Milwaukee Archdiocese, SCHS promptly informed local law enforcement about the situation and they have been involved ever since. Gary Craanen had been employed at St. Catherine's for over 30 years. During his time here, the school never received a complaint about abusive behavior involving him. Nonetheless, we will always do everything in our power to protect our students, which is why we acted swiftly upon learning about this very serious matter.

Sincerely, Christopher Olley

Two days later, Gary Craanen retired from the position that he held at Saint Catherine's for over 30 years.

To this day, Craanen operates Uncle Puff's Photography in Wisconsin on <u>etsy.com</u>.

***

I've been told that (Father) Francis "Frank" Bruno is aware of my pursuit of him and has made threats to me through those same people – none which have followed through. Bruno has since retired from the New Jersey State Department of Corrections, and while I have aggressively sought him out, he remains elusive. I'm confident our paths will cross though, and when they do, he will be confronted. He's getting sloppy. In March 2012, Frank Bruno was seen on the campus of my children's grade school and in the affiliated church. A photograph was taken of him and emailed to me.

Frank Bruno has never been charged for his alleged crimes. Being at Saint Gregory the Great is not a crime. Being in church is not a crime. Being around the grounds of Saint Gregory the Great school is not a crime. However, Saint Gregory the Great is my parish and since I had absolutely no cause to call the police to say "there is a guy that has been alleged to have molested children in the 1970's at my church" (given the statute of limitations being expired), I did the next and only thing I could morally do; I contacted the pastor of Saint Gregory the Great via email ending with the following:

"...IF I see him at Mass or on the grounds of SGG I will walk up to him and ask him to leave. I'd he refuses, I will forcefully and physically remove him; consequences be damned." Bruce

I didn't choose to make this public, the pastor did.

A few days after I sent the email to the pastor, the Hamilton Police Department knocked on my door at about 12:30 p.m. looking to speak with me regarding it. I was told to call Detective Sgt. James Leigh at headquarters. When I did reach the Detective I was asked about the email. He advised me that the pastor and his business manager were "concerned with the tone" of the email and that it sounded "slanderous." Detective Leigh was candid that the police normally do not get involved in slander matters. He asked if I had proof of the claims made against

Frank Bruno, and I explained the objective of my book and how Bruno fit into it. He asked if any of the alleged crimes occurred in Hamilton and I told him that I could not pinpoint the exact locale of alleged acts, but I was convinced that they at least some of them happened in the Mercer County area. He asked me if I was serious about the email I sent to the pastor and I replied "yes."

The pastor and his business manager have all of my phone numbers and no one hesitates to call me when they are being called out on my website (as has happened in the past). So I'm left to ask, what was the motivation behind calling the police and not me directly? From the time the email went out to the time the police came and knocked at my front door (alarming my family – and believe me, I heard about it when I got home), I had been trying to get my ring blessed by the pastor that week and had been in contact with the pastor (and under his roof) and his staff no less than four times, and not a word mentioned.

I then made an offer to the Detective. I told him that I would give him a copy of the chapter of the book that detailed the claims against Frank Bruno. I told him I would provide email (with the consent of the senders) of the claims against Frank Bruno. I told him that I'm willing to sit with anyone to discuss the claims against Frank Bruno. Anyone including Frank Bruno.

I honored that offer. At 4:30 p.m. that day I delivered, in its entirety, the complete chapter of the book detailing the allegations against Frank Bruno and others. The promise made to me from the Detective is that this is to be filed away and not shared with anyone until the book's release.

Why did I do this?

When I contacted the Bishop via email four weeks prior to tell him that he "really should call me" about a concern – he ignored the email. Did I say what he "really should call me" about? No, but he knows my areas of concern, if he isn't going to call, he should at least have someone else call. So I'm left to look into the allegations against one of his priests alone and this could take time. If the Hamilton Police Department and Detective Leigh see fit to "open a file" on these claims, at the very least, it's one step further than the Diocese of Trenton has done collectively. I welcome it – have at my files.

The Catholic Church, the Diocese of Trenton, the bishops from Ahr to O'Connell have all refused to acknowledge that the mistakes of the past are still so very present with the victims.

This research has led me to realization, a hunch if you will, of just why we don't feel as much outrage as we should. It's a simple thing that really dawned on me last year; we don't see the victims in the news as children. We at times see them as adults, alcoholics, drug users and emotional wrecks. This is what we see. We see adults. We don't see the child that was raped. We don't see a 12, 13 or 14 year-old infused with alcohol. We see the end result and while it's a sad sight, the impact is lost years later.

I'm the one that gets the visit from the police (and rightfully so, they were doing their jobs by responding to a call) - but one has to wonder who is being protected against whom? Am I the bad guy in this? I have not drawn any conclusion; I'm just left to wonder.

***

Prisoner number 000669605C is remanded to the Adult Diagnostic and Treatment Center in Woodbridge, New Jersey, where he will most likely die. He stays mostly to himself, in denial and without remorse. His name is John Banko and he was the first Catholic priest in New Jersey to be convicted of sexually abusing a child.

Banko was convicted of first-degree aggravated sexual assault and second-degree endangering the welfare of a child for the attacks at Saint Edward the Confessor Church in Milford, New Jersey. Leading up to this conviction, Banko was already serving 15 years on a 2002 conviction for sexually assaulting an altar boy at the same church in the 1990's. The second conviction resulted in a consecutive 18-year sentence.

A report by Banko's doctor at the Adult Diagnostic and Treatment Center, New Jersey's prison for sex offenders in the Avenel section of Woodbridge Township, concluded that Banko exhibited a pattern of compulsive criminal sexual behavior even though he continued to deny the attacks.

His arrogance intact, at his trial he was steadfast in his belief that his celibacy vow did not include homosexuality.

He has refused repeated requests to provide a comment for this book. Should he outlive his sentence, he will come back to Mercer County living in plain sight of schools and playgrounds. When local pastors were made aware of this, they feigned concern but dismissed the urgency with promises of prayer. What they fail to grasp is that the protection of our children depends on more than Hail Marys alone.

***

According to Monsignor Joe Rosie, Father Jerry Brown lives in a small town in southern New Jersey. The Diocese of Trenton is fully aware of his exact address (or have direct access to it). No one's talking though. He's well into his eighties and not subject to any sexual predator registration process or law. He has not shown up on the known databases of predator clergy members, and lives this farce called "prayer and penance." There was one telling slip of a comment that Monsignor Rosie let out the day we met. He said to me that while the Diocese keeps track of those with credible accusations against them in a shared file (or database), those not associated with the Diocese (but residing within – say a member of an outside order) are not tracked. This tells me that the Diocese (or the plural dioceses) is at least taking measures to try and keep an eye on those clergy with credible accusations against them. Then why aren't they going one step further to enlist the aid of the community, who has more than a casual interest in knowing, by publishing those names? In the cases of a Jerry Brown, the dioceses must take steps to ensure that the surrounding neighborhoods know that a predator, not just a retired old priest, is in their midst. Brown was never prosecuted and lives off of a stipend provided by the Diocese of Trenton.

***

Theodore Cardinal McCarrick is retired and lives in Washington, D.C. He is an active, albeit unofficial ambassador of the Vatican for many oversees trips involving Islamic countries. In an interview on MSNBC in December 2011, he told mediator David Gregory that the true path to healing the sexually abused is complete transparency, which he asserted the Church has faithfully adhered to since 2002.

According to neighbors, the Cardinal still visits the New Jersey shore each summer.

***

Father John Bambrick survived the efforts of the Committee of Ten to have him transferred from the Catholic community of Saint Joseph, Toms River, but did nothing to ease the tension between the flock and the administration.

Bishop David M. O'Connell assured me in a letter that no one has any retaliation to fear by speaking his or her mind when the Committee of Ten presented him with our official list of issues surrounding Father Bambrick. We pointed out to him that people feared coming forward because of their jobs. In writing he reassured us that there would be no consequences – he had not met the likes of John Bambrick.

In the year following the efforts to have him removed, John Bambrick did retaliate against Union organizers by instituting a policy that each teacher must be certified within his or her core competencies within two years' time or face dismissal.

In December 2011, the Bishop received an email blitz from dozens in the Saint Joseph community in direct response to Father Bambrick denying Mass of the Dead for long time alumni and supporters of the Parish and in January 2012 he dismissed a popular religion teacher who offered suggestions (not opinion) on how to discuss the Obama Administration's mandates on Health and Human Services. On all counts the Bishop backed the priest's decisions.

In January 2012, Father John Bambrick expressed his desire to be transferred from the community of Saint Joseph. The Bishop honored the request. John Bambrick was assigned to Rome.

***

Maureen Fitzsimmons and Monsignor Walter Nolan met with me in 2008 at the meetinghouse on the grounds of Saint John's Roman Catholic Church in Allentown, New Jersey, and I told them the story of my attack at the hands of Jerry Brown. They listened with sympathetic ear and we prayed together. At the end of the 90 minutes I spent with them, I asked Nolan for his blessing – something I had not asked a priest for in over 20 years. Blessing bestowed, I left.

It took me a few years to realize that what Patrick Newcombe said about Nolan and Fitzsimmons was frightfully true. Not one pen or pencil was raised to take a single note in the hour and half I spent in that meeting. If, as Nolan claims, they didn't know how to handle such things in the 1980's and 1990's, the lessons of 2002 Boston must have taught them that documentation was essential. Clearly they were dealing with claims under Bishop John Smith that his Excellency did not want in writing. Nothing in the protocol changed from then until now. Meet with the victim, offer counseling, take no notes, throw in some prayers, and confuse the inquirers.

One week after the meeting in the Pastoral Center with Patrick Newcombe, Monsignor Walter Nolan was fired from his duties as Executive Director of the Office of Child and Youth Protection. Nolan was replaced by Monsignor Joseph Rosie and was allowed to retire.

In all that I've written, spoken of and covered for the past eight years, not one religious priest, monsignor, bishop or even cardinal comes close to being as revered as Walter Nolan. He is a pastor without peer who was brought to the priesthood with a tragic past. His parishioners and the many he baptized and wed love him. He is compassionate and fatherly to the many young kids that listen to his every word. He had his faults as well. He blindly followed the orders of the hierarchy and whereas he should have acted to protect those sexually abused, he placed his standing within the Diocese of Trenton first.

In Philadelphia, Monsignor William Lynn stands trial for endangering children by allegedly transferring predator priests from parish to parish without informing the resident pastor of the newcomer's history of deviant behavior. In large part he was more concerned with protecting Cardinal Anthony Bevilacqua.

At the very least, Nolan did the same; at worst, his behavior is criminal. I don't need to justify my accusations and claims with words pressed in a book. I lived it.

Ms. Fitzsimmons remains employed by the Diocese of Trenton.

***

Bishop John M. Smith officially retired in December 2010 and according to a close family member, is physically ill and unable to travel without escort. In the summer of 2011, the Holy See assigned the now Bishop Emeritus to spend five days at the Jesuit Retreat House in Parma, Ohio, to interview priests and parishioners about how they perceive the sitting Bishop of Cleveland, Richard Lennon as a spiritual leader.

Such an investigation, known as an Apostolic Visit, is rare by the Holy See, according to at least one attorney familiar with church law. The review, which Lennon has said he requested, comes in the wake of his reconfiguration of the eight county diocese, which saw the closing of 50 churches since August 2009. The critics of Lennon claimed the closings and consolidations were race-based. Monsignor Rosie took part in the Apostolic Visit as well and the Holy See overturned Lennon's decisions and edicts in the spring of 2012.

Neither Smith nor officials from the Trenton Diocese returned phone calls or responded to emailed questions. The Bishop now resides at the same residence he assigned to Father James Selvaraj to in 2005.

***

Terence McAlinden has not been defrocked as of the date of publication but Bishop O'Connell was true to his word and had him removed as the sitting pastor of Saint Theresa Roman Catholic Church. As of May 2012, no less than six other victims have made accusations towards McAlinden. His laicization is still pending in Rome.

***

Lorenzo D'Oria suffers from HIV but lives a full life in Florida. He enjoys a wonderful and loving relationship with his parents, brother and sisters. Because Lorenzo was allowed to narrate his own story, I found it only fitting that he be afforded the opportunity to close out his chapter. In his own unedited words:

What am I doing today??I am currently retired and living on SSDI. I have HIV and Hep C, the treatments of Interferon left me with what I call a 'mushy brain' Actually it's Chemo Brain. That makes things foggy..so to speak. My Drs give me methamphetamine which have pleasure receptor blockers so my mind is speeding and my body doesn't feel it. This can make life difficult because you never know if you'll be able to sleep, God forbid you take your meds too late. The HIV has taken a toll on my body and in certain ways I'm maturing faster than I should be. In other words those of us who are long term Survivors of HIV are going to wear our bodies out faster than they should. I had to stop working in 2006. That was when I got really sick. I was teaching the 6th Grade International Baccalaureate Program in an underprivileged school with Insanely poor people, many of immigrant backgrounds. Before that I taught 5th grade for 5 years as a bilingual teacher in the BABES program, which is a bilingual immersion program for native English and Spanish speakers. I was also certified in Spanish k-12. MY dream job, from which I was 1 step away from was to be a High School IB Spanish teacher. That would have allowed me to teach on a College level.

Religion? I'm a nondenominational Christian. I have been attending The Church of the Holy Spirit Song, sort of like the MCC, but somewhat less gay. I don't usually attend Catholic events, however when I do it's like I never left. You can take the boy out of Catholicism, but you can't remove the parts of me that remain Catholic, although I'm estranged.

I have had four partners since HS. Men with whom I have shared my life. I buried the first, Ronald in 1986 at the age of 26. He was the first Person with Aids in the USAF.I was with him for 5 years. The second,

Michael died in 2001. We were together 5 years and he eventually became Schizophrenic. After that I was single until 1999 when I moved back to Florida after getting my dual degree of Spanish and Elementary Education at The College of NJ. I graduated in 1999.

I was with "Bear Man" for 6 and 1/2 years. When I got sick I felt he was repulsed by me and I asked him to leave , although he would not have otherwise. He was honorable, but I did not want to be with someone who was repulsed by me. Actually I think he was afraid I was going to die. AS it turned out, later on I was informed that I had miraculously made it back from the abyss. I was never aware that I was in any danger of dying. The truth is that I have died three times and have no fear of death. I don't have to take anything on Faith! LOL! Isn't that an advantage!! The stories that accompany the events are all different, but I can sat that one time I had absolutely no control over it and cried out "Jesus Save Me!" and I was brought back, but not until after having been admonished that I didn't belong there and that my time would come and I would know that it was my time. Also that I'd be welcome back there then.

As of recently I am single. I have dated and was with one man recently for a year until he turned out to have addiction issues I can't deal with. The future? I'm hopeful to meet a partner again. I am not some bitter old queen. I am vibrant, hopeful and upbeat about life in general. I'd say I've come a long way. I still believe in God and Jesus. I still have some questions on some of the Sorrowful Mysteries but something tells me that I can comprehend more than one might imagine! Big Hugz!
Lorenzo

***

Patrick Newcombe remains in poor health but is no longer alone. He has found the happiness that had eluded him most of his life. In 2010, he became engaged to "Lisa", who stands firmly by his side. Patrick calls her a "wonderful lady" that understands him and is willing to help him deal with the possible consequences of the abuse he suffered.

We stay in distant contact through social media. He spends most days trying to live a productive life. No longer able to work, due to health problems that he does not discount, came from his childhood of sexual abuse.

Patrick maintains that three priests - Frank Bruno, Terrence McAlinden, and James Scott - abused him. Scott was the recent Paterson Diocese settlement for which Patrick received five-figures. It was Patrick that contacted attorney Greg Gianforcaro about his legal liabilities concerning helping Chris Naples; he was aware of the fact that his settlement was with Trenton not Paterson. It was at this point that Patrick found out that after he reported the abuse by Scott in 1990, it took the Diocese until 1996 to actually "send him to a rehabilitation center because former Diocese of Trenton attorney Michael Herbert told Newcombe to "let sleeping dogs sleep. Patrick, you signed a confidential settlement agreement with us in 1992 and we shouldn't even be talking about this." Newcombe maintains that it was his call to Paterson that prompted them to insist Scott enter a rehabilitation facility, but the priest refused. The last James Scott was heard of, he had moved to Florida. The Paterson Diocese claims to have no knowledge of his exact whereabouts, but still sends him a support stipend each month.

Included in the lawsuit/settlement between Trenton and Newcombe was Monsignor Vincent S Treglio. Newcombe claims that Treglio knew of the abuse and crimes and did nothing. He too, is living in Florida with James Scott.

Patrick Newcombe is bitter with Monsignor Walter Nolan above all else. He told me in an email in January 2011:

When I originally contacted Nolan in 1990 I told him about the following people Frank Bruno (abuser) Terence McAlinden (abuser) James Scott (abuser) John Scully current pastor in Trenton (knew of the abuse) Francis (Patrick) Magee he walked in on me and Bruno, and was the Pastor of St. Martha's. So he knew of the abuse, someone in Ireland who committed suicide has charged him himself. A kid I knew back then initials are T.Z. - it's in the transcript also accused him in Trenton. Richard Lyons he knew of the abuse, Vincent Treglio he knew of the abuse... They all knew.

Patrick spends his days now keeping up on current events and has found his faith once again with God:

I belong to a great Church (not Catholic) but I have spent some quality time with the Pastor told him my story. He apologized on behalf of Christianity as a whole and over time has earned my trust. This church family has adopted me and I look forward to attending not only church, but the outside functions. I blamed God for 30 years for what happened to me, it has only been recently that I realized He had nothing to do with it.

When I asked Patrick about any lingering effects he starts with the nightmares which make it impossible for him to even consider going back to sleep. This goes on to this day. He still battles with his addictions to alcohol and drugs, both first introduced to him by the abusing trio of priests, Frank Bruno, Terence McAlinden and James Scott. He will go years without a drink or a drug and then he says the triggers start, brought on by his past.

As of mid-2012, he remains sober and depends on the love and support of his family, friends and church.

***

As of late 2011, Pope Benedict XVI has ordered Father James Selvaraj back to his home Diocese in India. Father Selvaraj currently lives in Mercerville, New Jersey. He refuses to run to this day.

***

William "JR" Giebler was killed over the skies of Lockerbie, Scotland, as a passenger on Pan Am flight 103 by Abdelbaset al-Megrahi. At the time of his death, JR was a newlywed, having married only nine months earlier. In 2008, I petitioned the Mayor of Jackson, New Jersey, Mike Reina, to rename the street that JR grew up on. Maryland Drive is now William "J.R." Giebler Path.

JR rests at Saint Mary of the Lake Cemetery in Lakewood, with his mother Denise and one hundred yards from my father, Walter, and my sister, Rose. I visit them often.

JR features prominently in the Prologue, my first effort at putting pen to paper on this very personal journey. How fitting it is that the very last words of this book were written on May 20, 2012, where the breaking news of the day is that Abdelbaset al-Megrahi has succumbed to cancer. May God forgive my impertinence when I say "Allahu Akbar."

***

Finally, Charles W. "Chip" Mathews. You didn't read his name in the book, but you read about him. He was a simple and hardworking man from a caring and loving family in Bordentown, New Jersey. His brother Tim was a classmate of mine at Divine Word Seminary; Chip drove a truck.

What put Chip on Interstate 95, at that truck stop, at that minute, on that day, is for you to decide; I already have. Out of his right passenger side window, he saw his brother's classmate, obviously helpless, and his own protective instinct took over. As far as I know, Chip never told anyone what happened that day. He did what he felt was the right thing to do and went on with his life.

Chip's brother, my classmate, Tim, passed away on February 12, 2012. Needless to say his death stirred up a lot of memories for me. I entered the back of the church of Saint Mary in Bordentown and asked the first Mathews I came across if "the brother who was a truck driver in the 70's" was available. Bill Mathews, Tim and Chip's brother, said he was sorry, but Chip had passed away in 2005.

My heart sank a little. I said goodbye to both brothers at Tim's Mass. Father Raymond Lennon concelebrated the service; we embraced tightly afterwards. It had all come full circle.

Afterthoughts

"I cannot do what you do, and you cannot do what I do, but together we can do something beautiful for God."

+Blessed Mother Theresa

Many pages ago I asked, "Where did it all go wrong?" Now we need to ask, "What can we do to make it right?"

Did you ever try to fight City Hall? The old expression says that you can't. Well, try Rome, or even Trenton for that matter.

As I'm preparing to wrap this up, I turn on the television and see the same issues playing out across the pond, where the head of the Irish Catholic Church refuses to resign all the while attempting to distance himself from a 1975 secret inquiry into one of the country's serial priest pedophiles, and more recently, from the controversy ignited by one of his priests who "accidentally" displayed gay porn during a PowerPoint presentation to parents of children preparing for First Holy Communion. Ongoing at the same time, just across the bridges from New Jersey, is the criminal trial of Monsignor William Lynn, charged with endangering children by keeping accused priests in ministry by secreting archives containing sexual abuse complaints against them while serving as secretary for the clergy in the Philadelphia Archdiocese. While Lynn has testified reluctantly and awkwardly during his trial, Cardinal Sean Brady of Ireland had this to say about his own circumstances: "I accept that I was part of an unhelpful culture of deference and silence in society and the church, which thankfully is a thing of the past."

Is it? No, unfortunately it's not. It's more than just a passing storm. It's the Church's very long, very defining, mid-life crisis. But the beleaguered Cardinal did hit upon a thing or two, namely that as much as it would prefer to continue operating how it has historically, the Catholic Church can no longer hunker down around itself, but must face and more importantly, yield to the larger social conscience which now has its own set of expectations for the Church going forward:

The church is undergoing nothing less than an epochal shift: It pits those who hold fast to a more traditional idea of protecting bishops and priests above all against those who call for more openness and accountability. The battle lines are drawn between the church and society at large, which clearly clamors for accountability, and also inside the church itself.[45]

How has the Church responded? Boston wasn't "ground zero" for the Church's child sexual abuse scandal any more than Ireland or Philadelphia is. Rather, it's a battle that starts here, at home, within our local diocese. In the Diocese of Trenton it comes down to this: A toll-free number and a shadow email address on a Diocese website and in a Diocese newspaper, anemic efforts by any standard. Why? It's relatively simple: The Diocese of Trenton is still out to protect its own and that's because "its own" are still living. As long as Bishop John Smith is still breathing, the current Bishop will not so much as give his predecessor's past transgressions a fleeting nod. What's right or wrong has nothing to do with this. Bishop O'Connell will never break ecclesiastical protocol by trouncing the reputation of the beloved Bishop Emeritus nor extend an open invitation to victims that would prove much too costly for his

Diocese, in terms of scandal and dollar figures. Litigation would result in school and parish closings and with the Catholic population within the Diocese approaching 1,000,000 strong by 2022, the hierarchy deems this a wholly unacceptable option. So still exists a sense of perverted loyalty within the Church where holy men will continue to collude for the supposed "greater good."

The perversion of justice lies not in the acts of brutality, violence and rape of children - those acts stand alone. The perversion of justice lies not in the shifting of predators from parish to parish - those are acts of cowardly men who are foot soldiers that kowtow to the color purple. The perversion of justice lies in the continued deceit masked as "letters of the law," be it canonical or civil within the statutes of limitation. Bishop David M. O'Connell knows the law enough to realize it's on his side and as long as he is the law of the Diocese of Trenton, he will use it. But at what cost?

When I sat with Monsignor Joseph Rosie in early 2011 and asked him why the Diocese continues to pay a stipend and insurances to those priests who are in a state of prayer and penance, he said two very telling things.

First, the Monsignor said to me that the Diocese has a "record" that lists all of the credibly accused clergy within the state. This leaves me to wonder do the other dioceses in New Jersey have this list and why the Monsignor didn't say that the local and state authorities also have this list. What is this "list" and who's on it? Don't the dioceses within New Jersey, all who vociferously claim that they are committed to the safety of children, owe it to the residents of this state to make these people known?

The second thing that the Monsignor said was that those in "prayer and penance" are paid a stipend and given insurance so that the Diocese can "keep an eye on their whereabouts." The problem is that this is just not feasible for a diocese to effectively watchdog; there are no 24/7 resources available to monitor these predators, who by nature are used to, and thus quite savvy at, secreting their behavior. They're farmed out, they're "retired" and they live largely on the generosity (or ignorance) of those in disbelief that a good priest is capable of such heinous crimes. It was the Monsignor himself, in his March 2011 meeting with Patrick Newcombe, who acknowledged the deficiencies by stating that all the Diocese of Trenton could do was write letters and direct these predators not to conduct themselves as priests.

At a very early point in my professional career, an officer in the United States Navy said to me, "you bring me issues; bring me solutions."

To set the tone for meaningful transparency, the sitting Bishop must release the names sealed in the 2002 agreement between the Mercer County Prosecutor's Office and Bishop Smith. He also needs to release the names of each and every credibly accused Diocese employee and religious affiliated with the Trenton Diocese at any time, in all church bulletins and the Monitor newspaper and update it regularly. The release of information must be comprehensive, listing not only the names, but also the accuseds' current status (laicized, "prayer and penance," deceased) the municipality they currently reside in, or if their last place of residence was within the Diocese but their current whereabouts are unknown.

The Essential Norms for Diocesan Policies Dealing with Allegations of Sexual Abuse of Minors by Priests or Deacons, approved by the Vatican in December 2002, requires each diocesan bishop to appoint a review board, which will function as a consultative body to the bishop. The Trenton Diocese has this loosely in place, only to check the audit square. As presently comprised, it has no teeth. In May of 2012, the policy listed on the Diocese website is outdated with contact resource names. Bishop O'Connell needs to appoint an independent public board of review to each and every case that comes to the Diocese's attention. Board members should reflect a cross-faith selection of professionals (not just Catholics from within the Diocese), and include laypersons as well as nuns and a representative from law enforcement from the county of the accuser. The Bishop would be wise to choose Father John Bambrick to chair this Board. A stunning nomination from me, I know, but all differences aside, Father Bambrick is objective and sympathetic to the abused as well as still a "company man." Those having their cases heard should be in attendance with legal counsel, and should be allowed personal support from any other person of choice; these are stressful circumstances and intimidation is easily felt.

And the public has some homework to do, too, on remaining fair-minded. Not every person accused is guilty. The zero tolerance policy for child sexual abuse among the clergy has morphed into zero tolerance of innocence, where those under the harsh lights of accusation are literally skewered in the media: guilty until proven innocent. There are too many Father Selvaraj's out there, falsely accused priests who languish for years in process limbo, their reputations destroyed, cut off from the financial, legal and even moral support of the dioceses they serve. As hard as it is to wrap one's head around the concept, there must also be recognition that even those priests whom evidence suggests may have committed sexual abuse are still entitled to due process. A charity organization, *Opus Bono Sacerdotii* ("Work for the Good of the Priesthood)," was established to provide spiritual support to any priest going through a difficulty; guilt or innocence doesn't matter here - the organization is concerned with ensuring priests get the same treatment any American would get if they stand accused. This is a good thing.

Bishop David O'Connell is an educator and a Canonist. He has the obligation to his priests to defend their presumption of innocence and preserve their due process. He also has the obligation to the children and his faithful to administer swift and just punishment to those rightfully accused. A tough line to walk, but one he was called to ministry for by God.

During Christmastime of 2011, I knelt in the confessional of Saints Peter and Paul in Philadelphia and confessed to Father Ed Burke. I had sinned and my life had been threatened (not all in the same transaction). It was time for me to reconcile with my God. After we spoke he said to me, "your penance is to say a prayer for those accused." This was an extraordinarily challenging thing for me to even comprehend, much less to actually do. This priest was telling me that in order to obtain absolution for my sins, I had to leave the confessional and kneel in front of the Blessed Sacrament and pray for the very men that not only abused children, but those that covered it up. This confessional was under the same roof that Joseph Cardinal Bevilacqua and Justin

Cardinal Rigali mandated and oversaw the massive cover-up in the Archdiocese of Philadelphia for which Monsignor Lynn now stands trial. I was not being asked - I was being told - to pray for the redemption of those who participated in a Holocaust of sexual abuse against children.

I did as I was instructed.

My prayer of penance was to sincerely ask God to have each and every one of the guilty and those that perpetrated their cover-up be forgiven by his Divine Mercy as they lay in their final hour, but that until then they suffer daily the trials and consequences of the evil they wrought.

Two questions are asked of me more and more frequently: "Have you lost your faith?" and "Do you believe that you were chosen to do this work?" I answer without hesitation. My faith is stronger than it ever has been. I believe in the one God that chose to give me the gift, the true gift, of the Catholic faith. It's no surprise that I've lost hope in the hierarchy of my Church, but as I reflect upon the events which led me here I realize that I never had faith in them; Bishop George W. Ahr turned his back on my family; Bishop John M. Smith turned his back on anything that was not already hooked to an established precedence; and Bishop David M. O'Connell has yet to prove himself a true advocate for the abused. My confidence in spiritual leaders dwindled at a young age, and with the passage of time, hope for closure and justice has faded as well.

Do I believe that I was chosen to do this work? I believe that a certain chain of events in my life placed me in a position to put these stories and thoughts on paper. I believe that God gave me a mind that retains the smallest of details and I believe that He gave me the gift of being able to tell a story. I believe that God saw to it that the influence of advocacy of the Sisters of Mercy was instilled in me. I believe that God placed His hand between Jack Banko and me in the form of my friend, JR Giebler. I believe that God placed His hand on my shoulder and freed my arm to fight off Jerry Brown. I believe that truck was at the Connecticut rest stop for a reason. I believe that God saw no further purpose in my continuation at Divine Word Seminary beyond three years, and I believe that He saw to it that I met Monsignor Lawrence Donovan to facilitate my exit. I believe that I was called in a different way. I do not go so far as to deign that I was "chosen" for this purpose, for to say so invokes a special providence from God that I am not worthy of attracting nor capable of achieving.

While I have been conditioned to separate my devotion to God from my faith in the institution, that doesn't mean that I don't pray for the survival of the "one, holy, catholic and apostolic church" into which I was baptized. Scandal is nothing new to this Church. It existed from the very beginning, with Judas, one of the leaders Jesus himself hand-picked. Judas betrayed Christ and had to be replaced with Matthias, and we must trust that through the doctrine of apostolic succession, God will replace traitorous leaders with worthy replacements who will provide the Church with spiritual and moral direction and who have the courage to challenge and deal forthrightly with corruption among their own ranks.

In January of 2012, 10 years after the *Boston Globe* expose, Cardinal Sean O'Malley of the Boston Archdiocese stated that his efforts to revive the faith were based on "our firm conviction that Christ does not abandon his Church." I, too, believe the Catholic Church will endure. I connect this belief to Jesus Christ promising the same to Peter when he entrusted him with the stewardship of the Church: "And I tell you, you are Peter, and on this rock I will build my church, and the gates of hell shall not prevail against it." (Matthew 16:18). Read in conjunction with the Lord's promise that he is with us "always, even to the end of the ages" (Matthew 28:20), I shudder at the immenseness of God, desperately wanting to believe that there is hope for faith renewed.

That hope starts anew each and every day with Bishop David M. O'Connell.

Acknowledgements

With any project of this magnitude, no man is an island. He surrounds himself with support and energy that propels him through a darkness that seems to have no reassuring light. Then an email comes that says "I love you" or "I'm proud of you" or simply, "Thank you."

This book is as therapeutic for me as it was for those that survived and bravely told me their stories. Reassured that they stood with so many, they told me the most intimate details of the most horrific points of their life. I didn't give them a voice, they always had it; I merely gave them the venue.

I'm nowhere without the support of all of my friends, and most especially the Campion, Doran, Tattory, Cadigan, Barletta and Petersen families. A word of support expressed at just the right time when the creative well went dry, a night out to escape the solitude of another chapter, or a round of golf to just get out and get moving, were Chicken Soup for this writer's soul, validating the effort, and for me, defining the very essence of the word friendship.

This book is so largely rooted in my past, particularly my school days, and I would be remiss without acknowledging these loyal classmates and mentors from that time period who are still in my life: Scott Neuner, Ken Jones, Detective John "Jay" Lee and those that supported me from Divine Word Seminary - most notably, Gene Fleming, Pete [last name withheld] and Tony Conte, as well as the Reverends Edmond Bolella and George Martin.

So many people generously lent their talents and refused compensation. The Sisters of Mercy from Mount Saint Mary and Georgian Court University and the priests and monsignors of the dioceses throughout all of New Jersey who cannot be named herein for obvious reasons. I cannot fathom the belief of one aging monsignor that said to me "silence will be (my) undoing at my judgment." He spoke these words to me close enough to the hour of his passing and I truly believe that he looks down on us today, enjoying his eternal life.

Cindy Bauerle spent hours transcribing notes and recordings and then thanked me for allowing her to be a part of this project. Jennifer Stampe added so much to this book and coupled it with humor, respect and thoughtfulness – I treasure our relationship.

Beauty, intelligence, humor and compassion transcend the body and being of Linda Vele Alexander. Each moment spent with her on this project was useful and productive. To say this book is "nothing" without her research, writing and editing is a drastic understatement. She breathed creative life back into the book at least as much as she did to me. I will be forever in her debt for her support and care and forever in thanks to God for leading our paths to cross.

Forty years ago, I handed in a composition to my seventh grade teacher, Mrs. Dunn. She looked at it and put a heart of the top of the paper. She told me that I had a talent and should keep writing. My 12 year-old heart jumped at the attention and support of the prettiest teacher at Saint Mary Academy. All these years later, Mrs. Dunn is no longer

Mrs. Dunn, but Denise Purdy-Thompson and just as beautiful as she was in the late 1970's. She, along with Joanne and Julie Groff, fostered a love for reading and writing, without this book could not be possible. A generation after I left their classrooms, they still have a powerful influence over me and I love them all as I would my own sister.

My personal sense of accomplishment in writing this book, really, is that I put forth the stories of the victims of priest sexual abuse. To me, that was the mark of success and beyond that, I don't know if I ever considered my own expectations for it otherwise. With that being said, I could not end these acknowledgements without relating the circumstances of its endorsement from my biggest critic.

My life took an immediate turn for the better on November 20, 1989, with the birth of my son, Matthew Novozinsky. A source of inestimable fatherly pride, Matt shares with his younger sister and brothers the designation of everything that is right in my life. He read the Prologue, walked up to me and said "Dad, this is good. This is really, really good." This was my validation of critical acclaim; he was as proud of me as I am of him, and all of my children, each and every moment of each and every day that I am graced by God with the joy and privilege of being their earthly father. Those nine words were unequivocally THE most transcendent words spoken to me during the past eight years of my research and writing, and I most humbly thank him for it.

-Bruce Novozinsky 2012

Endnotes

I have made all efforts to properly cite the sources that informed my research. All errors are strictly unintentional. I will rectify any oversights on my website at www.novozinsky.com, along with a personal note to the slighted party.

The following are acknowledged sources:

1. Web source: www.georgian.edu/lakewood_nj/index.htm
2. Roland Burke Savage, *Catherine McAuley: The First Sister of Mercy*, (M.H. Gill and Son LTD, 1955), 393.
3. Web source: www.mercymidatlantic.org/history.html
4. Web source: www.sistersofmercy.org/
5. Phil Brennan, "Homosexual Culture Undercuts Priesthood," www.newsmax.com, April 5, 2002.
6. Sources vary
7. Web source: apostolicsuccession.org/
8. Matt Carroll, Sacha Pfeiffer, Michael Rezendes; and editor Walter V. Robinson, "Church Allowed Abuse by Priest for Years," *Boston Globe*, January 6, 2002.
9. Id.
10. www.pulitzer.org/archives/6732
11. www.pulitzer.org/citation/2003-Public-Service
12. Dahlia Lithwick, "But Why Isn't Bernard Law in Jail [Part 2]," *Slate*, December 19, 2002.
13. Cardinal Law resignation letter, December 13, 2002
14. billoreilly.com
15. novozinsky.org (no longer active)
16. *Child Sexual Abuse in the Archdiocese of Boston*, July 23, 2003, retrieved at www.bishopaccountability.org/downloads/archdiocese.pdf.

17. David Gibson, "Is Penn State Like the Catholic Church," *Religion News Service*, November 10, 2011.

18. *The Nature and Scope of the Problem of Sexual Abuse of Minors by Catholic Priests and Deacons in the United States*, 1950-2002, retrieved at http://www.jjay.cuny.edu/churchstudy/main.asp.

19. *The Causes and Context of Sexual Abuse of Minors By Catholic Priests in the United States*, 1950-2010, retrieved at http://usccb.org/nrb/johnjaystudy/20.

20. Bill Donohue, "Straight Talk on the Catholic Church," *New York Times*, April 11, 2011.

21. Mark Shea, *Catholic & Enjoying It*, John Jay Report Stuff," May 20, 2011 as retrieved at www.patheos.com/blogs/markshea/ (blog).

22. Thomas Doyle, "'Arrogant Clericalism' Never Assessed in John Jay Report," *National Catholic Register* (online), May 21, 2011, retrieved at http://ncronline.org/blogs/examining-crisis/john-jay-never-assessed-arrogant-clericalism.

23. Arthur Jones, "John Jay Sex Abuse Report Cites Wrong Culture as Culprit," *National Catholic Register* (online), May 18, 2011 retrieved at http://ncronline.org/blogs/john-jay-sex-abuse-report-cites-wrong-culture-culprit.

24. Paul Vitello, "Prospective Catholic Priests Face Sexuality Hurdles," *New York Times*, May 30, 2010.

25. Id.

26. James Martin, "John Jay Report: On Not Blaming Homosexuals," *America,* May 17, 2011, retrieved at http://www.americamagazine.org/blog/entry.cfm?entry_id=4229.

27. www.spiekerconnection.com/portfolio/angel-news.pdf

28. *The Joy of Sex* is an illustrated sex manual by Alex Comfort, M.B., Ph.D., first published in 1972. An updated edition was released in September 2008.

29. Diocese of Trenton website, www.dioceseoftrenton.org

30. www.richardsipe.org

31. Id.

32. Id.

33. George Archibald, *Journalism is War*, (Highway, 2009).

34. Jeff Diamant, "Newark Archbishop Shielded at Least 4 Priests Accused of Sexual Abuse," *Star Ledger*, December 5, 2010.

35. Obituary of Brian Egan, *Birmingham News*, January 20, 2011.

36. "Confessions of a Safe Sex Slut"

37. *Catholic World News*

38. benedictinesisters.org

39. Giaquinto press release retrieved at www.bishop-accountability.org

40. www.bishop-accountability.org

41. Erin Duffy, "New Bishop Addresses Concerns of SNAP Protestors," *Trenton Times*, March 8, 2011.

42. David O'Reilly, "Hospice Operator Fires Counselor - It Dismissed the Priest after Learning He Had Been Accused of Sex Abuse and Suspended in New York," *Philadelphia Inquirer*, January 5, 2006.

43. www.bishop-accountability.org

44. Elizabeth F. Loftus, "The Reality of Repressed Memories," retrieved at //faculty.washington.edu/eloftus/Articles/lof93.htm.

45. (No author) "Times Topics: Roman Catholic Church Sex Abuse Cases," *New York Times*, retrieved on March 12, 2012 at topics.nytimes.com/top/reference/timestopics/organizations/r/roman_catholic_church_sex_abuse_cases/index.html (updated regularly).